M000304397

Conversations with Greil Marcus

Literary Conversations Series
Peggy Whitman Prenshaw
General Editor

Conversations with Greil Marcus

Edited by Joe Bonomo

University Press of Mississippi   *Jackson*

www.upress.state.ms.us

The University Press of Mississippi is a member
of the Association of American University Presses.

Copyright © 2012 by University Press of Mississippi

All rights reserved

Manufactured in the United States of America

First printing 2012

∞

Library of Congress Cataloging-in-Publication Data

Bonomo, Joe.
  Conversations with Greil Marcus / Joe Bonomo.
    p. cm. — (Literary conversations series)
  Includes index.
  ISBN 978-1-61703-622-4 (cloth : alk. paper) — ISBN 978-1-61703-623-1 (ebook) 1. Marcus,
Greil—Interviews. 2. Music journalists—United States—Interviews. 3. Authors, American—
20th century—Interviews. 4. Rock music—History and criticism. I. Title.
  ML423.M164
    781.64092--dc23   2012002778

British Library Cataloging-in-Publication Data available

Books by Greil Marcus

Mystery Train: Images of America in Rock 'n' Roll Music. New York: Dutton, 1975.

Lipstick Traces: A Secret History of the 20th Century. Cambridge: Harvard University Press, 1989.

Dead Elvis: A Chronicle of a Cultural Obsession. New York: Doubleday, 1991.

In the Fascist Bathroom: Punk in Pop Music, 1977–92, New York: Doubleday, 1993. (Originally published as *Ranters and Crowd Pleasers*)

The Dustbin of History. Cambridge: Harvard University Press, 1995.

The Old, Weird America: The World of Bob Dylan's Basement Tapes. New York: Henry Holt, 1997. (Originally published as *Invisible Republic*)

Double Trouble: Bill Clinton and Elvis Presley in a Land of No Alternatives. New York: Henry Holt, 2000.

The Manchurian Candidate. London: British Film Institute, 2002.

Like a Rolling Stone: Bob Dylan at the Crossroads. New York: PublicAffairs, 2005.

The Shape of Things to Come: Prophecy and the American Voice. New York: Farrar Straus Giroux, 2006

When That Rough God Goes Riding: Listening to Van Morrison. New York: PublicAffairs, 2010.

Bob Dylan by Greil Marcus: Writings 1968–2010. New York: PublicAffairs, 2010.

The Doors: A Lifetime of Listening to Five Mean Years. New York: PublicAffairs, 2011.

AS EDITOR:

Stranded. New York: Knopf, 1979.

Psychotic Reactions and Carburetor Dung (by Lester Bangs). New York: Knopf, 1987.

With Sean Wilentz, *The Rose & the Briar: Death, Love and Liberty in the American Ballad.* New York: Norton, 2004.

Best Music Writing 2009. New York: Da Capo, 2009.

With Werner Sollors, *A New Literary History of America*. Cambridge: Harvard University Press, 2009.

Greil Marcus's books have been published and reissued throughout the world, often in updated editions. See Chronology for details.

Contents

Introduction

"There is an infinite amount of meaning about anything," Greil Marcus said to an interviewer. "And I free associate." For more than four decades, Marcus has explored the connections among figures, sounds, and events in culture, relating unrelated points of departure, mapping alternate histories and surprising correspondences. He is a unique and influential voice in American letters, and a collection of his interviews is overdue.

Marcus was born in 1945 in San Francisco, California, and he lived there and in Palo Alto, Menlo Park, and Berkeley, where he settled and wrote until 2010 (he currently lives in Oakland). He received his B.A. in American studies in 1967 and, a year later, his M.A. in political science, both from the University of California at Berkeley. In 1968 he published his first piece, a review of *Magic Bus: The Who on Tour*, in *Rolling Stone*, where he became the first records editor. Renowned for his ongoing "Real Life Top Ten" column, Marcus has been a writer for a number of magazines and websites, and is the author and editor of eighteen books. His critique is egalitarian: no figure, object, or event is too high, low, celebrated, or obscure for an inquiry into the ways in which our lives can open outward, often unexpectedly. When Marcus listens to a song, reads a book, or watches a film, he hopes to be surprised, allowing cultural associations, suggestions, and evocations to materialize on the surface of his thinking, whether he's essaying the Sex Pistols, Bill Clinton, Appalachian balladry, Elvis's legacy, a contemporary American novel, or last week's Top 40 hit. His work is characterized by native curiosity and precise patience borne out of respect for these as-yet-unheard correspondences, for the ways in which assumptions about a given text might prismatically move through that text to project revelation and discovery.

Little of Marcus's personal life is revealed in these wide-ranging discussions. Skeptical of the autobiographical impulse, Marcus remarked to Tony Fafoglia in 1988:

I think that if you want to use the word "I" in a piece, you have to earn the right. I don't mean that you have to be around a long time. I mean that in terms of the writing of a given piece, you have to justify leaping out, and you have to see that somehow the authority is backed up. You can't just assume that the reader ought to give a shit about you or anyone else.

Two years later, in a conversation not included in this book, Marcus was struck by interviewer Lorenzo Buj's interpretation of a line in *Lipstick Traces*: "Lost children seek their fathers, and fathers seek their lost children, but nobody really looks like anybody else. So all, fixed on the wrong faces, pass each other by." Buj pointedly asked Marcus if he is one of these sons or fathers. Marcus replied, "Well, to explain that passage I'd have to get very personal,"

and I'm not going to do it. That is one of those things that any writer stumbles on. That's a line I wrote, and I wrote it because it made sense of what I was trying to explain and describe at that point in the book, with no personal motive for me at all. . . . And it was only later, rereading that passage that I realized that was probably the most autobiographical or confessional line in the entire book.

A decade and a half later, Marcus remarked to Oliver Hall, "I just have a very strong sense of privacy. There are things about my family background that I find actually interesting, and sometimes I talk about them, but I don't think my life itself is very interesting."

Marcus sifts these "things" in his important 2008 memoir "Tied to History," revealing a complex past as the source of lifelong critical passions. "I'm perfectly aware that there is this theme running through all of my work, and I know what its sources are," he acknowledged to Asbjørn Grønstad and Øyvind Vågnes in 2010. "I know what its personal neurotic sources are, and I've even written about that recently. I took me a long time. I didn't think that it was anyone's business or that anyone would care. But then there was an occasion to do it, so I did it." The occasion was "Telling Childhood: New Stories about a Strange Country," an event in 2006 at the Richard Hugo House in Seattle where a group of writers gathered to discuss childhood. "As time for the talk approached I realized I had nothing to say," Marcus told me. "I knew nothing in particular about childhood, it wasn't something I thought about. So my own childhood was all I had to work with. I don't write about myself, and I'm not particularly interested in myself, so this was not exactly something I was inclined to do. But it seemed to reach people very directly, including my own brother, oldest except for me, Bill Marcus, who died in 2007." Marcus read the talk again a year later at the New York University Humanities Center in a series organized by Lawrence Weschler. Wendy Lesser ran the piece in the Spring 2008 issue of the *Threepenny Review*.

"Usually people write memoirs—this is my sense anyway—out of a great sense of self-importance," Marcus remarked to Robert Loss at *PopMatters* in 2010, "or because it's a way of justifying themselves in public for things that really can't be justified. Most memoirs are exercises in self-congratulation." Yet "Tied to History" is anything but narcissistic. In the essay, Marcus reveals that his father Greil Gerstley died in the Philippines typhoon that sank the *USS Hull* destroyer in 1944; Marcus's mother Eleanore was three months pregnant with Greil. In 1948, she married Gerald Marcus, and Greil was adopted and his surname changed. The tragedy of the *Hull* and of Greil Gerstley's fate was never discussed in the family, a covert narrative which came to define Marcus. "The situation never changed," he writes in "Tied to History." "When I grew older, the habit of not speaking about the past became a kind of prison. I didn't know how to break out of it. I didn't ask, and nobody told." This absence, he writes,

> lay behind what I ended up doing with my life: rewriting the past, pursuing an obsession with secret histories, with stories untold—with what, to me, were deep, fraternal connections between people who never met: such people as the Dadaist Richard Huelsenbeck in Zurich in 1916, the revolutionary theorist Guy Debord in Paris in 1954, and the punk singer Johnny Rotten in London in 1976.

Marcus's fixation with the past originates in this shadowy memory. "I used the cultivated mystery of my own past as a spur to reconstructing events both as they happened and as they didn't—as they might have," he says, adding: "I became a writer, and this is always the route I've traveled."

Marcus learned more about the *Hull* incident one evening when he watched a television documentary; later, he learned more from a historian who shared with Marcus harrowing firsthand accounts of *Hull* survivors. Referencing the opening sequence of David Lynch's *Blue Velvet*, its imagery associated not with any individual's past but with American culture at large, Marcus acknowledges that as he now possesses the facts of the tragedy, he "can make sense of them, or hold them in my mind, only as scenes from movies—the likes of *The Cruel Sea*, *Victory at Sea*, the documentaries *The World at War* or *Why We Fight*—or from the movie that, someday, someone might make." He adds: "But if any such movie were ever made, the story that I have, as a personal story, would be even less mine than it is now—and the truth is that, now, it isn't mine at all. It is a contrivance—it is a story that I might now remember, but don't." In "Tied to History" Marcus essays the random ways in which the past evolves into the present, and the ways in which what we create in the present—whether it's a public act or a private secret—evolves into a future that is impossible to know.

Marcus is interviewed often, usually on the occasion of a new book. In choosing the fourteen pieces included here I selected among interviews ranging from 1980 to 2011. A conversation with Marcus is marked by a complex and lively engagement with issues that, given its origins in popular culture, never strays into rarefied ether. "Real ideas," he argued to Thom Jurek, "are exchanged in plain language." Marcus has been blessed with smart, well-prepared interviewers; his answers are erudite and carefully composed, conversational and meaty. It's helpful to the reader that Marcus speaks in paragraphs, and that he's well versed in the vernacular: his answers are driven by a voice that's inquiring, intelligent, and never condescending. He's funny, too.

In conversation, Marcus might discus a current book or column as well as his critical methodology and broad approach to his material, signaled by a generosity of spirit leavened with aggressive critical standards. "I try and write as if the distinctions that are always being thrown in our faces between high culture and popular culture, fine art and pop art, are meaningless," he told Brent Brambury, "because I don't hear them, I don't see them." To Mark Kitchell: "My role as a critic is to intensify the experience other people might have with a given incident or object." To John King, in an early interview: "I can't write about music in a purely aesthetic manner. It doesn't intrigue me." He was quick to insist to Fafoglia several years later that, "The last thing I want to do is lead someone not to enjoy something they in fact already do enjoy."

In editing *Conversations with Greil Marcus* I strove to maintain balance among decades, books, and well-known and obscure subjects, to select interviews that moved between a book under discussion and expansive, interrelated issues, and to minimize the inevitable repetitions that occur over decades. There are radio interviews here as well as print and online interviews, and I've blended recognizable sources with the less well-known, conventional formats with the unconventional. It's interesting to watch Marcus react in real time to hot-button issues of the era (i.e., federal funding for the arts, censorship, "We Are the World," Reagan/Bush), name and honor his influences and contemporaries, wrestle with his ambivalence with rap and hip-hop, and defend his steadfast and frankly surprising dismissal of the New York punk scene of the late-1970s, an unorthodox position that places him at odds with many cultural observers.

Keith Richards has said that rock and roll is music for the neck down; Marcus has spent the better part of his career expanding that definition. Though he's considered by most people a music critic—"Most of the time music is where I start," he concedes to David Weich. "Something musical makes a breach, opens up questions that I wind up pursuing"—these interviews illuminate Marcus's considerable breadth of interests and knowledge. He's equally poised discussing film, literature, or politics as he is Dylan, punk, or indie rock; his expansive co-interview with noted scholar Werner Sollors on the occasion of *A New Literary History of America* serves as a primer on American studies. Mark Kitchell's interview from 1984, published here for the first time, is a wonderfully conversational, lengthy account of Marcus's undergraduate experience with the Free Speech Movement at University of California at Berkeley, an event to which Marcus acknowledges comparing everything in his life. The extended interview at RockCritics.com from 2002 is especially lively, given that various readers emailed questions to which Marcus responded, and the resulting range in content and tone of the questions—some deferential, some provocative—leads to a spiky, vigorous conversation.

No single collection of interviews with Marcus can be comprehensive; his interviewers are too numerous; his erudition too broad. The possibilities for conversations are abundant: for the record, I hope that future interviewers ask Marcus about the cultural value of Flannery O'Connor, the novels of Larry Brown, Marcus's Bay Area neighbors Green Day, collage artist Winston Smith, Sherwood Anderson's *Winesburg, Ohio*, Davis Grubb's *The Night of the Hunter*, and Michael Chabon's *The Amazing Adventures of Kavalier and Clay*. Regardless of the subject, Marcus is pointed, provocative, obstinate, witty, and discursive in these interviews, never sacrificing a thoughtful response for a canned answer, always eager to do a conversation justice, to explore the deep mysteries his subjects embody.

I have many people to thank in editing *Conversations with Greil Marcus*, first among them Greil himself, who was enthusiastic and obliging from the initial stages of the book to its completion. Early in the process, with help from his daughter Cecily, he sent me print and radio interviews, several of which would've been exceedingly tough to locate given their short circulation life, and directed me to others; he also generously offered to fact-check the manuscript. His cooperation was invaluable. I'm grateful also to the many people who've asked Marcus thoughtful questions over the decades, to Walter Biggins, Anne Stascavage, and the staff at the University Press of Mississippi, to the staff at Founders Library at Northern Illinois University, and to all in low and high places who helped during the arduous permissions process.

Above all thanks to Amy, who was here from the very start of this book a long time ago, and whose love, support, enthusiasm, and critical eyes were crucial along the way. Thanks, favorite.

JB

Works Cited

Brambury, Brent. "Interview," *Brave New Waves*, CBC Radio, broadcast November 16, 1989.

Buj, Lorenzo. Longer unpublished version of "An Interview with Greil Marcus," originally published in *Border/Lines*, Winter 1990/91.

Fafoglia, Tony. "Making Too Much of a Song: An Interview with Greil Marcus," *Listen Up*, December 1988.

Grønstad, Asbjørn, and Øyvind Vågnes. "Interview with Greil Marcus and Werner Sollors," *Journal of American Studies*, 45: E16, 2011.

Hall, Oilver. "Greil Marcus: Interview," *Perfect Sound Forever*, March 2005.

Jurek, Thom. "Interview," *Metro Times* (Detroit), March 14–20, 1990.

King, John. "A Critic on His Music," *OutTakes*, January 16, 1981.

Kitchell, Mark. "An Interview with Greil Marcus," unpublished, 1984

Loss, Robert. "High Stakes Criticism: An Interview with Greil Marcus," *PopMatters*, April 26, 2010.

Marcus, Greil. "Tied to History," *Threepenny Review*, Spring 2008.

Weich, Dave. "All These Inches Away Where Greil Marcus Began," *Powells.com*, 2001.

Key Resources

The following are important interviews with Marcus that because of space limitations I could not include in the book (listed in order of publication/broadcast).

Interview, National Public Radio, broadcast December 9, 1980.

"A Connoisseur of the Void: A Conversation with Greil Marcus," Gary Kamiya, *Frisko*, Summer 1989.

Interview [with Phil Proctor and Peter Bergman of Firesign Theatre], *Roger Steffens Show*, KRCW-FM Los Angeles, CA, broadcast April 20, 1989.

Interview, Terry Gross, *Fresh Air*, National Public Radio, broadcast June 19, 1990.

"Hearsay & Heresy: An Interview with Greil Marcus," Chris McAuliffe, *Tension* (Australia), August–September 1990.

"An Interview with Greil Marcus," Lorenzo Buj, *Border/Lines*. Winter 1990/91.

"A Hunka' Hunka' Burnin' Text: Greil Marcus on Dead Elvis and Other Pop Icons," *Lingua Franca*, August 1991.

"Anarchy in the U.S.: Music, Film, and the Breakdown of Society," Ted Drozdowski, *Boston Phoenix*, November 15, 1991.

"Rock of Ages: Berkeley Writer Greil Marcus Talks about What Elvis, Madonna, Nirvana, and Jesus Have in Common," Gina Arnold, *Express: The East Bay's Free Weekly*, February 21, 1992.

"Fictional Elvis," Julian Stringer /1993, *Million* (U.K.), July–August 1992.

Interview, Gabriel Roth, unpublished, 1993.

"A Surfer on the Zeitgeist," Andy Beckett, *Independent* (U.K.), May 23, 1993.

Interview, Ray Pratt and Sarah Vowell, KGLT-FM Boseman, MT, broadcast April 28, 1993.

"Down the Rabbit Hole with Greil Marcus," J. W. Bonner, *Green Line*, September–October 1993.

"The Critic at Large: An Interview with Greil Marcus," Dave Haslam, *Puncture*, 1st Quarter 1994.

"Lipstick Traces," Andrew Goodwin, *SOMA*, Spring 1994.

"Bob Dylan's Invisible Republic: Interview with Greil Marcus," Paolo Vites, *Jam Magazine* (Italy), 1997.

"'A writer writes to be read': Interview with Greil Marcus," Nate Seltenrich, Rock-Critics.com, 2004.

"Interview: Greil Marcus," Christopher Gray, *Phoenix*, January 21, 2009.

Chronology

1945   Greil David Gerstley born June 19 in San Francisco, the only child
        of Greil and Eleanore (Hyman) Gerstley. Gerstley dies in the Philip-
        pines typhoon that sank the *USS Hull* destroyer in 1944. Eleanore
        marries Gerald Marcus in 1948; Greil is adopted and his surname
        is changed. Family grows to include three more boys and one girl.
        Marcus lives in San Francisco until 1950, Palo Alto 1950–55, Menlo
        Park 1955–63, Berkeley 1963 until 2010 when he moves to Oakland.
        Raised as a Stanford fan, immediately switches allegiance to Berke-
        ley in 1963 when he attends University of California at Berkeley.

1966   Marries Jenelle Bernstein, June 26.

1967   Receives B.A. in American studies (individual major) from the Uni-
        versity of California at Berkeley.

1968   Receives M.A. in political science from the University of California
        at Berkeley. Publishes first piece, a review of *Magic Bus: The Who
        on Tour*, in *Rolling Stone*, where he becomes the first records editor.
        Becomes music columnist for the *San Francisco Express-Times*.

1969   Daughter Emily born December 10.

1970   Begins five-year contributing editorship at *Creem*.

1971   Teaches American studies honors seminar at University of Califor-
        nia at Berkeley.

1972   Daughter Cecily born April 12.

1974   Writes television column for *City* (San Francisco)

1975   Publishes his first book, *Mystery Train: Images of America in Rock
        'n' Roll Music* with Dutton. The book comes out in revised editions
        in the United States in 1982, 1990, 1997, and 2008, and is published
        in the U.K., Germany, Spain, Greece, the Netherlands, Japan, Italy,
        China, and France. Begins a five-year stint as a book columnist for
        Rolling Stone.

1978   Begins writing "Real Life Rock" column for *New West* (later *Cali-
        fornia*) (Los Angeles), reprinted in *Music Magazine* (Tokyo).

1979   Edits *Stranded* with Knopf; editions appear in 1996 and 2007. Joins Board of Directors of Pagnol & Cie, operators of Chez Panisse restaurant in Berkeley.

1981   Serves as book columnist for *California*.

1983   Begins writing music column for *Artforum* (New York). Named to Board of Directors, National Book Critics Circle. Serves until 1989.

1986   Begins writing "Real Life Rock Top Ten" column for the *Village Voice*.

1987   Edits *Psychotic Reactions and Carburetor Dung*, by Lester Bangs, for Knopf. The book is published in the U.K., France, and Brazil.

1989   Publishes *Lipstick Traces: A Secret History of the Twentieth Century* with Harvard University Press. The book is published in the U.K., Italy, Germany, Spain, France, Portugal, and Turkey. Begins writing "Real Life Rock Top Ten" column for *Artforum*. Co-curates exhibition *On the Passage of a Few People through a Rather Brief Moment in Time: The Situationist International, 1957–1972*. Musée national de l'art moderne, Paris, at the Institute of Contemporary Art, London, and at the Institute of Contemporary Art, Boston.

1991   Publishes *Dead Elvis: A Chronicle of a Cultural Obsession* with Doubleday. The book is published in the U.K., Germany, Japan, Austria, and France. Begins writing a cultural column for *San Francisco Focus*.

1992   Begins writing "Days between Stations" column for *Interview*. Named to Executive Board of College of Letters and Science, University of California at Berkeley; serves until 1998. Member of Critics Chorus in Rock Bottom Remainders, all-author rock 'n' roll band.

1993   Publishes *Ranters and Crowd Pleasers: Punk in Pop Music, 1977–92* with Doubleday, published in the U.K. as *In the Fascist Bathroom: Writings on Punk, 1977–92*. The book is published in Germany and Brazil. Soundtrack for *Lipstick Traces* released on Rough Trade Records.

1995   Publishes *The Dustbin of History* with Harvard. The book is published in the U.K., Germany, and Argentina.

1997   Publishes *Invisible Republic: Bob Dylan's Basement Tapes* with Henry Holt. The book is published in the U.K., the Netherlands, Italy, Germany, France, and China. Appointed Regents Lecturer in American Studies, University of California at Berkeley.

1998   Curates *1948—From the Permanent Collection* at Whitney Museum of American Art, New York, January-March.

1999   Theatrical adaptation of *Lipstick Traces* staged in Austin, Texas, and New York City by Rude Mechanicals of Austin. *Dead Elvis* reissued by Harvard. Begins writing "Real Life Rock Top Ten" column for Salon.com.

2000   Picador USA reissues *Invisible Republic* as *The Old, Weird America: The World of Bob Dylan's Basement Tapes*. Publishes *Double Trouble: Bill Clinton and Elvis Presley in a Land of No Alternatives* with Henry Holt, also in the U.K. Appointed Chevalier de l'ordre des arts et des lettres, République Française. Teaches undergraduate seminar "Prophecy and the American Voice" at Berkeley, and again in the fall as Anschutz Distinguished Fellow in American Studies at Princeton, where he also teaches a faculty seminar on Harry Smith's *Anthology of American Folk Music*.

2001   Restaging of *Lipstick Traces* in New York City, and later in Columbus, Ohio; Iowa City; Minneapolis; Seattle; Los Angeles; Raleigh, North Carolina; Chicago; and Salzburg, Austria.

2002   Publishes *The Manchurian Candidate* with British Film Institute.

2003   University of California Press publishes *The Manchurian Candidate*. Begins writing "Real Life Top Ten" column for *City Pages* (Minneapolis).

2004   Edits, with Sean Wilentz, *The Rose & the Briar: Death, Love and Liberty in the American Ballad* with Norton. Soundtrack to *The Rose & the Briar* issued by Columbia Records.

2005   Publishes *Like a Rolling Stone: Bob Dylan at the Crossroads* with PublicAffairs. The book is published in the U.K., Germany, France, Italy, Japan, and Spain.

2006   Publishes *The Shape of Things to Come: Prophecy and the American Voice* with Farrar Straus Giroux. The book is published in the U.K. and France. Begins writing "Elephant Dancing" column for *Interview*. Teaches graduate seminar "Prophecy and the American Voice" at University of California at Berkeley. Teaches seminar "Practical Criticism" as Ferris Professor at Princeton. Presents "Obsessive Memories" at "Telling Childhood: New Stories about a Strange Country" at the Richard Hugo House in Seattle. Eleanore Marcus dies December 25.

2007   Teaches lecture course "The Old Weird America: Music as Democratic Speech, from the Commonplace Song to Bob Dylan" as Distinguished Visiting Professor at the New School in New York, and again in 2009, 2010, 2011, and 2012.

2008   Begins writing "Real Life Rock Top Ten" column for *The Believer.* Appointed Una Lecturer, University of California at Berkeley. Teaches seminar "The Old Weird America" as Winton Chair Fellow at the University of Minnesota. Publishes "Obsessive Memories" as "Tied to History" in the *Threepenny Review.*

2009   Edits, with Werner Sollors, *A New Literary History of America* with Harvard. Publishes updated and redesigned twentieth anniversary edition of *Lipstick Traces* with Harvard. Edits *Best Music Writing* with Da Capo Press. Teaches seminars on cultural criticism at the New School, New York City, and again in 2010 and 2011, and at New York University in 2010 and 2011.

2010   Publishes *When That Rough God Goes Riding: Listening to Van Morrison* with PublicAffairs. The book is published in the U.K. and Germany (editions in France and Italy not yet published). Publishes *Bob Dylan by Greil Marcus: Writing 1968–2010* with PublicAffairs. The book is published in the U.K. and Italy (editions France and Germany not yet published).

2011   Publishes *The Doors: A Lifetime of Listening to Five Mean Years* with PublicAffairs (editions in U.K., France, Germany, Spain, Italy, and China not yet published). Picador USA publishes revised edition of *The Old, Weird America*. Gerald Marcus dies March 25.

Conversations with Greil Marcus

A Critic on His Music

John King/1981

From *OutTakes*, January 16, 1981. Reprinted by permission of the author.

Not many rock critics have made a name for themselves. The musical form is over twenty-five years old, yet most reviews still consist either of strings of superlatives ("the awesome vocal is propelled by thunderous guitars and a pounding bass") or snide putdowns ("Dobrewski sings like an albino orang-utan in heat"). Intelligent, vivid writing is all but unknown.

It does exist, however, and Greil Marcus proves it. For twelve years he has written about the music and the world it affects; he writes regularly for everything from *Rolling Stone* to the *Village Voice* to *New West*, the California magazine where his "Real Life Rock" column appears.

He has also published two books recently. One he edited: *Stranded* (1979), for which he had twenty rock critics write essays on the one album each would take to a desert island. One he wrote: *Mystery Train* (1975). The latter is nothing less than the finest study done of popular music's complex role in American society.

"Well, then, this is a book about rock and roll—some of it—and America. . . . It is an attempt to broaden the context in which music is heard; to deal with rock and roll not as youth culture, or counter culture, but simply as American culture."

This goal would not even *occur* to most rock critics, but—using Elvis Presley, The Band, Sly Stone, and Randy Newman as examples—Marcus succeeded in showing how rock ties into American life and American dreams.

"Echoing through all of rock and roll is the simple demand for peace of mind and a good time. While the demand is easy to make, nothing is more complex than to try to make it real and live it out. . . . Finally, the music must provoke as well as delight, disturb as well as comfort, create as well as sustain. If it doesn't, it lies, and there is only so much comfort you can take in a lie before it falls apart."

Marcus is a critic of the music, yet he is also an unabashed fan. His love of the music stretches back to 1955 [sic] when he first heard "All Shook Up" on the radio, and he is still drawn to music that, quite simply, grabs him. "Neil Young's played the same goddamned guitar riff for fifteen years and I'm still not tired of it. . . . The rock version of 'Hey Hey, My My' sounds like someone is taking the amplifier apart."

Marcus was a twenty-three-year-old political science major at the University of California, Berkeley when he began writing for the underground *San Francisco Express-Times*. It was an era of constant rioting and student/police confrontation, and the music on the radio—from the Beatles' "Revolution" to the Jefferson Airplane's *Volunteers* to the Rolling Stones' "Street Fighting Man"—reflected the tumultuous atmosphere. Marcus: "Some of us always used to say that rock and roll isn't music. They'd say what is it? We'd say 'life itself.'"

At thirty-five he still lives in Berkeley, but it's north Berkeley now, in a tastefully furnished hillside home surrounded by oak trees. Although the critic has an almost scholarly look about him, his tastes have not softened at all; in *New West* he constantly surveys the New Wave and "postpunk" music coming out of England, and he is planning a book on the British music scene. "Obviously, one of the things that draws me to punk stuff is that once again the music has become politicized. I looked over at the Sex Pistols and the Clash, and in some ways that scene was very familiar to me."

John King: You're a very powerful writer: you constantly employ strong metaphors and sharp, decisive juxtapositions. Is this ever done mainly for effect?

Greil Marcus: I've been accused of hyperbole, but I don't write anything that I don't believe. Often when I'm dramatic I regret it later because it looks fake even when it isn't.

I'll give you an example. . . . I was writing about John Lennon after he was killed, and the day that I was writing the article a friend of mine called and told me a story.

The night John Lennon was shot, about 8:30 that night in New York—remember, he was shot around 11 p.m.—Captain Beefheart was being interviewed by a journalist. In the middle of the interview he suddenly stood up, held his hands to his ears, and began shouting, "There's a terrible noise!

Stop it! There's a terrible noise! It's horrible!" He ran over to the wall, held his head against the wall, *pounded* his head against the wall, yelled, "Stop, stop, stop the noise!"

Finally he calmed down and turned around to the interviewer and said, "Something terrible is going to happen tonight. I don't know what it is. You'll read about it in the paper tomorrow. I can't talk to you anymore." And he left the room.

Well, that's an incredible, dramatic story. Now I don't believe in people being psychic, but I've had enough experience with Captain Beefheart to know he's not an ordinary character, so I believed this story and I tried to use it in the article I was writing . . . and I couldn't do it, because I didn't believe in it *enough* to make it credible. It didn't come off.

In that sense there's something really dramatic that I didn't believe in and so I couldn't use. It's not a matter of ethics; I just couldn't pull it off.

JK: Do you also find it difficult to write about groups or trends that don't inspire you?
GM: Of course. I don't waste my time writing about why I hate Journey, or why the Jefferson Starship is beneath contempt, or why I haven't listened to a Grateful Dead album for God knows how many years. There's just so much interesting stuff to write about—and most of it to me is very difficult to write about, to put down, to catch. Why bother with the rest?

JK: Then you don't feel any responsibility to write, say, a column on the urban cowboy phenomenon?
GM: No. While Kenny Rogers might be interesting in a sociological sense, he's not interesting musically. I have to have both: I can't write about music in a purely aesthetic manner. It doesn't intrigue me.

There's a punk group now that's real big in England called Adam and the Ants. All the British papers are full of them because they represent a punk revival. That may be interesting—the idea of reviving something three years after it arrived—but you can't listen to their records.

JK: Much of your recent writing has dealt with New Wave, especially English groups such as the Clash, the Gang of Four, and the Sex Pistols. Has listening to punk and postpunk over the last few years changed your ideas about what's "good" or "bad" in rock music?
GM: I don't think the arrival of punk has significantly changed my tastes.

Like most critics, my reaction when punk came along was Oh boy! Yes it was new, and yes there were all these new questions being posed, but first of all we liked the music.

Most critics value intensity, harshness, surprise, anger, and bitterness in music. They value them instinctively and emotionally, but also intellectually. It just wasn't difficult to relate to the new music.

But it's not as if I underwent a born-again experience and suddenly realized that Van Morrison was a pasty-faced melodic wimp who I shouldn't listen to. What I really want out of music is passion, music that makes me feel more alive. When all is said and done I can probably get that out of Van Morrison better than anybody. So I'll always listen to him, even if I can't find some way to link him to punk.

JK: Both you and Robert Christgau (of the *Village Voice*) have written about the disappearance of a rock "center," an artist or style that captures everyone's interest. Has the fragmentation in rock—and in the listening audience—always been there? Has it grown worse since punk came on the scene?

GM: I don't know if it's gotten worse—it's gotten more rigid, more ideological. Because punk, if nothing else, was an ideology. About rock, about popular culture, about class. . . .

When I talk about centers, it just means having something that everyone has to have an opinion on, some common ground for conversation. There really have never been more than two centers: Elvis and the Beatles. The Sex Pistols almost became one simply because they were so publicized, but, in a way, they got publicized past rock. Punk became a general international giggle before it became a rock issue.

And yet the Sex Pistols are clearly the most significant band of the past five years.

JK: Punk and New Wave have been lauded by most critics, but it's only recently that they've begun to achieve any commercial success. Could part of this be that, while critics turned to punk in relief after the dry spell of the mid 1970s, most listeners no longer take a vital interest in the music they hear? They didn't care if it sounded tired?

GM: To me, music is most effective in a social context. This has to be self-evident: I can't create that. What a critic should do is help people to see more in the music than they would otherwise. But you can't give someone vision.

The reason you can sit and talk for hours about a piece of music or a group is because somehow a connection has been made between what you want to do with your life and what this piece of music is. For instance, The Band gave me a sense of what the possibilities of life in America were—what they felt like, how much fun they could be, etcetera. They brought a social context in there; not always an overt one, but it was implicit in their music. Without that, there isn't much to write about.

JK: Rock seems to have been fundamentally different as a cultural force in America during the '60s.
GM: Right. These connections I've been talking about weren't arcane—they were obvious. There may not have been many people talking about it or writing about it, but they were seen by everybody, and that deepened the music. It *also* deepened the social activities that were taking place alongside the music.

The vast bulk of rock consumers today want something that's familiar and safe, and says that nothing is changing or will change. That's very different from what my friends and I wanted out of rock when I was seventeen or twenty-two. We wanted music that indicated things *were* changing.

The whole time sense was different then. The Beatles and the Stones released several albums each year; Dylan would play Berkeley every few months. Everything was moving much faster.

The audience now has become—I'm probably over dramatizing this— rigid, and passive, and they don't want to be surprised. It's disturbing that the Rolling Stones can put out an album [*Emotional Rescue*] that's really worthless, and it goes straight to No. 1. And it's not the Stones' fans that are buying the music, but people going for the name and the dusty reputation. They've become this bedraggled myth of male toughness.

JK: I think that's what I hated most about that album: I read an interview where Jagger said that they could do much more than boy/girl songs, but that no one wanted that from them.
GM: They've retreated. "Gimmie Shelter," which I think is the greatest song they or anybody else has ever done, is ten years old and it's never been off the AM radio. It is too true, too powerful, and too good. It will be played when no one can remember a single track from *Emotional Rescue*.

He's been saying that for ten years: "We want to do something interesting, and new, and not the same old thing, and maybe the next album. . . ." He acts as if there's some law, or that if the Stones made a *new* album. . . . I'll tell you what the Stones' problem is, what Jagger's problem is. Once they made what they considered to be an experimental album, their psychedelic record . . .

JK: *Their Satanic Majesties Request.*
GM: Right. And it was a big flop. Everybody hated it, they hated it, and it didn't sell that well. And it terrified them!

JK: *Some Girls* was a much better album. Do you think the Stones were spurred at all by the punk challenge? A bunch of kids saying they couldn't cut it anymore?
GM: I think that album came from all these people saying, "You fat old men are worthless," and Jagger and Richard saying, *Oh yeah?* Half afraid it was true and the other half saying, "Don't give us this garbage! We've been around for fifteen years and we can do better than the punkers with one hand."

JK: How does it feel to watch mediocre groups and albums rise to the top, to lash out at them, and to laud new groups or new sounds, and to see nothing change? Do you ever become discouraged?
GM: Oh no. I'm not trying to make anyone's career. I see myself as someone who's messing around with issues in popular culture, and I'm trying to provoke the reader into a response.

Rock criticism doesn't have much effect: Every rock critic in the world, organized as a conspiracy, couldn't sell a million copies of a Captain Beefheart album. It is possible, however, that this conspiracy might help artists like Beefheart get recording contracts and attention.

When I write an article, and it's a good article, about some unknown group, it will awaken some minds in a receptive audience. That's what I want.

An Interview with Greil Marcus

Mark Kitchell/1984

This interview was conducted in September 1984 as background for Mark Kitchell's film *Berkeley in the Sixties* (1990). It was not published. Used by permission of the author.

Greil Marcus: The Free Speech Movement was a big shock. It was confusing, it was surprising, it was exciting, it was a day-by-day event than lasted almost three months. It was astonishing. Following that was the so-called "Filthy Speech Movement." I'll never forget Mario [Savio, political activist and a key member in the FSM] coming back from Selma to find the campus in an uproar. The Filthy Speech Movement was contrived, made into a big deal by Clark Kerr [president of the University of California], not by Art Goldberg [UC Berkeley student and FSM leader], who was doing his damnedest to make it into a big deal. "We're from the working class, these are the words we use in the street, why can't we use them here on the campus?" No one was paying any attention. They had a rally, twenty people came, and then Clark Kerr and Martin Myerson [acting chancellor after FSM] delivered this statement saying, "We can no longer administer this campus, everything's been destroyed, we resign," and everybody went, "What? What?" Nothing had happened.

So Mario comes back to find everybody running around with their heads cut off, and he gets up and gives this speech on Sproul's steps [Sproul Hall, campus administration building] trying to diffuse the crisis, because it was a phony crisis and saying that it was totally orchestrated by Kerr to get the regents to give him more power and say, "Come back, we'll give you power." He kept referring to it as the "Sexual Intercourse Movement"; it was really hilarious. So that was the first decline.

Then in '66 over the ROTC issue, the recruitment by ROTC on campus. A few people got themselves arrested and it was contrived into a student strike that was a failure. And everybody was going around campus either quoting Marx or Hegel, who says, "Everything happens twice; first is trage-dy, then is farce," or else quoting Bob Dylan, "What price do you have to pay to get out of going through all these things twice?" And that strike was the opportunity for the emergence of probably the most pathetic of all campus leaders, Michael Lerner, who was just a cosmic jerk. He got up and made this really stupid speech with a whole pregnancy metaphor that made the forty-five people who were standing in the rain to hear it laugh.

But the worst thing had really happened on the anniversary of the Sproul Hall sit-in in 1965. Mario was in England, and so to commemorate the sit-in, people wanted to have some sort of civil disobedience, but there was nothing, there was no issue to be disobedient about. So it was decided that people would not sit in at Sproul Hall, they would "mill-in." So people sort of milled-into the building and milled-out of the building, and then there was this big rally. And what they did for the rally—and I don't know if you've heard about this—they had huge papier maché mock-ups of Mario and Clark Kerr (or maybe it was Edward Strong [former chancellor of UC at Berkeley]) and then someone got inside the papier maché mock-up of Mario and gave his famous speech through the mask while the Kerr figure stood by in fear and terror. It was kind of funny. And then, since there really *were* some issues, like the war, to talk about, the person (I don't remember who it was) in Mario's mask, or in this contraption (it was enormous) gave a speech attacking the Vietnam war from inside the Mario mask. So we'd gone from real people to masks within a year. It was just bizarre. It was totally surre-alistic. And everybody was wondering, "Who's talking? It isn't Mario. Why doesn't he take it off and talk?" And the person never did.

Things went on to the point where, except in moments of real terror (of which there were plenty), you lost any sense of what was going on. I remem-ber during People's Park [public park created on university land to prevent development], I was standing on one side of a playing field. The campus was under attack, there was fighting. And on the other side of the field was an Alameda County Sheriff with a tear gas gun. I was standing, I guess, fifty yards away on a knoll with a couple of other people. And we just sat there looking at each other. Finally, he raised his gun and fired it at us. And we stood there, because we were interested to see just how good his aim would be, how close he would come. We weren't scared. He wasn't. We were a chal-lenge, so he shot—not a bad shot. We looked at the tear gas bomb a couple of yards away, kicked it down the knoll and walked off. It was nothing.

I don't mean. . . . The day of the People's Park battle, the *real* battle, was absolutely terrifying. I'd seen a lot of tear gas. I'd never seen anything like that. And nobody believed that they were using, well, first they said it was bird-shot, then they said it was buckshot, then they said it was bullets. But people were coming up with gunshot wounds and saying, "That can't be a gunshot wound; they wouldn't be doing that; why are they wearing flak jackets? Hmm, that's interesting . . ."

It got to the point where, well, there were doubts about People's Park, at least after the fact, or even while it was going on, that somehow this was to have an excuse. After the Columbia incident in 1968, we had to have trouble on campus to show that we were still Number One! It was like *football!* I can't remember the name of the guy who led it. . . . But he said, "Let's do a Columbia!"

"What? What's that?"

He said, "Well, you go from one building to another, hit and run."

"Oh, that sounds like fun. Let's do that."

It was a puerile collegiate competition, which it had never been before. And I guess what I was trying to say to you on the phone was that, one of the reasons FSM . . . Well, people forget that during May '68 in Paris, everyone went on vacation during the weekends. They'd be fighting in the streets like crazy all week, but when Saturday came, everybody went home, went to the country, went to the beach, came back Monday and went back to fighting. It was hilarious.

I don't care how much experience people said they had, whether it was in Mississippi, or at the Palace Hotel, Auto Row, Bank of America, nobody knew what the fuck was going on with FSM. It was spontaneous. Some people who were trained Communists, like Art Goldberg and Bettina Apthecker, had some idea of how you dominate, how you lead, how that's done, but FSM had more to do in terms of spirit with people like Mona Hutchins. Do you know who she was, or is? Mona and I went to high school together. We weren't in the same school, but we were involved in the same high school political group. She was the head of her chapter at, I think, San Carlos High School.

Mark Kitchell: Was she in the Young Republicans then?

GM: I don't know if it was the Young Republicans. . . . Was that her group on campus, or was it the Young Americans for Freedom? It was a conservative group. She was the leader of the conservative group on campus. Well, in high school, Mona had gotten her chapter of this high school political group to pass a resolution favoring the legalization of abortion, which in 1963 was just unbelievable! So there was a movement by the local John Birch

Society, which was very powerful on the Peninsula in those days, to have her expelled. There was a fucking school board meeting, a public hearing over this issue, which of course . . . it should never have been a public issue at all, but it was. And I went, and I spoke and Mona spoke and we fought, and that school board was going to fucking expel her! Well, we won. That was a girl with a lot of nerve.

She turned up that summer on the front page of the *Chronicle* because she was arrested for riding on the outside of a cable car. From time immemorial, everybody knew that women were not permitted to hang on outside of a cable car. Everybody knew that was against the law. She was the first woman who had ever tried to do it, and she was immediately arrested. They took her down to the Hall of Justice and they found out that there was no law. From that day on, women were allowed to hang on outside on the cable cars. That's the kind of person Mona was. And she immediately dove into the Free Speech Movement because no one was going to push her around. And that was the beginning of it. You can't push us around.

When I was a freshman, before FSM, people used to joke that the motto of the university, "Fiat Lux," really meant, "Fiat You," that the university didn't give a shit about anybody. That bubbled to the surface, but what I'm trying to get at is . . . Well, Mona left when civil disobedience went too far for her, when people like Goldberg and Bettina became too dominant, she dropped out of FSM and went to the Colorado School of Mines. I don't know what happened to her after that.

It drew in people who just wanted an outlet for that spirit. That's part of what Mario must have meant about "breaking through to reality." Because, what went on during FSM was real, it wasn't student politics and it wasn't the issue, "Should the university be a sanctuary for these forays into the community?" That really wasn't the issue. The issue was, "At this moment, we live here. Are we going to have the right to determine the nature of the community in which we live?" That's what the issue really came to be, I think.

And that's why people discovered that they were able to fight for themselves and not, "We're going to go out and risk getting arrested for the sake of black people," which is all fine and good, but it's a very different thing. No one knew what the fuck was going on. No one knew what would happen the next day.

I remember the first sit-in at Sproul Hall, I didn't know what the hell I was doing there. I didn't know why I was there. This is early on. The first one, which people finally left after a couple of hours, I guess. After the table thing. Everybody went in to say, "I, too, manned the table." Hundreds of people. I sat around the police car for God knows how many hours, mainly because it was so interesting. The speeches were wonderful. They were great. But I didn't know what I was doing there. I wasn't there because I hated the university and I didn't like being a computer card. I loved the university. I had a wonderful time as an undergraduate. I thought it was the greatest place in the world. I got a great education, I had good teachers, I met interesting people, it was a beautiful campus. I learned very quickly that the most important thing about going to the University of California at Berkeley was to find out how not to stand in line. And I figured that out real quick. You need your reg card signed, you make an appointment with the dean, you talk about how you're sort of sad and you're homesick and by the way, sir, would you sign my reg card? "Oh, sure," he says and it takes five minutes.

I loved it. I didn't think the university was a cold, mean, oppressive place. Just the opposite. When I met Linda Artell, we were in the American Studies Seminar, and we had a special room in the library where we could study, this little elite group of sophomores. And we'd study there until three or four in the morning, when the library was locked and we'd have to climb out of the third floor of the library on a rope to get back to the dorm. I had a great time. The university wasn't a bad place. It was run by fools and it was run by people who wanted to exercise power over people who they hoped would have none. That's what was bad about it. I'm sure a lot of people felt alienated in the way that leaflets talked about. I never felt alienated. Being part of FSM was not alienating, it was the opposite. It was transcending any possibility of alienation. You're not alienated when you're involved in something. You're not alienated when there's something you want to do. You're not alienated when you're interested in what might be happening at noon.

I'll never forget coming out of a class at noon and saying to whoever I was with, "Let's go down to Sproul Plaza and see if anything's happening." There'd been all kinds of stuff going on. So we walked down to Sproul Plaza and there's this police car in the middle of the plaza with all these people sitting around it. Looks like something's happening!

That was not alienating. It was fun! The papers all said, "Well, this is just the '60s equivalent of a panty raid." Obviously it wasn't. It was much more fun than a panty raid could have been. It was, if you wanted to make a panty raid analogy, it would have to lead to a three-month-long campus-wide orgy where everybody's having a wonderful time, which panty raids don't lead to; they lead to rape. Or they did. People forgot about that when they made the panty raid analogy. There were some notorious, appalling panty raids in the fifties that led to mass rapes, covered up. There was even a novel written about them, a terrible novel.

But what I'm trying to get at is that it was an experimental activity in which people discovered themselves, and when Mario gave his famous speech, people discovered poetry, and when that incident happened in the Greek Theatre, people discovered drama, and throughout it all, people would be studying and they'd come out of their classrooms, and they'd see the stuff they'd been studying come to life. Whether they'd been reading Camus, or Shakespeare, or Ionesco, or Melville, whatever. All these sorts of cosmic issues of responsibility and action and will and necessity and fortune, providence; there it was!

When it was over, there was a great feeling of exhaustion, but there was also an era of good feeling that lasted about two months. That's all. People felt very close to each other. People were so proud to have been a part of this. Machiavelli talks about having pride in your city, loving your city as if it were an actual person, and people felt that way about Berkeley for a short time afterwards. People really loved their professors for the vote that they made, and people really hated their guts for the way they immediately backed off and washed their hands of it. But I don't think anything like that, in terms of the sense of discovery, happened afterward. It was a matter of organization, and either something was well-organized and it was worth doing, like Stop the Draft Week, or it was not well-organized and it wasn't worth doing, like the '66 student strike. Shit.

What I remember about People's Park was the violence. Just violence and more violence. Not that it wasn't worth fighting about, but we simply organized around the violence. I had National Guardsmen camped on my front lawn. That was interesting. Another Bob Dylan song, "The National Guard stands around the door," or whatever the line in "Maggie's Farm" is. But again, it was that déjà vu.

I think something new and remarkable and, in a certain sense, complete, happened during FSM. And in many ways, what happened after it was an attempt to recapture not the success of FSM, but the feeling of it. There was a way of speaking people exercised during FSM and for a couple of years afterwards, and that is, whenever anybody got up to give a speech, and Frank Bardacke always did this, he would get up and he would say, "I'm going to give a speech about such and such. First, I'm going to raise this issue and then I'm going to raise that issue, then I'm going to discuss the ramifications of them and I'm going to show you what conclusions we're going to draw." And then that person would actually proceed to do that. There was no manipulation, there was no fanciness, there was no stylization, it was straight talk, and it was presented as straight talk and was listened to as straight talk. That was the form of speech, of discourse.

Later, it became, "What can I say that will get these people out there to do what I want them to do? What bogeyman can I raise to scare them?" Now, that's perfectly legitimate, but it's a change. I've given speeches like that myself. But it's a different way of speaking.

When the Third World Strike took place, nobody really thought about whether there really ought to be a Third World . . . whatever it was, a Department, Institute, I can't remember exactly what was being demanded.

MK: It was an argument about whether it should be a department or whether there should be a college.

GM: Yeah, a department or college. I don't think people thought real seriously about whether there should be a department or a college, or for that matter, whether it should be either. It was an opportunity to fight and we wanted to fight. Now, it no longer had a campus context, the whole fucking country was going down the drain, and this is where we live, so this is where we fought. That still makes sense to me. But it was not the best of all issues to struggle over, I don't think. And that was a very violent strike, because there were a lot of blacks and a lot of Chicanos for the cops to beat up.

MK: I can remember looking at the footage, and it's like a pas de deux going on at Sather Gate every day.

GM: Oh yeah. You'd show up at Sather Gate, the sheriffs would show up at the front of the campus. You'd shout at them, a few people would start throwing rocks, then the sheriffs would charge and beat the shit out of people, who would back off and throw more rocks. I mean, the same thing happened every day, it was just hilarious. During that strike, there was an illegal rally on the steps of Sproul with illegal sound equipment. The rally started.

I was sitting on the Terrace quite far away. I was tired, I didn't want to be in the crowd that day. And suddenly, the cops came up and shut off the sound, and from where I was sitting, I could see the billy clubs going up and down, lots of them, lots of people being beaten, but because there was no sound and a trick of the acoustics, just because of the way the sound traveled that day, and there was no amplification, you couldn't hear anything. In other words, people were being really beaten, but you couldn't hear any screaming, you couldn't hear any yelling. So you just saw these truncheons going up and down, sort of in slow motion, with the soundtrack cut off. And it was, like, aesthetically interesting! "Look at that! Isn't that interesting." Then you think, "Hey! I'm not in a movie theatre! I'm only a hundred yards, or fifty yards away!"

The displacement, the disassociation, really became overwhelming. I think in many ways, it was an attempt to get that spirit back, and that spirit was a function of a long struggle, a three-month, day-by-day, what-the-hell-are-we-gonna-do-now? What's this all about? "Why am I doing this?, or why am I not doing it?" if, on a given day, you were disgusted or fed up.

I remember thinking in, maybe it was around October during the Free Speech Movement, "This is pointless, this is stupid, this is a game and I'm sick of it! I don't want to think about it anymore!" And my cousin from Philadelphia, a conservative business school graduate student, who had no interest in politics then or ever, saying to me, "All we ever talk about is this goddamn Free Speech Movement!" And what he meant was, he was interested in spite of himself, he couldn't help it. He said, "I didn't come here for this! I came here to study business administration, but all we ever do is talk about this! We argue about it all the time. Won't it ever end?"

No, it didn't, for quite a while. Sorority girls, who weren't supposed to have ideas, were yelling and screaming at each other over this. It was great! That's not alienating, it's the opposite. A situation was created in which people were no longer alienated from the school, each other, the world, or whatever. That was wonderful.

MK: I think there's a basic thing that still excites people when they think about the sixties, it's that sense of the possibility of change, and if there's anything different about our generation, it's maybe that we experienced the sense that you could change things.

GM: Yeah, and you could do it right then. You could say, "No, we don't want to live this way, we want to live that way." And some other people don't want you to live that way; and therefore you have to fight them, and then you find out if you can live that way. What you discover is that while you're fighting, yes you can live that way, and in fact the way you wanted to live, you didn't even really know what it was going to be like, it was an abstract notion. And suddenly, it's no longer abstract. People were really free when they were fighting that fight in a way that they weren't free in later fights. There's an old sixties saying, which is something like, "The Revolution ceases to be the moment you have to sacrifice yourself to it." That doesn't mean that it's not a revolution if people die in it, it means the moment you have to say, "Well, I don't really agree with this, but I'll go along because it's the only way to win."

When your own subjectivity has been lost, when you no longer say, "Hey, wait a minute! I don't want to fight about a Third World College. I don't want to fight about the piddling difference between a department and a college. This is stupid."

"NO! THE STRUGGLE! SHUT UP! PUT YOUR BODY ON THE LINE." That's sacrificing yourself to the revolution. Nothing like that went on during FSM. My god, the disputes. There just wasn't manipulation. There were a lot of attempts at it. It didn't work.

There was a horrible little sit-in, I think, December 2, previous to the big one. . . .

MK: This must have been before Thanksgiving. . . .

GM: Yeah, it was an abortive sit-in. It was called off. It was an embarrassment.

MK: Tell me about it.

GM: Well, it was. . . . I can't remember the proximate issue. I could look it up, but . . . It wasn't any big deal. People were called in, people sat around for a little while, and people left. People were fed up. And it could be that the people who led it were so insincere that that was communicated. In other words, "We gotta have a sit-in! We gotta do something to keep this alive." That was the motive. So, let's have a sit-in. Well, a sit-in wasn't a good idea because it had already been done. And there wasn't . . . The big sit-in was not a sit-in, it was a take-over. It was a sit-down. It was serious.

MK: Dancing in the administration building?

GM: It was crowded. I mean, I wasn't there, I wasn't arrested. Like I told you on the phone, I was just part of the crowd. Nevermore. But that's what the Free Speech Movement was.

MK: Why didn't you go in?

GM: Because, at that time, I was just too fucking fed up with it all. I just thought the big sit-in was another abortive sit-in. I thought this was one more last gasp. And I was wrong. The arrests that night galvanized me in the same way that they galvanized thousands and thousands of other people. I was out there carrying my picket sign at seven that morning. I'd guessed wrong, and I found out right away and I was glad to find out right away.

What happened was what happens in politics: something happens, you don't understand it immediately, and that's what happened with that sit-in and me; but then when you do understand it, there's this great sense of liberation. And the strike was just marvelous fun. It really was. I had to spend three hours picketing the engineering building with three other people. I don't think we stopped one person from going in. That was really a thankless task. So we went back to the strike headquarters. "Couldn't we go to Dwinelle [Hall]?" So they sent us to Dwinelle and that was a lot better.

The administration had gone too far. I don't think . . . I certainly didn't expect that anybody would be arrested. That they would be so stupid as to do what they did. The smart thing would have been to let the people sit there. They would have come out, but the papers were playing it up too big, they had to do something. There was Pat Brown, he was in trouble. And of course, he really was in trouble. But that's what it was about.

MK: Well, I don't know whether to keep on honing in on specific incidents. . . . In a sense, I want to get to something bigger, that goes to the heart of my vision of what the film is about. You talk about the Free Speech Movement as discovery, as liberation, as taking control over your lives. In a way, the word that wasn't used a whole lot then—it was too academic—but there is a certain sense in which people talk about the sixties as "authenticity," "personal authenticity."

GM: Well, in a way. Authenticity means, in Arendt's terms, acting without masks, and that just goes back to that thing I told you about where, a year later, someone was giving a new speech through Mario's mask. The word didn't come to my mind at that moment, but that was what my revulsion was about. It couldn't have been less authentic. And I think as time went on, people began to act out roles that they had accepted or chosen, or fallen into, without giving a whole lot of thought to why they were doing this. People really had to think during those three months because it was so new, because it was so scary and confusing, because there were so many arguments and fights going on all the time.

My roommate and I were living in a dorm and we covered the door of our dorm with the leaflets that were handed out every day. There were dozens, and not just about FSM—mostly for FSM, but for every conceivable political group. There was just a huge increase in political interest of all kinds during that period. It got to the point where our door was maybe an inch thick in leaflets. Just one after another. And somebody on our floor wrote at the bottom of the door, "End of Ho Chi Min Trail." I didn't even know what the Ho Chi Min Trail *was* then. I had to have someone explain it to me. And then the same guy one night lit the door on fire. He lit a match to the leaflets. And there was a lot to burn. We woke up and there were flames shooting into the room. It was very spectacular. That's just one version of the arguments that went on constantly. Because *everybody* was involved, whether they were pro or con or whatever. Later there were some people who went to rallies and went on demonstrations and some people who didn't. It was more cut and dried.

The great theory of radicalizing people—get them somewhere where they'll get hit over the head with a club, and they'll be radicalized. . . . Well, there's a hole in that theory, and that is, just because someone has been manipulated into a place where he or she can be hit over the head by a cop, should that person then, on rational terms, change his or her politics? Not necessarily. Maybe nothing real happened, therefore no real change should happen. There was a demonstration once in Berkeley, where the people who were organizing it, who were manipulating it, made a mistake. That is, they had printed up the leaflets denouncing the police brutality in breaking up the demonstration *before* the demonstration took place. And those leaflets were accidentally distributed at the beginning of the demonstration. So people are standing in the crowd on Telegraph (where there had been many confrontations and great violence and all that) and people are reading . . . "Is this an old leaflet? What's the date? Hey! That's today! What police brutality? There hasn't been any police!" That really happened. It was great. I left.

MK: This is all so very, very true. All this manipulation and the media fastening . . . With Ron Dellums [Berkeley City Council member], we were talking about how the media could never get the ideas, they always fastened on the confrontations. They would polarize things, but they could never hit at the ideas that were going on behind it, and I'm sure a lot of people on the left, the Michael Lerners and Jerry Rubins and so on, were manipulating people, figuring that once they did get hit over the head with a billy club and were pushed into a confrontational situation, that would wake them up. There's a certain total disregard of any ideas in there, too. But the flip side of that—and this is so difficult and it's what I'm trying to get out in the film—is, it wasn't just *Politics* politics, it was such a complex mixture of *personal* and political. You could look at it in a more formal sense as two sides of the same coin, the Movement on the one hand and what emerged as the counterculture on the other. There's a tremendous sense in which people began, in something like the Free Speech Movement, to question and challenge one aspect of society and then begin to question everything. A whole sense of politics as having to do with everything in your life, and a search for personal authenticity.

GM: Yeah, that's true. On the other hand, I don't really buy it. I think, in some ways, the counterculture really was the result of a whole lot of money in the economy, a whole lot more money than anybody ever expected to be there, or knew what to do with. I don't think hippies were political. I think hippies were antipolitical in the worst way. They were passive and there's no such thing as passive politics. The hippies were the Movement's silent majority in a lot of ways.

I remember going over to the Haight, once it began to get publicized, to look around and see what it was. It looked pretty stupid to me. It was boring. It was very tiresome. Someone like Tom Farber [Berkeley writer] would probably see it very differently, I think, but what I'm trying to talk about, the kind of freedom that was discovered in certain periods, I don't think there is a counterculture analogy to that. I look back at the Free Speech Movement rather helplessly, as an experience by which I measure other experiences. I mean, I don't reify it into, "Ah, that was the Golden Time and nothing will ever be as good" or anything like that, but so often when something interesting and alive comes along, something that strikes me as interesting and alive, I find myself just naturally comparing it. To me, punk was very analogous to the Free Speech Movement. Obviously not in any structural way, but I found the same kind of spirit and experimentation going on in the music that I found going on walking and talking in the Free Speech Movement. It seemed very similar to me. And the counterculture certainly never did. Maybe because of the dope, which never interested me.

MK: Well, essentially, all that you say is very true about the hippies, but the counterculture is something much more vague and difficult and multifaceted.

GM: Oh, sure. I mean, if you had asked me in 1968 if I was part of the counterculture, I'd say, "Sure." Of course I was. I listened to different music, I read different books—different from the mainstream culture—I still do. But the idea was always weak in its conception. "Counterculture." It basically means, "You do this, and we'll do something else, but we'll define ourselves against you." It should have been called a "Contestatory culture," a culture of contestation. I suppose that's more what it felt like to me. "We're going to replace your culture with our culture," it was more like that. That was more interesting.

MK: In a way, I've had to do the same thing as I think we're doing here, which is to keep on taking it deeper and deeper, and I think when two sides of the same coin, political or cultural rebellion, where it comes home is a very complex mixture of some kind of broader political and social change and a lot of personal change.

GM: Yeah, but look at some of the shibboleths, some of the slogans of the time. "Everyone who's arrested for possession of marijuana is a political prisoner." Remember that? It wasn't true. It wasn't true! "The Pigs are our Enemies." That wasn't true either. They were the proximate enemies, they were the only people we could get our hands on, they were the only people who would actually come out and fight us, and so, if you want to fight, that's who you fight, but it was not true. Stuff like that.

It was so easy to ride along on those poor excuses for ideas. One of the problems with the Movement was that it. . . . Particularly people like Jerry Rubin, who were always spouting these things, "Anybody arrested for possession of marijuana is a political prisoner. . . ." They believed that, and since it wasn't true, there was no way they were going to get anywhere standing on a completely false analysis. The fact was that most people who were arrested for possession of marijuana didn't give a shit about politics, they just wanted to smoke pot. It is possible to go from a trivial incident like being busted for marijuana to the idea that I'm not permitted to live my life the way I want to live it, and the way I want to live it is to smoke a lot of pot. Well, if I'm not permitted to do this relatively trivial thing, what other things might I not be permitted to do? And maybe that would lead someone to question the organization of society and really begin to live in a different way, and to begin to think in a different way and so on and so forth. That's all possible, but that's something that happens to some people and not to others.

Well, what fascinated me about almost any confrontation that took place at Berkeley, was the way it always unfolded. You start with some little issue, ROTC on campus. Can ROTC recruit on campus? Maybe yes, maybe no. What should we do about it? Well, by the second day, people were no longer discussing ROTC on campus, they were discussing the U.S. Army. By the third day, they were discussing the U.S. government. By the fourth day, they were discussing the whole nature of democratic politics in our society. By the fifth day, they were discussing the nature of reality. And that was always wonderful to see people go from the smallest, most local kinds of issues to the largest questions and to do so honestly, with great enthusiasm, to be caught up, and to begin talking philosophy as if it was ordinary conversation.

Marx writes about how politics had to realize philosophy, history had to realize philosophy, had to be the realization of philosophy. And he wrote about how during the Paris commune, you could find workers who had never had a philosophical thought in their lives, talking about what was going on in Paris in philosophical terms, because it became the natural speech. Philosophy was being realized in ordinary life.

Well, that's what was happening here, too. And it was just great, it was delightful! That was utterly authentic. In some ways I don't really like the word authenticity, but when you can go from reading a book to living it out, without trying to, then you've reached a real high level of authenticity. In some ways, I'm speaking philosophically in the bad meaning of the term. I'm saying, the struggle was won as it was practiced. The struggle was about itself. The freedom people fought for, they found while they were fighting. When you're not fighting, it disappears.

People used to talk a lot in Berkeley—my friends, political theory students—about workers' councils, which Hannah Arendt had written about in *On Revolution*, which we all got real interested in, and these were the autonomous groups that sprang up throughout the twentieth century in every revolutionary moment in Europe. In 1905 and 1917 in Russia they were soviets, in Germany in 1919 they were Räte, 1918. In Turin in 1920, the official government basically collapsed, people came together, formed groups and created power; they didn't seize power, they created power, and they replaced the state until they were either co-opted by the Bolsheviks or stomped out by bourgeois governments. And we all said, "Wouldn't that be a great way for politics really to be?" And Arendt was saying, "Oh, this is the true revolutionary organ" because revolution was never able to institutionalize itself in councils, the true revolutionary spirit could never be sustained. Well, the fact is that council politics, which reappeared also in Hungary in 1956 when the whole Hungarian state apparatus utterly collapsed and disappeared, councils sprang up all over the country, took over all functions of social organization and government, and federated within days. It was great.

The energy required to sustain council politics is beyond belief. It's a twenty-four-hour a day job for everybody. It means twenty-four hours a day of arguing, talking, going out and cleaning something up, making food; it means no rest, no sleep. You can't live that way. There's no way to institutionalize that. FSM, by the end, was just like that. There was Haircut Central, Food Central, Dust The Table Central, Jail Central, Legal Central. . . .

MK: So there was a vision you had of the way the world ought to be and the way the world ought to work?
GM: Yeah.

MK: And you decided it was an impossible dream?
GM: No, I didn't decide anything. It became. . . . You can't institutionalize a spirit, and I'm arguing . . . I'm making in some ways a very anti-political argument. I said, I think people were always trying to recapture the spirit that they found during FSM, or that they heard about when it became a legend. I don't mean that people weren't *really* against the war. I don't mean that what we did didn't really help stop the war; of course it did. It was real on that level. I don't mean that some people didn't really feel that there ought to be a park. . . . And the issues were real. I'm not trying to say, "Oh, it was all an illusion," or anything like that. Far from it.

I was down in Oakland for Stop the Draft Week because I wanted to stop the draft, I wanted to stop the war, and so did everybody else. It helped, and so did thousands of things like it. But if we're really trying to talk about what happened to people during these moments, what they were about in a political and personal sense, they were about experiencing freedom, rather than trying to build freedom.

MK: Was it just a vision of politics as constantly being a leavening . . . Leavening the status quo, the institutions, without ever building on that?
GM: I don't think it was a vision of that sort at all. I don't know that it was a vision. What I'm saying is, when I was talking about workers' councils, we spoke of those things as if they were possible institutions. We missed the point that what made workers' councils remarkable was that they basically *weren't* institutions, and could never be. Weber, who we were also reading at the time, makes his famous argument about the institutionalization of charisma, and how charisma becomes bureaucratized. You start with a charismatic figure and then his aura, his magic is turned into a structure, and that structure endures as long as it can squeeze out a little of that charisma and govern. And when it can't, it becomes utterly immobile. You see that in the Soviet Union. Why do you think they've got Lenin in the glass crypt for? Anybody ever stole a sacred relic? All there'd be left would be a bureaucracy. That's how that works.

MK: Now, is this something that you've come to feel is one of the central problems? Do you still see this going on? Society moving inevitably towards. . . . It's not even on that level. It's the whole thing that Marcuse was working towards articulating, of repression becoming more and more internalized. Is our society getting to the point where now revolutions have to be just to liberate people?

GM: Those aren't revolutions. The self-help business of the seventies is not revolutionary. Human potential is not revolutionary, it's narcissistic therapy. That's all it is. No. I mean, societies go in various directions. Some become utterly immobile and become more and more repressive in a very active and specific way, like Russia. Some societies turn themselves into welfare service agencies and essentially wither away and become very boring, like Sweden. Other societies may very well lead to a state of complete collapse, as ours might. I don't know what direction our society's going in.

You could have a revolution in this society when it began to fall apart. If, for example, in the next five years our banking system completely collapses, then there's going to have to be an enormous increase in state power and repression, or there's going to have to be a whole lot more collapse. One or the other. It'll be interesting to see what happens. Revolutions generally happen, as Arendt said again, when power is lying in the streets. People come along and pick it up. That's certainly what happened in Russia in 1917. A society collapsed and there was a small group of smart people who were tough enough to take advantage of it. The Bolsheviks didn't make the Russian Revolution.

MK: In a lot of general questions that have to do with what you think the sixties were about, you keep characterizing it as freedom, something temporary. . . .

GM: Not necessarily temporary, I mean, in the sense that it comes to an end and then it isn't any more. I don't mean that, but something that's more organized around moments than . . . Something that doesn't even desire its own permanence. I've always been fascinated with the way things that don't institutionalize themselves are dismissed, forgotten, not taken seriously. The Free Speech Movement did not, in any authentic way, institutionalize itself. It happened, and then it was no longer happening, and therefore it was a trivial event. Well, it wasn't a trivial event, it was an *enormous* event, but because it left behind no structures, it was easy for people to forget and dismiss. God knows how many times I have read that the Columbia sit-in, or whatever it was in 1968, the Columbia student rebellion in 1968, was the beginning of the student movement in America! Or was the first sit-in on a college campus! I mean, I read these things and I'm just dumbfounded. In *Rolling Stone*, there was a long article by David Horowitz and Peter Collier on the Weathermen, and it talked about how the Weathermen essentially began during the Columbia revolt in '68, and they referred to it as the ". . . first mass arrests on an American college campus in the sixties."

I called up David and I said, "Are you out of your mind? You live in Berkeley!" I was really pissed. Then I called up Jann Wenner, who was *here* then, who covered the Free Speech Movement for *Newsweek*, and I said, "Jann, how could you let that get by? We have our old college name to uphold!" He was very embarrassed, too. But, it's so easy to let facts float off in the air, if they don't leave behind institutions.

MK: Now, does this all live on? Do the sixties live on in people?
GM: Of course they do. People don't discard decades just because the media says, "Hey, it's now the seventies; hey, it's now the eighties."

MK: Do you have a sense of something bigger, that's more than just in individual people's memories or whatever, that there's a sense of something that began then and is still unfolding?
GM: Oh, sure! I only know what I think and what my friends think, I don't conduct any surveys, but all the people who I went through those times with, were utterly shaped by them, and they're still being shaped by them. The choices we make, the rage we feel, the dissatisfactions we have to suffer and the pleasures that we get are intimately connected to the values that we discovered at that time. In other words, what I'm trying to say is, that period shaped our sense of value, what's valuable and what isn't, what's real and what's fake. That'll keep unfolding as long as we live.

Decades don't die because they don't really exist. You know the Flipper song, "Life Is Cheap"? "Life is cheap, it's sold a decade at a time. . . ." It's really true, that is how it's sold, but that's not how it's lived. I *hate* talking about "the sixties." I hate talking about it as if it was this period, this self-contained historical anomaly, this weird time. I hate talking about the fifties. It was just when I happened to be alive. I was lucky enough to be alive during interesting times. I still am.

I used to damn near pray during the sixties, though, "Thank God I'm alive to see all this happening! This is really great!" I used to say that over and over again, like, "Dear God, thank you for giving me another day of life," or something like that. I wasn't really praying, but I would just say that out loud. "My God, I'm glad I wasn't born ten years earlier or ten years later. What luck!" I feel that way still.

MK: Those are patriot things you're saying.
GM: That's right. Sure.

MK: Fine, it's allowed! It's good and it's important that you're keeping it grounded in reality, and not the huge superstructure. Your own experiences. But there's some sense in which that time was some sort of movement, and again, it seems to be so mixed up with personal. . . . It seems to be the most personal kind of politics that you can imagine, and I somehow want to, in your own terms, take it from the personal sense to something that kind of grasps what the bigger thing was.
GM: Well, the bigger thing was that it was an absolute delight in the belief that the world could be made completely new. That's about as big as you can get. And if anything, that period saved me from cynicism. I'm a very cynical person by nature, and I have to carry a burden of that period, because I learned that the structures of power in this society are corrupt, and I'm never going to be able to unlearn that. It would be much more comfortable for me not to believe that. It would be much more comfortable for me or anybody to be accepting, to believe what I'm told, but I can't do that because I learned during that period that it isn't true.

But in terms of what I think you're driving at, the personal to the larger . . . I've lived a very conventional life. I was never a hippie, I was never into drugs. I was married when I was twenty-one and I'm still married. I have two kids, I live in a house, I've made my own career. I don't work for a company, I'm an independent writer. I've been real lucky, but . . . My marriage didn't break up because of feminism, my wife didn't become a lesbian. None of these sort of neat, sixties, seventies stories, I can't tell you any of them, in that sense. I didn't go live on a commune, I didn't go live on a farm, I didn't join a religious cult. I have lots of friends who did all those things, but I never wanted to do any of them and I never did. So, it's conceivable that if you just look at the bare, balsa wood framework of my personal life, I would have lived this way no matter what happened in the outside world. I'd have gotten married young, stayed married, had kids. But I wouldn't do the work I do. I wouldn't have anything to say.

We have to stop.

MK: Let me just ask this one little brief. . . . I just want to get as much of a sense of how I would think of you and characterize you. The ideas here, you're obviously very much concerned with the ideas as far as acting on them. There were a lot of people acting on their ideas. That seemed to be a thrust of the sixties. Were you somebody who tended to remain in the world of ideas, somewhat detached as far as action?

GM: No. I was on scores and scores of demonstrations, sit-ins, I was tear-gassed dozens of times. I don't know if you want to call that action. . . . I was never an organizer. I was never a leader. On the other hand, I do my work in public. I write, and what I do in my writing is I argue, and what I argue about are values. That's a form of action. I'm not a private person who is merely surrounded by books and who writes for himself. I don't write for myself, I write to communicate.

MK: So that's where the action in the struggle continues. In exploring those values . . .

GM: Trying to. . . . My role as a critic is to intensify the experience other people might have with a given incident or object. That's not how all critics see their roles. My role is not to tell people what's good and what's bad. I don't want to make too big a claim for it. My writing is. . . . In some ways, I really do believe that my writing is struggle, but it's not The Struggle, and it's not. . . . And God knows, if everybody only wrote, that wouldn't be so hot.

MK: What I'm trying to get at is, what's your personal thesis? And I know that's a very vague question, and it may obscure what I'm trying to get at more than it sheds any light on it. Well, we maybe can continue this later . . .

GM: Oh yeah. It's fun to talk . . .

Making Too Much of a Song: An Interview with Greil Marcus

Tony Fafoglia/1988

From *Listen Up*, December 1988. Reprinted by permission of the author.

Greil Marcus is one of the original batch of American rock critics. Marcus, along with Richard Meltzer, Lester Bangs, Robert Christgau, Dave Marsh, and Jon Landau were among the first writers to deal seriously with rock and pop culture in this country in the '60s. Marcus's credits are lengthy and distinguished. He authored the book *Mystery Train* which consisted of profiles on such pivotal American music figures as bluesman Robert Johnson, Elvis Presley, The Band, and Sly Stone. What set this book and Marcus's approach apart from others was his ability to place the work of these artists into the broader context of American mythology and culture. He also edited the excellent collection of writings by the brilliant rock critic, the late Lester Bangs, entitled *Psychotic Reactions and Carburetor Dung* published this year in paperback by Knopf. Marcus has also written for *Rolling Stone* and *Artforum* magazines. *Listen Up* spoke with Marcus this year about his ideas on the evolution of rock criticism, the role of the rock press and its influence on the music as well as his views on his own work.

Part One

Listen Up: I wanted to ask you about the evolution of rock criticism over the years, and if you have any idea as to where you think the origin of it started.
Greil Marcus: Well, people were writing interesting stuff about rock and roll from just about the beginning. Ralph Gleason in San Francisco was writing serious and interesting stuff about Elvis Presley in 1955. And Colin MacInnes, who wrote *Absolute Beginners*, was writing about '50s British

pop music in '57 and '58, and writing quite sophisticated, interesting stuff. But people generally didn't pay attention to that. Rock and roll fans didn't read it, and serious tastemakers didn't really pay attention. And I don't think rock criticism, as something that people thought about, as something that people thought even needed a name, started until about 1965, around the time when it became clear that something utterly new in rock and roll was happening, with the Beatles, when there was just this upsurge of experimentation and creativity, a kind of attempt to draw on all kinds of sources to make a new music.

I think the reason that rock criticism really took off then is that people who had been ten years old or so when rock and roll began, a little younger, a little older, were now in college, and so they were being exposed to all kinds of new books and authors and ways of thinking, a whole intellectual ferment, and they were reading Plato, and Walt Whitman, or William Burroughs, whatever they happened to be bumping up against. When you're eighteen, when you're nineteen, and you're reading stuff like that, it's absolutely overwhelming, and it seems to connect to anything, and when something else is going on that's overwhelming, say the Beatles, the Rolling Stones, the Byrds, then that's going to connect to everything that's around. I think all of that came together.

I know that's what it was like for me as a student. I first started writing about rock and roll in about '64 or '65, not stuff I published. I'd sort of sneak it into the papers I was writing for classes. But it's also about 1965 that Paul Williams in Boston, Jon Landau, also in Boston, Richard Meltzer, who was at Yale, all began to write about rock and roll with extraordinary seriousness, and also extraordinary playfulness. I assume you're familiar with Meltzer's *The Aesthetics of Rock*, which is the perfect example of this kind of heedless undergraduate all-encompassing synthesis: it, in a very extreme way, represents what a lot of people were fooling around with at that time. Richard was simply the most ambitious and irresponsible of all of the various people who were doing that then. But there were other people right about the same time. Ed Ward who is still a very active critic, began to write for Paul Williams's magazine projects. Richard Goldstein was beginning to do essentially straight and responsible pop reporting for the *New York Times*. I'm not exactly sure when he started doing that, '65 or '66, but he was probably the first rock fan to become a rock critic for a regular newspaper. In other words, Ralph Gleason was writing about all kinds of rock and roll for years before, but Ralph, a much older person, was essentially a jazz critic. But even so, before Richard Goldstein started writing for the *New York Times*,

Jann Wenner was writing a weekly column in the student newspaper of University of California at Berkeley. I forget the exact name of it. It was written under a pseudonym. His pseudonym was "Mr. Jones." But Jann was writing a column about pop music, about new records, about weird fantasies that new music inspired, reports of drug experiments. I'm sure that kind of thing was going on in other places too.

I know that for me, sneaking stuff into college papers, to see the first issue of *Crawdaddy* I came across, which I guess was in late '65, it was just remarkable to see that anybody else was interested in arguing and thinking about this stuff, or playing with it intellectually. That was really delightful to find that out, even though it was 3,000 miles away, and I had never heard of any of these people, and didn't really understand a lot of what they were saying, or know their vocabulary, it was a lot of fun. And that was the beginning of it for me.

LU: Do you feel that rock criticism has had an effect on the evolution of music itself? Do you feel that critics have had any influence on the history of rock music since that point in time?

GM: That's a really hard question to answer, because it has to be broken down into dozens of little subsections. I know that I have always worked on the assumption that I have no power. I don't want any power. I just want to figure out what it is I have to say, and find a good way to say it. And I certainly don't want to think that I'm going to wreck somebody's career, help somebody's career, or make someone not want to listen to something. The last thing I want to do is lead someone not to enjoy something they in fact already do enjoy. I found out much to my horror that sometimes the people I write about, various musicians, read what I have to say, and sometimes it actually has an effect on them, maybe an effect I might think good, maybe an effect I might think bad. I know that is probably truer of people other than myself, people who write for newspapers in major cities, people like John Rockwell, or Robert Palmer, Bob Christgau for the *Village Voice*, certainly Robert Hilburn of the *Los Angeles Times*. Those people have enormous power in terms of whether or not a band can get a gig. It even happens that a negative review of a band will be published in the *Village Voice*, and not an extreme one like this band is made up of Nazis and they all ought to be shot, it's just a negative review, and that band will lose jobs, or have shows cancelled. Much of it is in New York. And that's horrible! But that really happens, and probably happens much more so in the *New York Times* and the *Los Angeles Times*.

Certainly, I think there are some critics and writers that can help a band get a recording contract, that can help a band keep a recording contract. They might even be able to help a band get a certain producer. I'm sure if Band A is friendly with Critic B, and Band A says our label won't let us record with Producer C, if you can stick something in your paper, saying Producer C was *born* to Produce Band A, that would really help. I'm sure in some cases it does. I don't know if you want to call that criticism, but it is within the realm of what we're talking about.

I know that some critics, like Lester Bangs, really were respected by musicians. What Lester Bangs wrote about a given band was read very very carefully, and often had an effect. I think that was probably most true with Jon Landau when he was writing for *Rolling Stone* in '67, '68, and '69. Jon did not have a great deal of experience as a critic. He had a knack, and I've never understood how he did it, of writing with enormous authority, not as if he was a know-it-all, just as if he understood. He was tremendously impressive. I remember, he once wrote a piece about Eric Clapton, and described him as "the master of the cliché," and he essentially killed Clapton's career for a year. Clapton was so shattered by that that he just quit and said, "He's right, I've been faking it, I've got to find a way to make real music." That probably did have an effect. Whether it was a good effect or a bad effect, I'm not sure, but it sure as hell had an effect. And it certainly was criticism. I think the stuff that Jon Landau wrote at that time was kind of direct in effect. I know that Springsteen, for example, reads certain critics carefully. Whether or not that has an effect on what he does is not something I really know, but it would be kind of surprising if it didn't have an effect in some way. It's kind of tricky to try and figure out how. I think that some writers probably have a lot of power. Not power in the sense of being able to make a record a hit, there's no such thing. Various other areas in the record business have that kind of power. You can have every rock critic in the country write a major article on Captain Beefheart, yet they cannot make that a top 10 or a top 20 or even a top 100 LP. And if every rock critic in the country attacks Tiffany, they cannot bring that record down out of the top 10. There's no power over the charts in that sense. On the other hand, if you take a record that kind of might make it, and kind of might not, that needs a push, it certainly used to be true that a well-placed review in the right spot could make a difference between the relative commercial success and the relative commercial failure of a record.

I think to this degree critics have power: they have an undeserved, wrong, illegitimate, *awful* power to hurt the careers of unknown groups, who are terribly vulnerable. I don't mean that critics should never write negative things because they can hurt people's feelings or even people's careers. It's just stupid that other people pay attention to that, on that level. They have some power or some effect on some musicians in terms of how those people understand what they're doing. It's kind of a vague answer. I wish I could be more specific. There's probably way too much power. Once you believe that you have some kind of power, or what you write is going to have some effect in the real world, a concrete effect, well then, you might start to shut up. You might start to censor yourself, and you destroy your ability to write real criticism. It's a paradox because, on the one hand, all critics are driven by the writer's fantasy that the writer can change the world, and change the way people look at the world, and change the way people understand the world, and can have an enormous impact in the real world. Simultaneously, all criticism is based on the disinterested search for the truth about the given subject of that criticism, and isn't supposed to have any effect at all. So it's a touchy situation.

LU: In terms of your philosophical viewpoint in music, how do you approach the music in terms of your aesthetic? I've read a lot of your work, so I have some grasp on it. Why don't you talk about that? What place do you feel criticism has in terms of music and the function of the critic?

GM: Well, I've basically always said that if I have any concrete role at all, or goal, it's to expand the context or dimension in which people listen to music, so that music can be understood as an integral part of any person's life, rather than as a sideshow, or compartmentalized aspect, or just as symbols, or meanings of sounds. When I wrote my book *Mystery Train*, I was working very self-consciously to write about rock and roll as an American culture, not a youth culture. I continued to play with different contexts over the years. In terms of my aesthetic, I approach music as a kind of, more self-conscious, or God forbid, more professional fan. I listen to music in the car, I throw records on my hundred-dollar stereo. I have a good stereo, but I work in a room where 90 percent of my listening takes place. There I have a box I bought in a department store. And I just put stuff on, or the radio comes on, and when I hear something that intrigues me, or stops me, then maybe I'll make an actual effort to sit down and listen to it, or play it fifteen times in a row, or something. But I just let stuff bounce off, and then every once in a while I grab something and really try and listen to it.

I have always gone on a certain fantasy as an aesthetic. There is an infinite amount of meaning about anything, and I free associate. I listen to something, and it makes me think of something, and I see if I can make an argument, or a story or a metaphor out of that, and see where it goes. Lots of people have accused me for years of making too much of a song. I don't think you can make too much of a song. I really don't. You make a fool of yourself when you say, "When Mick Jagger wrote 'Gimmie Shelter' he meant. . . ." Who cares what he meant? The point is, what's happening to that song when it is out there in the world being heard?

LU: One thing I really appreciated about *Mystery Train* was the way you took the reader on side trips. It made me think about things more. I just wanted to get an idea of why you did that. If you could go back and do anything different with the book, would there by anything you would change? Would there be people you would include that you didn't include the first time?

GM: Well, no. That book is a book. It's something I wrote at a certain time, and I think it turned out pretty well. I had a chance to revise it once, and I didn't. I updated a lot of the back of the book, but didn't change anything in the main part, except to correct factual errors. And I am going to do another revised edition which will probably come out next year. I don't think I'll do much to the main part of the book. When I sat down to write that book, I wanted to write about people who would allow me to discuss music in America in terms of the large questions. But I also wanted to write about people who I felt hadn't really been written about before. And at that time, there really hadn't been anything of significance written about The Band, Randy Newman, and Sly Stone. Virtually nothing had been written on Harmonica Frank. That was kind of my fallback, I figured no one would have ever heard of him. I could say whatever I wanted, nobody would correct me. Nobody would say I was wrong. Nobody would know. Stuff had been written about Robert Johnson, but nothing I thought that was particularly good. Obviously, lots had been written about Elvis Presley, but I don't think anything distinguished had been written about him. And certainly no one had written *criticism* about him, just biography.

LU: Nothing about Sam Phillips either, in the way you dealt with him.
GM: Among certain rockabilly fanzine writers, I was not ahead of the game on that, I don't think. Not much had been done in terms of really sitting down and listening to those early Elvis records, and building a context for them. There had been some good things written on Elvis, and I talk about that they were in the bibliography, but nothing long and extended. And

these were my rules. And that's why, for example, I didn't write about Bob Dylan. There had been too much written about Bob Dylan. I had written a lot about him, and I didn't want to do it anymore. There were other people I considered, thought about writing about John Fogerty.

LU: I had the feeling you might have.

GM: I thought about writing abut Van Morrison as a sort of immigrant figure, but I had had enough. I was too tired. I think the book is now what it is. It would be pointless to change it. If I were a different person, if I had different tastes, if I had the knowledge of music I have now, not necessarily that I know more, but I know different things, I'm sure it would be different. I know if I were writing the book now, I would probably include more people. I'd probably write about at least two female performers, and three or four black performers. It would probably be a much broader and more catholic book.

Part Two

Tony Fafoglia: Do you have any interest in any of the new developments in black music like rap and hip-hop and such?

GM: I have not been as enthralled with hip-hop and rap music as I wish I was. When I first heard it, which was a number of years ago, '78, '79, '80, I heard groups like the Funky Four Plus One, and the early Grandmaster Flash records, "Adventures on the Wheels of Steel" and "The Message." That stuff was a complete knockout. I'd never heard anything like it before. It was so much fun, so full of humor. You could hear something you can hear many times in music, something that is always very special: You could hear the people discovering a form. You can hear their own thrill in finding out what they can do, whether it's with a voice, or an instrument, or a technique, whatever it is. That was just amazing. I had friends in New York that would send me out these records that, at that time, were pretty hard to find out here. But I got very tired of it very quickly when all there was to hear was same guy standing up talking about how big his cock was, or how tough he was. When that was really all there was to it, I lost interest in the rhythmic subtleties. It was just too oppressive. And I think this is a big blind spot I have. I'm sure there is much more out there than I've heard. But there's another problem: that is, for the last three or four years I've been preoccupied with this book I've been writing [*Lipstick Traces*], and I haven't been listening as seriously as I should've been. I've been listening very very hard to certain things that either strike me, or relate to the work I've been doing. That's why I was able to write that *Artforum* column and the column in the *Voice*. But I don't make any pretense of being able to cover the whole story or the whole scene. My *Artforum* column covered a very narrow spectrum, in other words it is what I happen to be listening to.

TF: How did Your "Real Life Rock and Roll Top Ten" column come about?
GM: I started doing that list when I was writing a column for *New West*, just because I thought it would be nice to have a list to go with whatever column I was writing. I thought it would be really boring to just have a list of ten records, so I began to stick in other things that in some way had some relationship to pop music, whether it was a book, or an article, or something I saw on TV, or a comment I heard. After awhile, I really began to enjoy making up those lists and making them as non-musical as possible, or at least as non–record oriented as possible. Then, I began to do those year-end top tens also for *New West*, or *California Magazine*, which were articles where I could actually talk about these things. They would never be all musical. In '82 I got fired from *California Magazine*, they killed the column. I really missed it. So I approached *Artforum* about doing the essay part as a column, because the Top Ten part just wasn't appropriate for them. Then about two years ago Doug Simmons of the *Village Voice* asked me if I wanted to make a column out of the original Top Ten, which would not be just a list, but he wanted me to talk about it some. It was his idea not mine. I thought it was a great idea, because first it would allow me to keep my nose in things while I was trying to finish this book, or force me to. And second it didn't seem all that difficult, it wouldn't take all that much work.

TF: In one of the issues of the *Village Voice* that carried one of your "Real Life Rock and Roll Top Ten" columns, there was a thing by Simon Frith that said that western rock and roll had reached another dead end, and that this time he didn't see any new avenues. It was a very pessimistic column.
GM: Yeah, I saw that. Well, I think he's basically right, but so what? I just don't know how to think about things in those terms. I read the column and I thought it was completely convincing, and it certainly summed up the way I had been feeling about what I'd been hearing. However, I don't believe that any of us are keyed into the world brain, as Lester Bangs used to call it, where all those decisions about the future are made. Would it have been possible for someone in 1975 to have explained to Simon, or me, exactly what was going to happen with the Sex Pistols over the next few months in

terms of this guy named Malcolm McLaren who is going to put this band together of these nobodies, and they were going to sing this really noxious obscene incompetent music, and try and cause a really big fuss, and try and upset people, and the music was going to have political themes and religious themes, and it was going to be very shocking? I think all of that could have been explained by any number of intelligent people, and I doubt if any of those people would have then concluded that an entire new chapter in the history of western popular music would then be written, and that it would affect thousands upon thousands of people, that it would lead to the making of hundreds of memorable unprecedented pieces of music, and that it would still be the basic direction that pop music would continue in ten years or more later. Well, that's what happened. So even if you have all the facts at your disposal it doesn't always mean that you know how it's all going to fit together. Sure, what Simon said made perfect sense, but I think I don't believe it because I'm more of an optimist. I don't want to believe it.

TF: That raises another question. It seems like over the years the punk/new wave movement did have an influence, and that parts of it, the least interesting parts, were co-opted. Even with all that, people still don't want to accept it.

GM: I think that's part of what has kept it alive. What's kept it going on to create new things is that there is that resistance. It sets up a certain frame of mind in the musician and in some fans, a sense of being forbidden, embattled, rejected, and that can be very productive. In some ways it can be just ridiculous, that a band like Pussy Galore can come along, and can stand up on stage and offer what is essentially, from one point of view, a completely unoriginal and unimaginative imitation of what Eater was doing in England from 1976 to 1977. Just stand on stage and swear a lot, and attract attention. That seems really pathetic and stupid. It's been done before so long ago. Forget what other people were doing in other art movements in other decades, it's just old hat. The fact is, I think, what Pussy Galore is doing is absolutely thrilling. It has a certain dangerous edge to it, a certain kind of glee, that I don't think other people have touched before. I think there is something original here. I don't quite understand how you can get up and run through the same old gestures and somehow it's different, but I think it is. What we're seeing now is the same old punk shit, more than ten years later, and there's something about it that is still scary, it's still cutting. It still puts you somewhere other than where you were when you started listening to the music. It moves you, and it makes other people disgusted. I think it's significant that the Sex Pistols, today, still make people upset. It is interesting that the *Rolling Stone* "Twentieth Anniversary of Ourselves" television special—which wasn't bad—they acted as if punk did not exist. That magazine was never comfortable with that stuff, and they still aren't. That is a real tribute to whatever the Sex Pistols were. It has not gone away, and it has not been co-opted. "Anarchy in the U.K." has never been co-opted. All you have to do is hear it on the radio to see that it is absolutely as strong as ever.

TF: When I said co-opted, I was speaking about the movement in its broader context, that is, not just music, but sort of watered down fashion. A friend of mine who was in Britain in '75 and '77 always found it interesting that the American scene was a lot less political, that the emphasis was, like with the Ramones, a matter of harkening back to the basic values of rock and roll: fun and moronic pleasures.

GM: I always found the British stuff, and some of the European stuff, a lot more gripping, more interesting than the American stuff. In fact, it took me a number of years to get over my anti-American prejudice, and appreciate groups like X for what they really were. It took my daughter, who is now eighteen, to show me that the first X album was a great record, any way you want to look at it. Or for that matter, the first Blondie record was great in a different way. But as pure punk, the stuff you don't have to make any excuses for, the first X album stands up to anything else. But in general, I found the New York stuff a tremendous bore. Whether it was the Ramones, or Television, or Richard Hell, or Talking Heads—their early records were of no interest to me whatsoever—the New York scene had nothing to do with what went on with the Sex Pistols, the Clash, X-Ray Spex, the Adverts, the Slits, and all the other groups I love. I still don't find it all that interesting. They had the same name, and I suppose they shared a certain minimalist back-to-basics attitude, but I think they came from a very different direction. I never heard anyone say, "I heard Tom Verlaine and Television, and suddenly I knew that I could play too."

TF: That's because Verlaine really could play. But you could say that about a lot of people that came out at that time. What did Graham Parker have to do with the Sex Pistols?
GM: Well, nothing.

TF: When he came out people said he was punk, but he sounded more like Van Morrison and the Rolling Stones rolled into some kind of new thing.

GM: He just happened to come along at that time. He happened to have short hair. He happened to like the Sex Pistols, but he didn't want to play that kind of music. When Elvis Costello first came along, when I first walked into my local record store and saw his first album, and they put it on, and I listened to it. I looked at the picture of that guy on the cover, that weird skinny guy that looked like he was about to fall over, and I listened to his voice, I was convinced that the whole record was a practical joke by Nick Lowe and Graham Parker. I thought there was no Elvis Costello. I just didn't believe it. That is what punk was all about. The fact that somebody like Elvis Costello could dare to appear in public looking like he did and saying the things that he said with that kind of vehemence, that just was not possible in rock and roll before. It was possible to be a nerd, to be Bobby Vee. But if you were Bobby Vee, you couldn't say, "I am an Anti-Christ," you'd say, "I wished you loved me," or "My heart is breaking." That is the difference punk made. With punk you could be Bobby Vee and say "I'm going to destroy the world and all the people that are in it."

TF: In *Mystery Train* you talk about the Kinks, who started out in the early '60s as a very popular band and by the late '60s had become a critically touted cult act. You used this as an allegory for what has become a common trend in popular music. Doesn't this pose a problem for popular culture, since, as Robert Christgau says, if music becomes fragmented among all these different groups, it's not popular culture? Do you see this as a problem for music?

GM: Yeah, I do. It bothers me, but on the other hand, I'm used to it. It's been like that for a long time. It does still mean something when there's a song that I like, or that I care about, and it's a real hit, nationally and internationally. And that means something different when it's a Pussy Galore record which is not [a national hit]. I miss that sense of largeness that you just felt—it was certainly true for me, even though it wasn't true for my friends who were Velvet Underground fans at the time—that almost anything that I heard and cared about was being heard and exciting millions of other people at the same time, and that was part of the excitement. There is something significant and special about popular culture, and if you're not going to find it in popular culture, God knows where you're going to find it.

TF: What influence did Lester Bangs have on rock critics?

GM: He had an enormous influence, and lots of different ways. When he was alive, there were, and there still are, a number of people who quite consciously imitated him. What they imitated was his wildness, his word play, the speed of his writing, and his outrageousness. I know that sometimes when I was writing, I would get stuck, I'd feel very stiff, so I'd read something of Lester's to kind of clear my head, and I'd sit down to start writing, and I'd write all this really awful shit that would just fly all over the page. It would be like hopeless imitation. There's a lot of that around with all these people writing rock criticism, which I guess is a sign that his writing will be around much longer. I think Lester has had an enormous influence in terms of keeping people honest. He worked very hard not to lie, either by commission or omission. He worked very hard to say what he meant, to find out what that was, and then to find a way to express that as strongly and as plainly as he could. He continues to have a huge influence on people in that way. He reminds us, whether it's me, or Dave Marsh, Bob Christgau, or dozens and dozens of other people, that we're stopping short, we're not pressing on with the subject as far as it ought to go, that we're covering up, that we're protecting ourselves, that we're not admitting our own stupidities, our own bigotries. Lester reminds people not to be pretentious. He was a genius at getting out from under his own pretensions, of hoisting the weight of the world on his shoulder, and then knocking it up in the air, and kicking it around with his foot. He was very good at that. I think the book [*Psychotic Reactions and Carburetor Dung*] ought to make a difference. There ought to be a lot of people who never heard of him, never read him, that discover him now.

TF: So what about bias in the major music publications? Are reviewers ever pressured by advertisers to give a record a good review?
GM: Well, I can't really tell you. It's been a long time since I wrote for a publication that was vulnerable enough for this issue even to come up. I can tell you that when I wrote for *Rolling Stone*, which was '68, '69, and then '75 to '80, that was not a problem, There were times when record companies made stupid clumsy attempts to influence or intimidate us. If it ever happened, I certainly don't know about it, and I know plenty of instances when we laughed, or told people to go fuck themselves. It certainly didn't happen then, and I can't say anything about what has happened since, because I haven't been there. I would really be shocked if it did happen. In terms of writers being dishonest, it is more subtle than that. There are many writers of all kinds, from obscure publications to major publications, who are friendly with publicists or A&R [Artist and Repertoire] people. They believe that those publicists and A&R people are their real friends, really like them, would be their friends even if they weren't writing about pop music.

I think in most cases that is not true. That isn't why those people are their friends. They're their friends because those writers can maybe help them out. I think these people are being cultivated. Publicists and A&R people are very good at introducing certain writers to certain performers, because they want those writers to become friendly with those performers. Once you become friendly with a performer, and you realize that this person may be a nice guy, has kids, likes kittens, who knows what, he ceases to be an abstract figure out there in your imagination. He becomes like Shylock, "If you cut him does he not bleed?" You find out he is a real person. And the next time you have to sit down and write about that person's record, and you want to say "This is an awful record," and you want to say so in the strongest terms, you won't do it. Well, that kind of stuff goes on. It is very important, from the record companies' point of view, that as many writers as possible be disarmed that way. I know for a fact that it certainly happened to me. I haven't become friendly with very many performers in the twenty years I've been doing this, very few. I have become friendly with some, and I know that I simply can't be as rough on those people as I would otherwise, unless I make a tremendous effort. Sometimes it means I just can't write about those people. I don't mean that every other writer would be affected by this dilemma as much as I am, but I would bet that most are affected more so. I know of very few writers that have ever said, "No, I can't write about that person I'm too friendly." I find it virtually impossible to write about anybody after I've spoken to them. That's one of the reasons I don't talk to musicians much. I wrote a negative review of Elvis Costello's *Goodbye Cruel World*. It probably was not as negative as it would have been if he and I had not become somewhat friendly before I wrote that piece. Afterward, he called me up and chewed me out for two solid hours. He was furious. I thought the situation was really funny, because he was not trying to intimidate me, he was mad, he disagreed, he thought it was a stupid review.

TF: I remember him saying at a later date that he thought that was the worst album that he'd ever done.

GM: He ultimately decided that I was right, or that other people who said similar things about the record were right, or else he came to the same conclusion. That situation came out okay. It proved that I could write a negative review of an Elvis Costello record, and he and I could still be friends. But that's another thing, once you become friends with some big star, or some little star, chances are that you don't want to lose that friendship. And these people are rather sensitive, so if you write something they don't like they never speak to you again, so you avoid doing it. I think there is a tremendous amount of dishonesty, but I would think it's more subtle than it seems and there is a whole lot less straight out pressure.

TF: One of the things that prompted that question was Robbie Robertson's solo album. I didn't think it was that great a record, but I read review after glowing review of the thing. I listened to it again, and still didn't hear it. For a person who listens to music from some sort of aesthetic, the whole thing can really be confusing.

GM: But don't you think that all the rave reviews that the record got were a product of people talking themselves into liking that record? I thought that record was a tremendous embarrassment, incredibly pretentious, and over-produced. It really sounded like a solo album by someone who couldn't sing. It had endless choruses to cover up the vocals. Everything bad about Robertson's style, and I don't think there was a whole lot bad about it, is there full-blown with nothing else. I read lots and lots of those reviews, and I don't think I read one that convinced me that the person who wrote it believed what he or she was saying.

TF: I think Christgau was the only one that called it straight.

GM: Well, he didn't like it. That made it easier to sound convincing. When a record company has a press-line writers can use, they're halfway home. Most people don't think. The line on this album was really great. It was "I haven't said a thing for ten years, because I didn't think I had anything to say." I'm not saying that Robbie wasn't telling the truth. I'm just saying that's a great hook for a piece, and that was the hook in almost every piece. Now, the response that you're opening yourself up to in a situation like that is for someone to say, "and he still doesn't." But most people do it that way. I was surprised, but there are just all these people out here who cannot accept that their heroes are going to go away. I was very surprised that John Fogerty's first comeback album was a big hit because I thought it was a pretty lousy record.

TF: The second was worse.

GM: Oh, much worse. But the first certainly did nothing for me, and it was hard to believe that all these people buying this record, making it number one, had never heard Creedence Clearwater Revival. That was another record that was terribly overrated. Again, it had a great line, "The guy has been beaten and stomped on by the record business, by the horrible monster Saul

Zantz, he lost all of his money, he's finally climbed out of the hole, and come back when everyone had written him off, and here he is again, and if you say anything mean about him he just might have a heart attack."

TF: What are the problems, as you see it, with the music media and with radio as a form for exposing music in this country?

GM: The problems with radio are very similar to problems in general in this country. Those are that people are no longer buying, selling, developing, starting, and closing down radio stations in order to make a long term investment, both in terms of money, and in terms of one's community. They're no longer looking at a radio station as a productive asset. They're looking at it as a financial instrument, in other words, as something that you buy, that you sit on, that you fiddle with, and that you sell in a couple years, usually for an enormous profit. There is very little attempt anymore to make a station a commercial success. They don't ask, "How do we do this so we can make a profit, and people can actually work here, and we'll all make money?" I'm just talking about plain old capitalism. Today's disinclination to produce and utter greed is decimating real programming.

In terms of the way people write, I tend to think there's a lot of people who go through the motions. Once in a while I read something that really makes me sit up and take notice. I read a piece by Howard Hampton about songs to be depressed by. It was the twelve most depressing songs of all time. It was great. But I think there's a tremendous amount of showing off that goes on, a lot of self-promotion. I think that if you want to use the word "I" in a piece, you have to earn the right. I don't mean that you have to be around a long time. I mean that in terms of the writing of a given piece, you have to justify leaping out, and you have to see that somehow the authority is backed up. You can't just assume that the reader ought to give a shit about you or anyone else. You have to earn the reader's attention, you can't take it for granted.

Interview

Brent Brambury/1989

From CBC Radio: *Brave New Waves*, broadcast on November 16, 1989. Transcribed by Joe Bonomo. © Canadian Broadcasting Corporation. Used by permission.

Brent Brambury: It was Benny Spelman who said, "Lipstick traces on a cigarette, every memory lingers with me yet." Let's talk about the first time you heard the Sex Pistols and "Anarchy in the U.K." Was that the first song you heard?

Greil Marcus: It was the first Sex Pistols song I heard. It was their first record, and when I first heard it there was a lot of noise coming over from England to California, where I live, about this strange new trouble festering in London and this unlistenable, outrageous music that was coming along with it. So I went into my local record store, bought the record, took it home and played it, and basically thought *That's nice.* It wasn't until the Sex Pistols released their third single, "Pretty Vacant," which is probably their easiest to hear, that it suddenly clicked for me and I thought, *My god, there's something wonderful here.* I went back, listened to "Anarchy in the U.K." and was just about knocked flat. So, I became a fan.

BB: When you introduce this book, you say "Real mysteries cannot be solved, but they can be turned into better mysteries." It would be misleading to say that [*Lipstick Traces*] was a book about music, because it clearly is not, but why does putting the Sex Pistols into a kind-of historical context make them, for you, into a better mystery?

GM: Well, because what I wanted to do when I began this book was to try and make sense of why the music the Sex Pistols made, and the music that was being made by people that came after them—everyone from X-Ray Spex to the Gang of Four, and many, many others all over the world—seemed to be so much more powerful, so much more lucid—even in the clamor—than any music I'd heard before; that, to me, was a mystery. To the degree that it can be made into a better mystery: what I meant by that was, there's a great story behind all this, there was a great wind of history, almost, blowing into that music and driving it. And that's the story that I set out to tell. *Lipstick Traces* begins with music, ends with music, and in the middle there are many, many strange tales of people forgotten, people virtually unknown even in their own time, stretching across most of the century, and even beyond it.

BB: Especially into the Medieval ages. Did you believe, or did you think, when you sat out to work on this mystery . . . that it would take as far afield as it ended up taking you?

GM: Oh, no, not in the slightest. I thought I was going to write a nice book about punk, and I would get to write about all my favorite bands, which of course I didn't. I got off the track very quickly, and discovered, I think, a new path, and it took me back to Dada, to the Cabaret Voltaire in Zurich in 1916, to Paris in the '50s and '60s, with groups that called themselves the Lettrist International, the Situationist International, groups that were trying to radically transform both art and society. And as you mentioned, it took me back to the Middle Ages to heretics, the Brethren of the Free Spirit, the Anabaptists, people who were trying to find a away to refuse, to deny and negate virtually everything that was taken for granted in their society—as did, I think, the Sex Pistols, as did the Dadaists, as did the Situationists.

BB: "Negate" is kind of the key word here, because everything that you look at has this negationist entity in itself. The first chapter of the book is called "The Last Sex Pistols Concert," so you begin at the very, very end and you show how the whole thing was sort-of built to self-destruct, that there was an inherent, encoded destruction in the Sex Pistols themselves, that this was the end of everything, and that even in the music itself, and the art, there was a sense that this was going to consume itself or it was going to "burst into flames"—to use the phrase from the *Village Voice* review—right in front of us on stage. Was that really understood in that concert at Winterland [the last Sex Pistols concert, in 1978] when you were there?

GM: Well, I don't know what other people understood; I'm not even sure what I understood that night. It was a very singular night for me, out of many, many years of concert-going, and I couldn't say, "Oh, this was the best concert I ever saw." It was not "best," it was not "worst." It was a kind of staged cataclysm and I think it was a cataclysm that, after a while, began to go beyond anyone's intentions in terms of what they might have wanted to stage, or might not wanted to. It was ugly. It was red—maybe that's the best way I can describe it. It was scary, and it was utterly gratifying to be in the presence of so much emotion, where you didn't know what was going to happen in the next second. And by that, you didn't know if the song you were listening to was going to blow up, or take you into a realm where you begin to fantasize, where you begin to have horrible fantasies of violence and destruction where you'd suddenly begin to think, *Now I know what it's all about.* Now, that's a feeling that people often have at great concerts; it's this sense of confirmation, a sense of seeing through all kinds of boundaries. And that was happening again, and again, and again that night.

BB: Was it the best spectacle you've ever seen?
GM: Well, it wasn't like a spectacle because there was no sense—for me anyway, and I think for many other people—of watching other people do things. There was a sense of being caught up and swept away.

A friend of mine told me a story about seeing the Sex Pistols on that same tour, a few nights before in Memphis, which I think sums up the way in which what the Sex Pistols were doing was not a spectacle. He said he was in a little bar. That's where the Sex Pistols were playing. Four hundred people. He said maybe two hundred were there to see the band, maybe two hundred were curiosity seekers. He stood in the back of the hall and in front of him were two very well-dressed people in their twenties from Ole Miss, the University of Mississippi. A sorority girl and her date. They were very dressed up; she was wearing heels—imagine this, in some grubby bar, God knows what brought them there. And they were being very diffident, and the Sex Pistols began to play "Bodies," their utterly scabrous song about abortion, about murder, about, really, a loathing for the body itself. And he looked at these people in the middle of the song, and he said the man was clenching his fists, he could see veins bulging on the guy's neck, he could see a vein throbbing in his forehead. He looked at the woman, and she had her face in her hands, and she was just weeping. Now that, to me, is not what is produced by a spectacle.

BB: You went through something similar to that when you were at Winterland, because you saw children in the audience and you said that you had the feeling that you wanted to knock down those children. First of all, you had the feeling like, *What the hell are these kids doing here?*, and then you thought, *I want them to get out of my way.*

GM: Well, it wasn't so much I wanted them to get out of my way, it was something, I think, much more violent, and deadly, than that. The music—

BB: I was being charitable!

GM: —produced in me really atrocious and appalling thoughts. I put that in the book and people have criticized me, not so much for having bad thoughts, as for mentioning that I have them. But one of the things that the book is about is the way in which thoughts of destruction, thoughts of violence, thoughts that really come close to murder, can at times be very close to creation, can lead people to get beyond the assumptions that have governed their lives, that lead them to say, "Well, this is the path that I should be on," and that many of the most valuable and the most stirring examples of art, of political action, often begin in a kind of swamp of emotion, despair, and disgust.

BB: And in that swamp there's also this need to break down, and to swallow. That's the thing that keeps coming back to me when I read *Lipstick Traces*. These movements are aiming at creating a vortex, at being at the center of that vortex. The shout that "I am nothing and I should be everything!" pervades through all of these movements. When you're talking about the Dadaists later in the book, you indicate how after the movement dissipated, and after the members either sank into obscurity or went off to do other things, they all tried to come back to understand what it was that had made that period of their life so exciting and so profound. And they were unable to do that.

GM: This is something that utterly fascinated me, about the Dadaists in particular, but really also about everyone else that I wrote about. I don't know a whole lot about what happened to certain Medieval heretics in the fourteenth century after they gave up the ghost, but in this century, the Situationists, the Sex Pistols, the Dadaists, many other people, had a moment when they felt that they were beginning life anew. Their life, everyone else's life. And then that moment passed. And you can write it off, you can say, "Well, it was an adolescent fantasy," but it just intrigued me the way that the Dadaists in particular—and these were well-educated people, these were extremely intelligent, thoughtful people—had been involved in something, and really nothing more than a few nightclub performances when they were in their twenties mostly, and then when the moment passed they turned their back on it, they said is was an adolescent fantasy, it was meaningless, it was stupid, "Now I'm going to get on to productive work; I'm going to become a serious photographer; I'm going to become a psychoanalyst; I'm going to go back to the church and write about God." And the people did all those things, and yet, for the rest of their lives, occasionally and then usually with more momentum, with a lot of real obsession, they began to say, "I was *formed* in that nightclub. I *lived* in that nightclub. I've never lived, really, since then. What happened to me? What was that about? Is there a way to find that spirit again?" And they lived under—let me put it this way—these people lived under a curse that they themselves had cast. And I think that anything that leaves that sort of mark, that sort of emotional scar, is probably pretty strong, is probably worth looking into.

BB: Do you think John Lydon has that same scar on him today, or do you think that he's able to write off what happened to him when he was a young man in the Sex Pistols, when he was Johnny Rotten, simply by saying, "It was all a commodity, it was all a marketable form"?

GM: Well, I think John Lydon, Johnny Rotten, is now in the same kind of position that Dadaist Richard Huelsenbeck—my favorite Dadaist, I think, because he was not really an artist, he was a noise maker and a trouble maker—was in the late twenties and the thirties when he wrote lots of articles condemning Dada, denouncing it, talking about how embarrassed he was at the strange things that he had done years before, and trying, really desperately, to put it behind him. If it was really so trivial, you have to ask, why did he keep saying, "It was so trivial" with more and more vehemence? Right now, John Lydon is trying to build himself or continue a career as a pop singer, and so it's absolutely necessary for him to say, "That was all trivial, have you heard my new album?" Maybe in twenty years he'll tell a different story.

BB: Tell me about Richard Huelsenbeck. You said he's your favorite Dadaist, and also you said that he is the figure that is kind of the specter that runs through *Lipstick Traces*, that he's in some ways the emblematic figure in the book.

GM: He is a character who was one of the original members of the Dada group at the Cabaret Voltaire in Zurich in 1916. He was the drummer; he sat behind the big bass drum and he pounded it. He liked to get up on stage and recite poems with a riding crop in his hand, which he used to threaten the audience. He was, from all accounts, an extremely unpleasant, scary, troublesome character who in later years would be denounced—again, and again, and again—by the people he'd worked with as, "I mean, this man is simply too much trouble." And yet, while he was doing all these strange things in the Cabaret Voltaire in the middle of the night, in the daytime he was studying medicine. After Dada, after he went to Berlin, started another Dada group, gave even more outrageous performances with people like George Grosz. He became a doctor; he set up practice in Danzig, now Gdańsk. He left Germany when the Nazis came to power, came to the United States and became a very successful psychoanalyst, lived a serious and productive life. And all through his life he focused, with evermore clarity, and with evermore despair, on a few days that he'd spent in a bar. I think, in some ways, his attraction to psychoanalysis was sort of getting a leg up on the kind of analysis maybe he knew that he'd be practicing on himself for the rest of his life.

BB: Do we have any indication what kind of psychoanalyst he was?
GM: Well, he was very close to Karen Horney, and he felt that Karen Horney's form of analysis—which took into account social conditions, politics—was far more profound than Freud's, which essentially argued that the entire world is located in the psyche, and that the psyche creates the world. So he was, in that sense, an anti-Freudian.

BB: We've already said that the Dadaists never got over what happened to them at the Cabaret Voltaire, but what, in fact, did happen? What were the performances like? What would be going on, what would you see?
GM: I think what you would see. . . . None of the Dadaists—I think this is interesting—were ever all that specific about what went on, they would describe at great length the feelings that they had on stage, the way in which they would suddenly feel possessed, they would feel taken out of themselves, they would describe the violence that often broke out in the cafe, the fights, the fights that sometimes came down on them, the fights that sometimes they tried to provoke. But if you simply read the program notes of what was put on in the Cabaret, it doesn't seem all that exciting. They'd read poems, they'd stage bits of plays, they'd play bits of Beethoven on the piano.

The Cabaret, I think though, really took off when they began to perform in masks. Marcel Janco from Rumania made up masks for each of the six members of the group, and he took their real faces and he cut them up, he damaged them, in a sense. This was going on during the war, during the First World War, and he—to me, anyway—made their faces look like they'd been blown up by bombs. People put on those masks, and suddenly they no longer had any responsibility for what they were doing, and they began to make louder noises, they began to recite more scabrous and violent poems, they began to break up the music. And people in the Cabaret began to react the way you react when you're confronted by something that you don't understand, the only thing you understand about it is that it's powerful, and it's threatening. I think, probably, what happened in the Cabaret Voltaire probably only happened for a week or so, even though it was open five months. So you can shrink the moment down even farther.

BB: You weren't the first to acknowledge the connection between Dada and punk, or, for that matter, between the Situationists, who you've mentioned already, and punk, but you did send yourself off to Zurich to investigate that connection. What were you hoping to find there?

GM: You're right. I was hardly the first to make those connections, but I was frustrated every time I would read someone say "Punk is like Dada," or "Punk has something to do with the Situationists," because no one ever really talked about that for more than a line or two. It struck me that if, for some reason, punk was something like Dada, then that might actually be interesting. But in order to find out if it was interesting, you'd have to find out what Dada was, you'd have to find out who the Situationists were, what they wanted, what they did.

Well, what I found—going to Zurich, going to Paris, talking to people who'd been involved with the Situationists, digging up musty documents I couldn't find in the United States, by Richard Huelsenbeck and others—was that it wasn't really terribly interesting if some punks had learned about Dada in art school, it really wasn't even all that interesting if Malcolm McLaren [manager of the Sex Pistols] was a fan of the Situationists, and used some of their slogans, some of their graphics, some of their ideas, to put together a rock and roll band. What was interesting to me was, that here were people— long separated by time, separated by place, who, for all that anyone knows, never heard of each other, didn't have to have heard of each other, who were trying to do very, very similar things, who were working out similar projects, maybe in a journal, as the Situationists did, in a little nightclub, like the Dadaists, in concert halls and in records, like the Sex Pistols. They were all trying to find a way—to put it in its most benign form—to demystify the world they found themselves in. To put it in a less benign form, to destroy it.

BB: Were these movements aware of how malignant the world was at this time? Did the Dadaists know that there were people in the audience who had just returned from the front of World War One, which is the beginning for a lot of people of the Modern age? Did the Situationists understand that they were dealing with a country that was schizophrenically divided by the rise of fascism in France? In fact, did the Sex Pistols know what they were doing when they sang "Belsen Was a Gas"? Were they aware of the possible offensiveness, historically situated, that they could create?

GM: I think that's what they were all about. I think they were more than aware of it; I think it was the whole notion that you could do something that would be so offensive it would actually begin to break down what people thought, and the ways they thought. That was what it was all about. In Zurich in 1916, you could hear artillery from the First World War. Not only were there people returning from the front in the audience at the Cabaret, most of the performers were draft-dodgers. They saw, I think, what they were doing every night in the Cabaret Voltaire as a kind of counterwar.

The Situationists, as you were just pointing out, came out of a country that had been occupied by the Nazis, that after the liberation by the Allies suddenly worked very, very hard only to put the noblest face on French resistance, when in fact the Situationists saw France as utterly bankrupt, and they set out to try and find a way to denounce, to deny, every claim that France and the rest of Europe was making on virtue, and to say, "No, there's nothing left, we have to start over."

The Sex Pistols. . . . I don't think that anyone could have written a song like "Holidays in the Sun" or, for that matter, "Belsen Was a Gas"—both songs about Nazis, about Germany, about the Wall, about concentration camps—without wanting to say, "Let's talk about the most important thing that happened in this century, and let's cut away all of these euphemisms, like the Holocaust, which sort of implies a Really Big Hurricane. Let's talk about murder." And that's what they did.

BB: You peg 1948 as the year that pop culture was born, in the English-speaking world. Why that date?

GM: Well, there was a tremendous sense of frustration when people came back from the war, or when the war ended, and people who had been at home had to return to ordinary life, when women who'd been working in factories, who'd been managing their own households with men gone, were suddenly shoved back in the kitchen, told they couldn't make a living anymore, were taken away from the friends they'd made. When soldiers came back from a life that had been lived with extraordinary intensity to ordinary, everyday boredom. When kids who'd grown up in the blitz, or in England, or who'd grown up knowing there were things they shouldn't talk about, were suddenly told, "everything's alright now, forget about it." There was a tremendous sense of frustration and a lot of building tension, and I think 1948 is the year it began to crack, the year that tension began to come loose.

And it came loose in endless forms. It came loose in the form of rampages by the early Hell's Angels, and it came loose in the form of "It's Too Soon to Know" by the Orioles, which sounds so quiet, sounds so mild, sounds so gentle, but, in fact, was the first time that black singers had begun to reach out to the mass audience—to the white audience, to the black audience—speaking in their own voices, with a lot of ambiguity, with a lot of distance, with a lot of doubt. I think, in a way, that that record makes the vortex we've been talking about, opens up a void, as surely as the loudest Sex Pistols song.

BB: If we're going to talk in terms of pop culture, isn't there also a kind of marketing aesthetic going on at the same time, where people are beginning to catch on to the fact that this stuff sells, that this suppressed wish, this sense of loss, can be sold back to the public in the form of their dreams?

GM: Well, I don't know; I think 1948 is a little early for that. What we're talking about, though, is the enormous postwar economic boom, where there was suddenly more money—more spending money—around then there'd ever been before, when the economies in the West, particularly in the United States, were full of abundance beyond anyone's dreams. And that, in the '50s, of course, would lead to an explosion of new kinds of culture—you can say, new kinds of commodities. But, we live in a capitalist world, and things are bought and sold. And what's remarkable is that those things that are bought and sold sometimes have a power to go beyond any attempt to say, "Well, this is just a commodity."

BB: Twenty years after the Orioles released that single, in France, there came a point in their history that almost led to bringing down the French government. How did something like that happen?

GM: Well, there was in France, in 1950, and I think we can smear 1948 a little bit and just talk about that era—the end of the '40s—where there was something that was called *le malaise de demi-siècle*, "the malaise of the half-century." And there was the sense in France that as the half-century turned, nothing was worth doing. There was a tremendous sense of pointlessness, a sense of despair, and boredom, that even sociologists were beginning to write books about. They were saying, "Something's wrong with French youth. They don't seem to want to do anything."

And it was about this time that a man named Michel Mourre, twenty-two, dressed up as a Dominican monk, went into Notre Dame at Easter high mass, got up on the podium before the ten thousand people who had come from all over the world to hear Easter mass, and announced that God was dead. This act inspired a small group of young people, a small group of French people, who called themselves the Lettrist International, and who banded together because they felt that even a tiny group could somehow begin—and this is how I think of it—begin a story that would lead to the abolition of everything they hated. Of governments, of phony culture, of repression, sexual and otherwise. And so they formed a group, and they lived together. They walked, they talked, they published manifestos, they did tiny little things. Now you brought up a perfect part of the story, whereby a kid with slogans painted on his pants, walking down the street, smashing into people, getting hauled off to jail, was the beginning of this story that led to a nationwide cataclysm. Maybe that's a facile way of putting it, but I think there's a lot of truth to it. I try very hard, in the book I wrote, to show how enormous events, and great art, can begin in the most trivial, puerile, stupid gestures. Tiny gestures.

BB: One of the propositions of the Lettrists was the perfecting of a complete *divertisement*, which seemed to me to be a very vague way of saying, "We're going to undermine everything that exists!" But at the same time, it echoes the definition of Dada, of modernity, that I think Lefebvre put forward in your book, which is "to the degree that modernity has a meaning, it carries within itself, from the beginning, a radical negation." So all of these things have within themselves the ability to destroy, or maybe better still, to envelope.

GM: Well, the Lettrists believed that as the world entered a time of abundance, and as they were sure this time of abundance would never end—that it would simply spread all across the world, that since the technological powers were now in place to banish hunger, to banish people desperate for shelter, desperate for clothes, that now abundance should be everyone's birthright—real culture, real everyday life in the future, was going to be a culture of leisure. Everyday life would mean leisure. So, the real job was not try and figure out how to make factories more efficient, the real job was to try and imagine a life that would be lived for pleasure, that would be lived for leisure, and you could have the kind of leisure that we're all familiar with, where you go into a store and buy a leisure product and take it home and use it, or you could imagine a complete *divertisement*, a complete entertainment, a complete nightclub, that the whole world is a kind of Cabaret Voltaire. That was the kind of fantasy that they began with, and that fantasy, that little utopia, that idea of complete *divertisement*, was what they used over the next ten, fifteen years, as the Situationists, to criticize society as it already existed, a criticism that was probably more vehement, exciting, romantic, fun, than any criticisms anyone else made during that time, any social critique, any political critique, any aesthetic critique.

BB: Did they understand the power of the slogan?

GM: Well, they certainly staked everything they had on the power of the slogan, just as they believed that changing the way you walked could be a first step toward changing your entire attitude toward the world. They believed that a single slogan, put in the right place, at the right time, could change the way people saw the streets they walked through. They had a project at one time—the Lettrist International—where they sat down and they tried to figure out the right slogans for the right neighborhoods. And they basically divided Paris up into a series of sectors, and they said, "Well, this slogan would really change this street, but it wouldn't have any effect on that street!" And they studied that; that was one of the things they did.

BB: Elsewhere in the book, you refer to voices that only have to speak to lose themselves. Is that why [*Lipstick Traces*] is the secret history of the twentieth century, because all of these voices had within them that innate, destructive power?

GM: Well, I think it's more that once a voice speaks—and by "speak" in this sense I mean speaks in public—leaves the realm of fantasy, is heard by the public, once that happens then you really have to take up the question of, "Well, what's it worth? What's going to follow from this? Is *anything* going to follow from it?" And, inevitably, what is going to follow from any shout, whether it's the shout of the Dadaists in the Cabaret Voltaire, the shout of Johnny Rotten in "Anarchy in the U.K.," the shout of the Situationists publishing in their journal, once any shout is heard, if it has any results at all, they're not going to be what you wanted, they're going to be different, they're going to be troublesome, you're going to end up saying, "No, that wasn't what I meant." And then you begin to say, "Why did I speak in the first place?" That's the nature of living in public, that's the nature of action. And yet, all the people I write about, I believe, were *desperate* utopians. They wanted a perfect world, which is also why they believed in perfect destruction. And you don't get a perfect world. You end up in despair and melancholy. And every one of the stories that I tried to tell, essentially you can kind of hear a gong clanging in the background, and finally there's just one ringing chord. So, in that sense, the voice only has to speak to lose itself.

In terms of what makes a secret history, well, if the book is a secret history, it's for two reasons. On the one hand, very simply, there are a lot of stories that I tried to tell that aren't much talked about, that have been forgotten, that have, in a few cases, virtually *never* been talked about. It's secret because people, in general, don't know about it. But there's another sense of a secret, and that is the sense of people whispering to each other, over the decades, more like, "There is a secret, pass it on." Every once in a while, somebody stops and says, "What is the secret?" You say: "You have to make it, to know it."

In other words, there is a sense that there is another form of action, there is another form of speech, there's another way of being in the world, other than the ways in which we've been taught, we've been shown. There is a chance to negate, to deny, everything around us, if only for a moment. That's the secret.

BB: I have to tell you, your terms of references are so broad, they're absolutely extraordinary. You go from texts by Henri Lefebvre and Michel Mourre and Marx, to *Sniffin' Glue* fanzine and to *Five Millions Years to Earth*, which is like a pulp science fiction film. How did you keep track of your own personal sources? We talked a little bit about the research you did, but how did you bring in all of these bits of your own experience to the book?

GM: Well, I try and write as if the distinctions that are always being thrown in our faces between high culture and popular culture, fine art and pop art, are meaningless, because I don't hear them, I don't see them. And I try and write in a way that a conversation between people who wouldn't have otherwise met—the characters in *Five Million Years to Earth*, and the people in the Cabaret Voltaire—can begin to take place, if only on the page.

In terms of how I kept it all straight, well, usually when I write a book I jump all over the place. This one I had to write from beginning to end, in sequence. Otherwise, I never would have kept it straight.

BB: You said the song by the Mekons, "The Building," is the first punk song, and the last punk song, in a lot of ways. Would you explain that?

GM: I call it the first punk song—it was recorded, I think, in 1981, which is, obviously, long after the heyday of punk—because it's so primitive. It's just the sound of one guy, sort of singing, and stamping his foot. So, it's a song that could've been recorded at any time in history when there was the technology to make a recording of anything. It depends on no genre, it depends on no instruments, it sounds ancient, it sounds like it could be hundreds of years old.

And it's the last punk song because it is, in a way, an elegy for all of the hopes, for all of the disgust, for all the anger, and all of the delight you can hear in punk. It's the last word: it's an old punk sitting in his room, half-drunk, wondering what the hell happened.

BB: Do you ever wonder if things will ever be as exciting, or as tumultuous, as they were in music in the late '70s?
GM: No, I don't wonder, because right before punk happened a lot of people were walking around with their heads down, wondering if things would ever be as tumultuous, as exciting, as they'd been in the mid '60s. And right about 1963, there were a lot of people wandering around, wondering if things would ever be as much fun as they'd been in 1955. So, no, I don't wonder.

BB: So, we don't have to worry, I guess.
GM: Well, I think there are lots of things to worry about. But that's not one of them.

Now We Are Engaged in a Great Cultural Civil War

Heidi Benson/1990

From *San Francisco Focus*, December 1990. Reprinted by permission of the author.

For two decades San Francisco–based writer Greil Marcus has used rock and roll and popular culture as the starting point from which to analyze the soul of America. He is one of the country's most astute and respected critics.

An early editor at *Rolling Stone* magazine, Marcus has written two books, *Mystery Train: Images of America in Rock 'n' Roll Music* and *Lipstick Traces*, a book that uses the punk movement as a springboard for a trip through some of the most extreme and ephemeral radical arts movements of the last century. He is currently a columnist for *Artforum,* and is writing a book on Elvis Presley's life after death. He has worked on an NEA-funded museum project in the past.

San Francisco Focus: Most literate and liberal people are astonished at the recent furor over the arts: dragging a museum director to trial for obscenity in Ohio, busting an art photographer on unknown charges in San Francisco, canceling NEA grants from Washington. Why have the arts become a social battleground?

Greil Marcus: It's important for people who like to think of themselves as broad-minded and educated to realize that they don't live in the same country that most of the other people in this country live in.

I remember being utterly shocked a number of years ago to read that something like 80 percent of the American public believed in the Biblical account of creation. I'm not saying the survey was accurate. It was published in the *San Francisco Chronicle* and I was horrified. It certainly threw the dispute between creationism and evolution into a new perspective.

SFF: So our basic value systems are completely different?

GM: Consider this. There's a picture that Annie Leibovitz took, of Debra Winger, in her book of celebrity photographs. I think Winger is wearing a skirt, but she's not wearing anything else, and she's sticking her tongue down the mouth of her German shepherd. It's a great picture! It's funny and it's sexy and it's surprising.

But someone wrote that the photo represented the essence of Satanism. I thought, "Wow! That never would have occurred to me. Satanism!" I might have expected comments like, "This is disgusting, this is obscene"—but it didn't strike me as satanic. But of course to people who believe there is a Satanist threat, it definitely is.

SFF: So what does that mean?

GM: Let's stop talking about this in polite terms. We are engaged in a cultural civil war.

It's a war over values. It's a war that was declared by the right, from positions of official power. It's got to be fought as if it's a war. It's got to be fought with a sense of danger, a sense of consequences, with a sense of risk, with a sense of casualties. Some people are going to lose.

SFF: If it's a war, how are artists supposed to fight it? They're trained to create, not to fight.

GM: Artists need to be able to say, "I'm doing everything I can to wreck this society, because it's corrupt. And I'm going to keep doing it. And nobody's going to stop me."

No civil war can be fought with a sense of wounded virtue—"How dare you take away my grant?" Forget it, that isn't the kind of speech that's needed to define this battle.

If you're going to talk that kind of language, you can't shake your fist and then put your hand out.

SFF: But realistically, how are artists supposed to support themselves?

GM: By living a life of little money, holding down temporary jobs, jobs they don't much care about in order to support themselves so they can do what they really do care about.

That's how artists have traditionally supported themselves. Or they have formed relationships with rich people, patrons, who have supported them, haphazardly, consistently, in whatever manner. That certainly is still going on.

Or they've managed to get small grants from private agencies—something, by the way, that the Reagan and Bush government has done everything in its power to discourage, by changes in tax laws, by making charitable giving much more disadvantageous than it ever was before. The government does not want money given to charity.

Some ask why the government shouldn't help support arts. Well, why shouldn't the government help support plumbers? Why shouldn't there be special stipends to train plumbers? Unless we live in a police state, people are going to make art. It's a basic human activity. It has to be furiously suppressed for it to stop. I don't believe anyone has ever made a good argument that government funding is necessary for art to exist.

SFF: But aren't artists persecuted enough? Don't they have a tough enough time of it?

GM: Yes, there is that idea that began in the nineteenth century about the tortured artist . . . the artist who never received his due—or only too late. There is a mantle of saintliness that artists wrap themselves in.

It's very romantic and it's very tiresome. It isn't true.

SFF: You're very critical of artists, aren't you?

GM: Art shouldn't be above criticism. Art shouldn't even be above vilification. Art shouldn't be above trouble. It can't be.

There is a belief now, spreading among artists, spreading among rock and roll songwriters, that because their stuff is being attacked it means it's powerful. It's not true.

It's possible that coming under attack may lead many artists to fight back and do things that are even more outrageous, more disturbing, more provocative, and truly powerful. That really *will* get under people's skin, that really will be troublesome in a way that I think artistic work today in general isn't. That's possible, and that would be great. That's what I meant about a cultural civil war.

SFF: When artists are attacked, they seem to have a hard time defending themselves, although both the Mapplethorpe and the 2 Live Crew trials ended in favor of freedom of the artist.

GM: Yes, but artists haven't responded the way they really should. The proper response, once they've taken NEA money to support themselves for projects as controversial as Serrano's *Piss Christ*, is not to say, "Oh gosh, I only meant this as a protest against the way religion is being exploited."

Come on! Don't come up with a great blasphemy and say you were only kidding. That's not the way out. That's not the solution to this problem.

SFF: Yet the art experts testifying in the Mapplethorpe trial defended his controversial work as studies in formalism.

GM: They brought up the Robert Mapplethorpe photograph of a finger inserted in a penis, discussing it in terms of light and shadow.

Come on! There's nothing to discuss in Mapplethorpe's work in terms of light and shadow. He's trying to show you pictures of things you haven't seen pictures of before, because he's interested in the way images work in people's minds. If you want "light and shadow" you can do the same thing with a couple of sticks.

SFF: So you would call that a trivialization?

GM: Worse. I would call it an act of base cowardice. Nobody believes that. I don't believe it for a minute.

SFF: So what is the proper response of the artist?

GM: The proper response is, "You ain't seen nothing yet."

SFF: Do you think San Francisco, a city known for its broad-mindedness, has served as a practice-ground for much of the avant-garde in American art today?

GM: I disagree with that completely. I think that since World War II, San Francisco has been a place where there has been a lot of artistic experimentation and a lot of invention and a lot of adventurousness in a context of tremendous contentiousness and conflict. But there's been a constant tension, at least up until the end of the 1960s, between invention and suppression.

I think of Lenny Bruce being busted here again and again, and being put on trial. I think of Lenore Kandel's book of poems which City Lights was busted for selling. I think of Michael McClure's play, *The Beard*, being busted. This is during the Vietnam War.

Until sometime in the 1960s, gay men could not dress in drag in public. You'd be immediately arrested for that. So Halloween in North Beach was the only time that men who enjoy doing it were permitted to.

There's been a *tremendous* amount of repression. I think this area is a place of conflict.

But I think that kind of conflict is not necessarily bad for art and bad for artists. I don't think to myself when I read *The Beard* that Michael McClure is a smart guy. I imagine an artist laughing to himself with glee as he wrote this play, saying, "They're never going to let me get away with this!" Because I think that kind of thing can drive an artist to go farther than he or she otherwise would.

The poem "Howl" was busted here.

SFF: It was also published here first.

GM: That's why it was first busted here, because that's where it was published. This is not a place that has a grand tradition of tolerance. That's just not true. This is a place where battles have been fought over art. I think that's a better way of looking at it.

And I think Phil Kaufman simply has to have been nurtured on that and has to have taken energy from that. Phil's work is a study in seeking out subjects that other people aren't interested in or would never even imagine could be made into a movie. *The Unbearable Lightness of Being* is probably the best example.

The Unbearable Lightness of Being is a very San Francisco movie, but I don't think it comes out of a context of tolerance. Let's face it, the novel by Kundera certainly didn't come out of a context of tolerance either. It came out of a police state, and that's what it's about.

Someone like Kundera wants to write a novel such as *The Unbearable Lightness of Being*, a novel about love and sex. He wants to write a novel about this Don Juan and all the conflicts he has because he's a Don Juan. And yet he's able to set it in a situation of grand political conflict and moral conflict, which elevates his hero and makes every sexual incident in the book seem of enormous significance. I think it's a lousy book myself. I like the movie much better. But the story allows the artist figure, the doctor in the book, to be a hero. And artists don't get to be heroes in this country in the same way.

I really do believe there's a tremendous amount of self-martyrdom being heard today among people who've come under attack either from the right or are having their NEA grants canceled—people like Karen Finley. I think she is now performing as a martyr. She's got herself a new subject. And she's even fallen into the old pre-avant-garde trap of talking about art as something holy.

SFF: But she is an important artist, isn't she?

GM: Karen Finley has an amazing power to make you squirm. She is able to reinvest obscenity with all of the displacing, upsetting, strange powers that obscene words used to have. Those words are not fun to hear, and they're threatening in that sense.

She has a great capacity to make you want to leave the room and not because she's screeching or scratching her nails on the blackboard. Whether or not that's dangerous is a completely different question.

One of Karen Finley's problems is that she insists on wearing this big banner around her neck that says A-R-T. I think she'd be a lot more effective if she said, "What I'm doing isn't art. I'm doing real life. I just happen to be in a room where other people come to watch me do it."

Because her enemies are able to say, "This woman shoves yams up her ass. This woman covers herself in chocolate. And she calls it art. How ridiculous!" So calling her work "Art" is not helping.

SFF: Do artists have a social responsibility because of the power of art to change the way people think and behave? Do they have a responsibility not to encourage antisocial behavior like suicide or attacks on women?

GM: Think of *The Sorrows of Young Werther* by Goethe in the eighteenth century. There was a wave of suicides all across Europe because of that book, because it glamorized and romanticized suicide. Think of "Gloomy Sunday" in the thirties, a torch ballad. It became a craze to kill yourself and leave "Gloomy Sunday" on the record player so that when your body was found, this seventy-eight was going round and round, the needle would be going "Click, click, click," and the cops would come and say, "Another 'Gloomy Sunday' suicide!" I don't recall the composers of that song were ever prosecuted for it.

SFF: Many people have raised these issues with the 2 Live Crew trial.

GM: But that case is really about keeping the black population of that county down, because Luther Campbell, the leader of 2 Live Crew, is a community leader. He's organized voter registration drives, he's organized funding for inexpensive housing for black people, he's emerging as a community leader in a black community that has had no leaders for a long time. So he's been targeted for that reason.

I don't buy the explanation of some people that it's been a top-down conspiracy against the black community. But I think it's been a matter of benign neglect, to use that horrible phrase of Daniel Moynihan.

I think many of the people leading this country are perfectly happy to see the black communities around the country destroying themselves, to see the life expectancy of a young black man drop every year, and to have it be a fact that for black men between the ages of eighteen and thirty—I may not have the years exactly right—murder is the number one cause of death. I think people are very happy with that.

Well, I don't see art reflecting rage at that. And if it were, I don't think that would be a reason it's being suppressed.

Luther Campbell and 2 Live Crew are being attacked because they're black and because they're singing about sex. But I don't think it's because they're tribalistic and fractionalizing. Just the contrary. They have a big white audience; they have a multiracial audience. I think that upsets the people who are after them far more than any sort of tribalism.

SFF: But why these crackdowns, this censorship now?
GM: We shouldn't be so shocked by it. We shouldn't forget that the kind of freedoms that we take for granted are very new. It wasn't long ago that Henry Miller's books couldn't be sold in this country. It wasn't long ago when *Ulysses* couldn't be published in this country. It wasn't long ago when there was no such thing as nudity in an American movie, in a general release movie.

People say, "We've made progress." But progress is not a legal concept. There have always been people who have never accepted the loosening of the strings that we've enjoyed over the last twenty-some years. And they have been waiting for a chance to tighten them up again.

And some of those people are now sitting on the Supreme Court.

Dead Elvis, or Long Live the King

Geoff Pevere/1992

CBC radio, broadcast on April 5, 1992. Transcribed by Joe Bonomo. © Canadian Broadcasting Corporation. Used by permission.

It's been over fourteen years since the death of Elvis Presley, but instead of being left to rest in peace, the King seems to pop up in the damnedest places. That's right; no matter where you look, Elvis is everywhere. In everywhere from baseball games to *Wild at Heart* and *This Is Spinal Tap*, you will find Elvis. From songs by Mojo Nixon to TV programs like *Twin Peaks*, Elvis refuses to lie down and play—let alone stay—dead. There are people spotting him in burger joints and on the moon; his image pops up in comic books, and is tattooed on people's flesh.

Greil Marcus is a critic and journalist who's covered rock and roll for many years, and who's written extensively about Elvis Presley. And the alive-and-kicking nature of Elvis Presley's posthumous career hasn't surprised Greil; he's even written a book about it, a book called *Dead Elvis*. Greil Marcus joins me from our studio in Berkeley, California, to talk about why the ghost of Elvis continues to haunt us all.

Geoff Pevere: Hi, Greil.
Greil Marcus: Hi, it's good to be here.

GP: Nice to have you. Do you remember when it was you first heard, or heard about, Elvis Presley?
GM: No, I don't remember the absolute first time. It was somewhere in 1956, and I had a classmate—I was in the fourth grade then, here in the San Francisco Bay Area— who was a rabid Elvis Presley fan. This was very early. This was before "Heartbreak Hotel" had come out; this was before he had become a national figure, before he'd ever appeared on national television.

And he played his first concert outside of the South in Oakland in 1956. And this classmate of mine went to the show. And I remember, very clearly, all of us in class, particularly the boys, making merciless fun of her for going to see this weird greaser. That was essentially it. But what was actually going on was that we were envious of her for having the nerve to do what we all really wanted to do, for having the nerve not only to go to this concert, but to step outside of herself, step outside of her inherited, middle-class—in her case, Jewish—New York City identity (her parents were from New York) and make a leap, and confront something new and threatening and different. I think even as little kids, we understood somehow that a lot was at stake with this.

And I remember for weeks after she came back, we teased her, and we taunted her. And we also tried to get her to tell us, without exactly asking her straight out, what it was like.

GP: Now, as you became older and started to think more seriously about music and its role in American culture, what was it about Elvis that began to fascinate you?

GM: Well, I'd been an Elvis fan in the '50s. I'd bought his records; I'd loved his music. But I kept my distance. And it wasn't until his comeback television show in pretty much Christmas time of 1968, when he appeared on TV sitting on stage dressed in black leather, with a guitar player—Scotty Moore, his original guitarist—a drummer beating on a guitar case with a couple of drumsticks, and sang his heart out, that I began to sense that there was so much more here than I had ever guessed. There was a great, heroic, potentially tragic story; I don't mean that I foresaw his horrible end. I don't mean that at all, but I mean someone who had gone so close to oblivion, and was now stepping back. That seemed, to me, quite a story. And it's then that I dove into his music, and really began to hear a lot of it for the first time. That's what set the fascination in my heart, and kept me going after he died, and made me so fascinated by the way in which thousands of people, all over the country and all over the world, were refusing to let this person go once he'd died.

GP: Now, Greil, I was eleven years old when the comeback special came on, and I remember watching it, and Elvis—to me at that point—was someone who starred in movies that a cousin of mine used to drag us all to every time she babysat us, and I was amazed when I saw that special because it was like seeing him for the first time. But I couldn't formulate what it was I found compelling about this man. Could you tell me what it was, when you first started to explore Elvis's music, what was it musically that you thought was so unique?

GM: What I guess captured me the most was the sense of absolute mastery, the sense that Elvis could take on a song and he could take that song, something someone else had written, something someone else had come up with, he could take it so far beyond itself, he could discover, as he sang, so many emotional possibilities, and they would go by so fast you would hear anger, you would hear sorts of things banging together. He could put more of himself into a song, so much so that it didn't seem quite real, it didn't seem as if a mere person could be singing.

At the same time, this person, this enormous talent, could take a great piece of material—again, that someone else had written—and bore your head off. He could bleed the life out of song. He could bleed the life out of his own material. And so, I was caught in the tension between the ability to summon and to portray, to dramatize, complete possibility, all the possibilities of emotional life and then to freeze that, to deaden it. And that rhythm that you can hear all through his career, from the very beginning to the very end, that's what fascinated me.

But I supposed ultimately it was the emotional richness, the treasures that seemed to rise out of so many of the songs that he sang, that really got me.

GP: When you think back over that career, what comes to me, anyway, is kind of less a sort of coherent trajectory to a career than a series of snapshots, and Elvis wore some radically different guises over the course of his career. There's, of course, the incredible, intuitive but intelligent young guy who's first recording at Sun Studios; the Elvis who gets scrubbed and goes into the Army; the Elvis of the movies, the '68 comeback special, the decline in Vegas. Did you maintain your interest in Elvis through all of these different stages in his career, Greil?

GM: No, I think in the last three, fours years of his career, I lost interest. I don't mean that I didn't read the little stories in the newspaper that said "Elvis gives away yet another Cadillac to someone he hasn't even met"; or, "Elvis checks into hospital for rest." I mean, I read those little news stories like anybody else, but, basically, I would get the new records as they came out, and I would play them, and I would hope that there might be some spark of life, maybe just a minute on a whole LP that said, the guy was still kicking. And sometimes there would be that kind of spark, and sometimes there wouldn't be. But I was, I think, without knowing it, waiting for it all to end.

GP: OK, it then did end on August 16, 1977—in a manner of speaking, of course, since your book argues that, in many ways, that was the beginning. But when he died, who was he? What did he mean to our culture?

GM: I think when he died, on the surface he was—well, I can sum it up by quoting a very early punk song about Dead Elvis, by a Dutch band. Can't remember their name; they might have been called the Punts. At any rate, their song was called "Elvis Is Dead," and I can quote you the entire lyric: "Elvis dead, Elvis dead, big fat guy is dead, dead, dead." That was the song. A real primal, early Dead Elvis punk song. And I think to a lot of the country that's what the story was, that someone whose time was past had finally collapsed, fallen down, in a sense. I remember Chuck Berry was on TV a couple of nights after Elvis died. He was being asked, "For what will Elvis be remembered?" And he said, "Oh, the '50s, teen music, bop-bop-bop." Chuck Berry wasn't sorry to see a white man who had gained the glory that a black man could *never* have had, a black woman could *never* have had, wasn't sorry to see that story end.

But I think beneath that, beneath this sense of ruin, and ugliness, and, in a sense, satisfaction, I think there was a sense that history really had changed because of what Elvis had done, because of who he was, because of the nerve he had to step out of the oblivion of obscurity he was born into. I think everybody knew that, and I think there was a sense of confusion and despair and fright, I think, for many, many people. It wasn't articulated, it didn't even *begin* to be articulated, for a long, long time and in a way it's the progressive articulation of that despair and fright, confusion and shock, over Elvis's death, in the form of songs, and stories, and strange artworks, that I've tried to follow in this book. I think it's been a long, long story; it's taken many years for it to achieve any kind of shape.

GP: I'd like to go to the moment when Elvis did die. Do you remember where you were, and how you reacted?

GM: Well, I reacted with denial. I was in Hawaii. I was on vacation with my family, and my father called me. I was working for *Rolling Stone* at the time, and he said, "*Rolling Stone* called, and they want you to write a piece on Elvis." And, I said something like, "They know I'm on vacation. Why don't they leave me alone?" And he said, "Well, they want you to write an obituary." And I said, "That's ridiculous. We're not a newspaper. We don't keep obituaries on file, we don't write them ahead of time like the *New York Times* does." And he said, "No, no, no—he's dead. He died. He had a heart attack," And I thought this was a joke. I really did. My father has an odd sense of humor; I didn't put it past him to come up with something like that in the middle of a vacation. And it took a while for it to sink in. And, in fact, what happened that day was that I had an absolutely horrible fight with my wife; I stayed up all night after having rented a typewriter from a little store in the middle of Maui many, many miles from where we were staying. Stayed up all night, and I wrote a piece saying that this event was going to be with us for a long time.

GP: And it has been. In fact, one of the things that your book suggests is that as a cultural force, Elvis may be something that is too big, and too complex, for us to comprehend all in one sitting, one viewing. When did that become apparent to you, Greil, that we were talking about a huge, huge cultural force?

GM: Well, I think it became apparent to me when I was writing that piece the night after he died. I was struck, as I wrote, of how the ways in which Elvis had been traditionally described—poor boy who made good; country boy who loses his soul in the city; outsider who becomes absorbed by the mainstream; rebel who throws himself against the dominant culture and cracks its wall—all these various, conventional ways of talking about Elvis Presley were completely inadequate. They didn't begin to get at what was actually happening in the music, what made that music special, what seduced, charmed, and transformed so many people all over the world. And I've been criticized with this book for saying just what you've said, that Elvis is too big to see all at once, that he is too big for a neat summation. Well, I think there are things in life that simply don't lend themselves to a simple, or even a complex, a unitary, totalistic explanation. And I think Elvis Presley's one of them. I think people come along, every once in a while, in various cultures who draw from so many aspects of that culture and create what you might call a "personal culture" that's so magnetic, that's so full of energy and desire and willfulness, that when it's made public it alters everything around it. I think Abraham Lincoln was a figure like that. I think Elvis Presley was a figure like that.

GP: In what forms would you say are the most interesting or the most significant that Elvis has adopted in death?

GM: Well, let me give you two answers. On the one hand, there's a fabulous perversity to the iconography of Dead Elvis. There is a delight in playing with Elvis in a manner that was never possible when he was alive: turning him into a killer; imagining him as a homicidal maniac; imagining that Elvis is like Hitler. There's a whole sub-theme running through Dead Elvis iconography of Elvis and Hitler; you see it on album covers, in songs, in comic strips, even in Don DeLillo's *White Noise* novel. So there is this strain of perversity, this gleeful sense that Elvis went to hell, that he's down there in hell, and even hell is changing because Elvis is in it. Hell is becoming, to quote the beer commercial, "a pretty cool place" with Elvis in it. The kind of place you might want to visit, if not necessarily take up permanent residence in. So there's the sense that "we can do anything with Elvis." I don't know if you know the movie *Eraserhead*, but there's a tremendous sequence near the end of that movie where Jack Nance, who is the guy with the huge hair standing up, falls through the looking glass, so to speak, and his head falls off, and it's lying there in the street. It's just rolling down the street, this head. And that's how I sometimes see Elvis after his death. He's just a head lying in the street, and people kick it around and it just bounces from here to there and it picks up detritus, whether it's dust, whether it's little stickers, whether it's bits of old records, and it carries them all with it.

On the other hand, I think the sense of loss that surrounds Elvis in death is an ongoing story. What I mean by that is that those who were Elvis fans obviously experienced some sense of loss when he died. Maybe it was the loss of their adolescence, as a lot of people have said, maybe it was the loss of finding out how their story and Elvis's was going to properly end in old age, now we would never know. But I think there's a much stronger theme that I find, particularly in music, of the sense of loss that people feel because they weren't around to see it happen when Elvis was alive. They missed it somehow, and yet they know that they're Elvis's children, and that they would not be making records, they would not be finding an audience, if Elvis Presley hadn't lived.

There's a group from Vancouver called the Odds, a pretty young rock and roll group. They put out their first album this year, it's called *Neapolitan*. And there's song on it called "Wendy under the Stars." It's about a seventeen-year old boy who's seduced by a thirty-two-year old woman, who loses his virginity on the night that Elvis died. And that's what the song is about. And it's about this woman saying to him, "Don't ever forget this night." Well, you know there's no way he's ever going to forget this night. And what's interesting about this song is the role that Elvis—a ghost immediately, he's dead, his ghost is present, he is guiding these two people through this sexual experience that neither of them is ever going to forget, that neither of them quite understands, and they act as if it's up to them to live up to his promise: "What would Elvis have wanted of us this night?" That's how the song works. So there's a sense of beauty and loss and pathos there that is not at war with the gleeful perversity of the other side of the story, but is intertwined with it.

GP: Do you think the fact that Elvis can be so many things in death to so many people is because of something inherent in Elvis, or because of a need in us to see him in so many ways?

GM: Well, obviously that question has to have two answers. It wouldn't be happening if we didn't have a need for a figure who is not just larger than life, but who's bigger than our ordinary world, who seems to be incredibly old and yet to still imply a future, who seems to be like a Buddha, like a silent, all–knowing presence. We need something like that. Those of us who have no religious beliefs at all still struggle toward transcendence, and so we've latched onto Elvis for that reason. But why have we latched onto Elvis and not Marilyn Monroe, or not JFK, not Sitting Bull? It's because I really do believe that there is more of a mystery in his best music than there is in the best music of other people. There is more threat, there is more promise, there is more delight, there's more fear in his music that you can feel. And that, I really do believe, is at the bottom of all of this. I think that other pop culture figures who have death cults around them *freeze*. Rudolph Valentino, James Dean, Marilyn Monroe—these people freeze very quickly into a single, iconic image. We think of Marilyn Monroe, we tend to think of the skirts billowing up in *A Seven Year Itch*. We think of James Dean, we see the guy in *Rebel Without a Cause* leaning against a car, the ultimate image of the American teenager. Perfect. We think of Rudolph Valentino, we see *The Sheik*. We think of Elvis Presley and nobody thinks of any single image, And certainly you ask any two people and something different will come to mind; he is an unstable figure who we refuse to let rest because he continues to embody so many possibilities, and embodies the fact of ruin and disaster.

GP: And the thing that I find really interesting, too, is that it seems that the predominant attitudes about Elvis Presley are more or less divided, pretty well polarized. I mean there is the corner that worships Elvis, and there is the corner that cannot seem to heap enough scorn and ridicule on Elvis, and it seems to me that's probably best exemplified by Albert Goldman's biography. Why is there such a strong need to dismiss Elvis in the culture, Greil?

GM: Well, I can't speak for other cultures. I don't know other cultures beyond that of the United States all that well; I do think I know something about the United States. The United States of America is a country built on conflict and division; it's built on fear, and it's built on hatred. That's hardly all it's built on, but those are essential elements of our national character. And there is a sense in which you cannot be an American until you can find other people who you can cast out of the commonality; that's what the Christian Right wants to do when they say "This is a Christian nation," which, of course, it's never been. It wasn't for the founders of the United States of America, and in law it's anything but today. But they say, "No, you must be a Christian, you must have a personal relationship with Jesus Christ if you want to call yourself an American." Well, Albert Goldman is a real American in the sense that he wants to exclude certain people from the commonality. And he has acted that out by saying, "There are people in our land who are scum." And those people, to Albert Goldman, are white, working-class hillbillies. They're people from the South. They're people without a lot of education. They're people who are "born stupid"—that's how he sees it. Albert Goldman's book is as—the word *bigoted* is not strong enough. It is as racist a book as I ever want to read, even though it was written by a white man about another white man.

GP: But is it an exceptional attitude? Or does Goldman tap into something that a lot of people might have been feeling about Elvis?

GM: Well, he taps into the scorn that so many people feel for white southerners. I was raised—I don't know quite how I was raised this way; my parents certainly never gave me any explicit bigoted messages—but I was raised, I grew up, let's say, with scorn and contempt for "rednecks," "crackers," "hillbillies." And it was something I had to struggle against and fight to overcome. It's a very, very common prejudice, particularly if you're taught that you're not supposed to hate black people—"Well, you gotta hate somebody, might as well hate the people who hate black people." Look at it that way. Albert Goldman tapped into what a lot of people felt, but he tapped into it the way David Duke has tapped into the fear and resentment of so many people. I'll make the comparison that explicit.

GP: The subtitle of your book *Dead Elvis* is "A Chronicle of a Cultural Obsession." Fourteen years later, as you have traced this, Greil, where is that obsession? Is it continuing to grow? Has it waned? Has it hit a plateau? How interested are we in Elvis now?

GM: Well, that's a difficult question to answer. I began to wonder if this whole thing wasn't about to fade away around a month ago when I read in the paper that one of Elvis's guitars, which had previously been auctioned off for four hundred thousand dollars, went for only a hundred and forty thousand dollars at the most recent rock and roll memorabilia auction. I thought, *Ah, the bottom's dropping out of the market.* Then, I picked up a copy of the *Village Voice* right about the same time, and there was an ad for a costume store—this was right before Halloween—and the ad said, *This Halloween, go as Elvis! As he was*—there's a nice picture of Elvis from the mid '60s looking very handsome—*or as he is today!*—and there's a picture of a grinning skull. And I thought, *Nope, nope, people are still having fun with him.*

Then I heard this amazing story about Boris Yeltsen. And this story takes place in the very worst days of the aborted coup in the Soviet Union last August. Right after Boris Yeltsen climbed off that tank, after he'd given a speech to the crowds that had assembled and said, "The future of the Republic is in your hands. You must stop the troops. The country is in our hands. The future is in our hands. Only *we* can save our country." After he'd done that, he went back into the Russian White House; he put in a call to John Major, the Prime Minister in Great Britain, and he told him he didn't know how much time he had left, he didn't know what was going to happen, but he wanted to make contact, he wanted to let him know that they were still resisting.

And then, he put on a record. He put on "Are You Lonesome Tonight?" by Elvis Presley. And I thought, here is this man, at a crossroads in history and he's listening to Elvis Presley. And what is Elvis Presley saying to him? Elvis Presley is saying, "You know, they say that all the world's a stage, and each of us must play a part." And I thought, well, as long as Elvis is continuing to sort of squirrel his way into the crevices of our lives like that, this story isn't near over. It may go underground, it may get quieter, it may even shut up for a while. But there are many chapters to be written if chapters as fine as that are still occurring today.

GP: My guest this evening has been Greil Marcus. Greil is the author of *Mystery Train, Lipstick Traces,* and his most recent book is *Dead Elvis.* Greil, thank you very much.

GM: Thanks a lot, it was a pleasure.

Punk: A Generation Later

Geoff Pevere/1993

CBC radio, broadcast May 26 and May 27, 1993. Transcribed by Joe Bonomo. © Canadian Broadcasting Corporation. Used by permission.

Part One

Geoff Pevere: Hi, I'm Geoff Pevere. The myth of punk music goes like this: it burned bright; it burned hard; and it burned out, and faster than you can say "never mind the bollocks." The truth is a little more complicated; the truth has to do with the spirit and an aftershock whose reverberations are still being felt. Punk, a generation later, tonight on *Prime Time*.

Way back in 1964, the British Invasion brought us the Beatles and many songs of hope and utopianism. In 1977 another British invasion brought us the Sex Pistols, and that invasion brought songs that were about anything but hope; it brought songs about, among other things, anarchy in the U.K. . . . When the Sex Pistols self-destructed after their American tour in 1978, some thought punk was dead; others believed that the safety pins had simply been sterilized, and punk domesticated as something called New Wave. Musically speaking, punk did live on in the sounds of the Clash, the Gang of Four, Essential Logic, Elvis Costello, and even Public Image, Ltd., the band that Johnny Rotten formed after the Sex Pistols spun apart. But punk was always about something more than the music; it was an attitude, a gesture of anarchy, and it affected the way we saw, and the way we were to see, pop music, politics, and culture.

Greil Marcus is a critic of pop music, politics, and culture, and he has written extensively about punk. His book *Lipstick Traces* stalked the spiritual roots of punk throughout the twentieth century. Greil's new book, *Ranters & Crowd Pleasers*, a collection of writings, articles, and essays, chronicles the lasting ethos of punk in both mainstream and alternative music, in

literature, and in politics. Greil Marcus will join me for the next two nights from our studio in Berkeley to talk about the punk aesthetic today. Hi, Greil.
Greil Marcus: It's good to be with you again.

GP: Well, it's nice to have you again. In *Lipstick Traces*, as we talked about, you traced what I have called the spiritual roots of punk, so what was left that you needed to explore about punk with *Ranters & Crowd Pleasers*?
GM: Well, *Lipstick Traces* started out as a book about punk; it was going to begin with the Sex Pistols and then "cover the territory," so to speak, and I would end up writing about all the bands that seemed to me doing such remarkable things: the Gang of Four; the Delta Five; Essential Logic; Kleenex and Lilliput, some of them very obscure bands from England and Europe but groups that seemed to me to be finding a completely new voice. Well, it turned out with *Lipstick Traces* the book became about something very different; it became a whole revision of modern history.

This book is really what I left out of *Lipstick Traces*. And that is for the most part, music. On the other hand, it's a much more explicitly day-by-day book about the period in which this music was being made—the late '70s, some in the '90s, but mostly the book covers the 1980s—and so the major figures in this book, along with the Clash, and the Gang of Four, particularly Elvis Costello, the people whose careers are really followed are Margaret Thatcher and Ronald Reagan, because to me they were the dominant pop figures of that decade, as well as, of course, the dominant political figures.

GP: We'll trace that in detail as we go along, but I guess a fairly elementary question: why do you think punk is so important?
GM: I think punk is, if not the only, the primary efflorescence of a freedom of spirit in the last fifteen, twenty years, in the culture, and in politics, and in social life. It is the one sign system that's come into being that tells people things don't have to be as they seem, you don't have to be what people have always expected you to be, new things, different things, are possible, and if you strike out on that trail of difference, of trying to live in a different manner, your life is going to be rougher, you may fail, you may be destroyed, or you may break through a wall that, before you heard, let's say the Melvins, as it was for Kurt Cobain of Nirvana in his little home town of Aberdeen, Washington, you will break through a wall you didn't even know was there.

GP: Usually, in conventional musical history, punk seems to be nicely compartmentalized, usually sometimes it's '76 to '79, sometimes it's just

'77/'78—but it's clearly not that. Tell me in what ways do you think punk has continued to manifest itself in culture over the years.

GM: Well, what I found looking at bands particularly in the last five, six years is that punk is never revived, it's not a period style. It's something that's always rediscovered, like a purloined letter, like a family heirloom in a chest in the attic or in the basement.

GP: When punk manifests itself today what does it have to say about contemporary culture, as opposed to the culture of the late '70s?

GM: I think that depends almost completely on who you're talking about. What is going on with Nirvana? Here is Kurt Cobain and Kris Novoselic and David Grohl of Nirvana, multimillionaires, putting on concerts to aid rape victims in Bosnia, not something that anyone else has thought to do, including our government. And yet here is Nirvana looking at their enormous success of *Nevermind* and saying, "Oh my God, the wrong people are listening to our music." I'm not saying this is a good attitude or a bad attitude, simply that it's there. And their response is to say, "When we sold four million, five million, ten million copies of *Nevermind*, we must have been doing something right, but we were probably also doing something wrong. But if we now have this audience, let's see how far we can go with it." So they have gone out and with Steve Albini made a very brutal punk record, that's how they've described it. Steve Albini said, "Every time we had a choice between going harsher and going softer, we went as harsh as we could." Well, now Geffen Records, the band's label, will not release this record. They say the band's committing commercial suicide. There's no question that the band wants to risk committing commercial suicide. They want to see what's going to happen. They're willing to take that chance. They're also willing to bet that maybe the audience out there that they've discovered all over the world can go farther than anybody thinks; they aren't talking down to their audience.

GP: I see. I found it interesting that *Ranters & Crowd Pleasers*, in fact, begins with a review of the Rolling Stones' *Let It Bleed* album, a review written in 1969. Now tell me, you describe this as the last music of the '60s. First of all, why does this qualify as the last music of the '60s, and why did you feel the need to start your exploration of punk with 1969's album *Let It Bleed*?

GM: There are a whole lot of reasons. Calling *Let It Bleed* the last music of the '60s was not a great stroke of critical acumen; the record was released in November or December of 1969. I know people can say a record released in 1976 or for that matter 1962 was the last music of the '60s, but this was definitely congruent. But that record was full of fear, full of trembling, full of dangers, full of premonitions of disaster; a whole utopian decade was heading for a smash-up. That's what that record said to me the very first time I heard it, which was before the infamous Altamont concert, not afterwards. I sat down; I wrote a piece about that record which was published just before the Altamont concert and it was one of the few times in the years that I've written about pop music where I actually made a prediction and was right. And I said, "What this record says is that the coming years are going to be very desperate, and it's going to change our lives in ways that none of us are going to want." And I was right. Maybe it didn't take great genius to see that, but I've never been much good at predicting the future.

Well, punk was in great degree, particularly when it began, a very self-conscious reaction to certain aspects of the '60s: the utopianism; the naiveté; the love-will-solve-all-problems; the handing around of flowers; the whole idea of the Summer of Love, which—rather brilliantly, in retrospect, anyway—if 1967 was the Summer of Love, people began to call 1977 the Summer of Hate.

I felt *Let It Bleed* by the Rolling Stones was not just a '60s album, it was an opening into the future, and it sort of threw open the door, and a lot of people turned around and said, "Oh my God, we don't want to look at that!" and immediately ran straight toward James Taylor and got through the '70s very nicely with him. And others looked at the horrors waiting in that world the Rolling Stones were singing about, playing about, and said, "OK, show me what you got." And we had to wait a while in politics and in culture to find out what that period got. So it seemed to me, this was a good beginning. Kick it off roughly, kick it off with the best of the past. I really do believe that "Gimmie Shelter," the first cut on *Let It Bleed*, is one of the four or five absolutely supreme rock and roll recordings ever made. I change my mind every once in a while about the other ones, but it will never be superseded. Whatever the form can be, this record is.

GP: Another album came out in 1969 that you heard echoes of years later in the music of the Clash, and others heard it in the sounds of Essential Logic, and that was Captain Beefheart's *Trout Mask Replica*. Greil, how significant was that record in sort of laying the groundwork for what you might eventually call punk aesthetic?

GM: Well, a lot of the early punks were the sort of people who were very self-consciously outsiders in their grade schools, and their high schools, at their places of work. They always had to pick something to like that nobody else liked. They had to dress differently, they had to talk differently. They weren't joiners, they weren't clannish people. They were the kind of people who stay in their rooms and never come out, except years later to shock the world as Johnny Rotten, or maybe mow down fifteen people in the street. Not necessarily a fine dividing line.

GP: Right.

GM: Well, one of the most willfully obscure, hard to listen to, and pompously avant-garde records of the 1960s or '70s, or anytime, was Captain Beefheart's *Trout Mask Replica*. If you listen to it you would find a whole world of voices speaking to you from all different directions, and you might feel both exhilarated and completely lost. It's a real masterwork.

On the other hand, I was playing it one night in 1969 and my wife swears it's what brought on a kidney stone attack. So it's not an easy record to listen to, but it was a huge favorite, it was a talisman in the pre-punk days, to Joe Strummer of the Clash, to Johnny Rotten. Today it's a record that Polly Jean Harvey of the band PJ Harvey, who's twenty-three years old—in other words who's considerably younger than the record itself—looks to as almost a text of what music can be, and where she might someday arrive. So, it's both the oddness and the determined refusal of any kind of normality in the music of *Trout Mask Replica* that makes it attractive to people. But also the fact that if you put it on at a party, half the people would leave. And you'd find out who your real friends are. That makes it punk as much as anything.

GP: Now, the word "solipsism"—which is, of course, where the Self becomes the preeminent reality—comes up a lot in the book, Greil. How did solipsism manifest itself in the pop culture of the '70s?

GM: Well the most obvious and really obnoxious way that it manifested itself was with the dread singer-songwriter movement of the early and mid '70s. I don't know if you remember that the Taylor family actually made the cover of *Time* magazine—James, and Alex, and I forget the other ones, I think there were two more—and they were called the Royal Family of Rock. And the idea was that these very rich, very confused, in some cases mentally unstable, white, extremely middle-class people were summing up the new America in the modern age. It was sort of a premonition of our present-day therapy-mania, I suppose. And you had a lot of people sitting around with very quiet music singing about their joys and sorrows.

And I don't mean that every piece of music made in the style was worthless, but it gave you the feeling that there was no larger world, that the world had been reduced to yourself and, should you deign to recognize them, your family, your close friends. That was it. And for some of us we wondered what we had done to be tortured like this for so long. And I think that the ultimate expression of this sort of solipsism came on a mass level, a great contradiction. Solipsism really means that you are the only person in the world. You *are* the world. Well, the ultimate in solipsism, of course, came with the great charity rock and roll events of the late '70s and early '80s, reaching its ultimate height with *we* are the world. You get a bunch of Hollywood stars, movie and music stars, together in a recording studio, and they announce that *they* are the World. It was just shocking, I couldn't believe it, the arrogance of it.

GP: Yeah.

GM: And the people having no sense that there was something really quite horrible about talking that way. The MUSE Concerts, for Musicians United for Safe Energy, really kicked this off. It was supposed to be about alerting people to the dangers of nuclear power; in fact it was about allowing the privileged among us—that is, whoever bought a ticket to the movie and the concerts—to bask in the glow of the likes of Carly Simon and Graham Nash, James Taylor, to be in the same room with these people. And the solipsism which came through there was in the notion that "if these people were worried about nuclear power, these rich, famous people, you should be too." Now that's not my idea of how politics changes countries, changes lives. That's demagoguery, and I don't question anybody's motives for engaging in these activities, and I suppose if "We Are the World" saved one life in Africa it was worth whatever cultural corruption it spread. And yet there was a kind of sickness, of presumptuousness, that ultimately excluded so many people from the world, even as the pretense was followed that the world was being saved.

With "We Are the World" it was very simple: if you bought the record, you too could become part of the world.

GP: Yeah, well I remember 1973. I was, like, sixteen years old, and I remember believing that it was Harry Chapin who had driven me to buy the first New York Dolls album, so I was primed a few years later, anyway.

GM: So, Harry Chapin didn't die in vain.

GP: [laughs] No, he did not die in vain, precisely. Now, by the '70s, though, of course, the process you're describing sort of stemmed from the fact that rock and roll had become a *huge* corporate enterprise. In one essay you say what it lacked was a center. What happened? I mean, how did rock audiences begin then to fragment in the '70s, Greil?

GM: Well, they fragmented for a number of reasons. The clearest reason is age. The rock and roll audience got bigger and bigger and bigger, and one of the dynamics of rock and roll, of course, is young people determined to have their own language, their own music, their own culture. In order to discover or invent that, they have to reject someone else's culture. But now this little dynamic is taking place *within* the arena of rock and roll; rock and roll is no longer something new, it's no longer something outside. So, it has to rebel against itself, and maybe in many, many different ways, in many areas, that causes a kind of fragmentation. When there is no figure that's number one, so present that everyone feels he or she has to have an opinion about this figure, then people cease to talk to each other in pop terms. The Beatles broke up, there was no longer any central figure of that sort.

We saw a weird phenomena in the mid '80s when over and over again there *was* such a central figure that everyone was talking about, and yet the other aspect of these central figures like Elvis and the Beatles in the past had been that they instantly inspired countless people to go out, make their own music, write their own books, take their own stands, say "I want to be like Elvis," and then suddenly discover what it means to be like themselves. That aspect of self-discovery, of imitation and self-discovery, was missing with the central figures in the '80s, and by those I'm talking about Michael Jackson, Prince, Madonna, Bruce Springsteen, people who were instantly publicized, overwhelmingly, so that everyone knew who they were, everyone had an opinion—"She's a slut, she's a goddess, he's a creep, he's the savior of rock and roll"—people could argue about that, but yet, those phenomena remained sterile.

There was only one Prince, there was only one Bruce, there was only one Madonna, there as only one Michael Jackson. These figures were not fecund in a way that the Beatles or Elvis or the Sex Pistols were; they were not *inspiring*. They created passivity in their response, rather than willfulness and desire.

GP: By the time that it had arrived and we were in the midst of that moment, how long did it take before punk's influence and impact would be felt on mainstream culture? How long did it take, and where was it first felt?

GM: Well listen, I first heard about punk turning on the television one Sunday afternoon, it must have been in January of 1977, maybe it was late '76, and there was a little news feature and the essence of it was, *Teenagers do even weirder new things in London,* and it showed pictures of kids with strange hair and safety pins through their cheeks, and stuff like that, and said [adopts mock newscaster voice] "This is a new cult known as Punk, the leaders are called the Sex Pistols." And so I said, "Oh that looks pretty strange." And I forgot all about it, until "Anarchy in the U.K." arrived in my local record shop a week or so later for five dollars for a single, and I said, "Why is that so expensive?" and they said, "It's been banned in England," and I said, "Oh it's been banned, I better hear it."

Punk *immediately* had an impact on mass culture, as "teenagers do even weirder new things"—on that level. But I think, in essence, punk has *never* had an impact on mass culture because mass culture is simply not equipped to understand, or simply respond to, anything like punk as anything more than a fad. Punk has had its effect under the rocks, after the rains, sprouting up like mushrooms, in the shadows, and I assume it will continue to function that way. There is a way in which if *Nevermind* by Nirvana is mass culture, the punk aesthetic—and this may be completely wrongheaded—says, "Well, we gotta steal it back." So I don't think that's really where it happens.

GP: In the late '70s many people were saying that bands like Fleetwood Mac were the reason why punk needed to exist. Punk was an antidote for the kind of music Fleetwood Mac was making, and yet you make a very interesting claim in your book for the *Tusk* album being a response to punk. Tell me more about that.

GM: Well, I think throwing Fleetwood Mac on the same garbage pile as James Taylor and Carly Simon is ludicrous.

GP: I agree.

GM: Fleetwood Mac began as a blues band; they never lost their edge, even during their sort of California period with Bob Welch, when he was singing all these songs about the Bermuda Triangle and stuff like that.

But in 1977, that's the year that the Sex Pistols really break as an international act of terrorism. That's the Sex Pistols' year. And in some ways the toughest record of that year is "Go Your Own Way," by Fleetwood Mac. And it was a flop; the single did not make it. It followed up the album *Fleetwood Mac* which was a big hit; it was the first single off the album *Rumors,* and it stiffed. It was as harsh and explosive and confusing a piece of hard rock as anyone had heard since the Who. After that, after *Rumors* then becomes a huge album, sells twenty million copies or whatever it sold, Fleetwood Mac comes along with *Tusk*. A two record set, the typical thing a big, mainstream rock band does after they've had a big hit; they get self-indulgent and sloppy. *Tusk's* first single is the title song "Tusk." It was recorded with the UCLA marching band, sounds like they recorded backwards underwater. There's just bits and pieces of tape loops flying around, and it sounds like this group of amateur musicians lurching toward a song that stays out of reach laughing at them, saying *Can't catch me, can't catch me!* This is what they released as a single? And they did what Nirvana is now trying to do; they said, "Can you keep up with us? Can we keep up with you? We're gonna try something radical and different." Lindsay Buckingham, who by that time was the real leader of Fleetwood Mac, had decided that what he was hearing in punk was what drew him to rock and roll in the first place, and here he was now a multimillionaire, a mainstream musician, who's expected to do exactly what he did the time before, and he did his best to confound those expectations.

I find this particularly interesting because I know something about the world Lindsay Buckingham came out of. We went to the same high school. I went a number of years earlier; I went to school with his brothers. His brothers were swimming stars and class presidents; they were golden boys, and Lindsay Buckingham, though you may say he's a golden boy, too—he's made all this money, he's rich and famous—he was not a golden boy in that family. He's the one who stepped outside of the future that was prepared for him in that high school, as a class president which he didn't become—this was a family dynasty, you have to understand—of the future in business, which he turned his back on and he became, for a number of years anyway, a failed, starving musician. That's not what he was raised to be. So that same spirit, coming out of this very comfortable, very appealing, really good place to go to school and to grow up—Menlo Park, California; Atherton, California—this guy had a "no" in his soul already, and in a way what *Tusk* was about was his attempt to discover that "no." Whether or not he found it, I'm not sure. But it was a poke in the eye with a sharp stick to anybody who thought that they had this band pinned down. And I think that "we really don't care" attitude was always there in the band.

GP: That brings us up to the end of the 1970s. And I'd like to bring you back tomorrow night to discuss how the punk aesthetic coped with the conservatism of the 1980s.

GM: OK.

Part Two

GP: In 1978, when the Sex Pistols self-destructed, it was assumed that punk had gone with them. But as we discovered last night, punk never really went away; on the contrary, it continued to inform popular culture, politics, and certainly mainstream music. Part of the reason for this was that punk was not just a fad, or just a nihilistic burst of noise, it was a refusal, a refusal of what was considered the norm, of what was considered blasé, and a refusal of the values that encouraged complacency. And by the '70s, the rock and roll culture that came of age in the '60s had stared to turn moldy, lazy, and narcissistic, it *was* complacency on parade. The utopianism of the Beatles gave way in the '70s to the self-serving folk rock ramblings of James Taylor, Harry Chapin, and Graham Nash. Punk thrust us back into the real world which wasn't as nice a place in the late '70s as someone like James Taylor would lead you to believe, and it didn't get any better in the 1980s. In fact, it seemed the most conservative of times: Ronald Reagan became president of the United States; Margaret Thatcher became prime minister of England; the Sex Pistols were history; John Lennon was murdered; and the gap between the "haves" and the "have-nots" yawned wider.

Greil Marcus is a critic of pop culture and pop music, and he's chronicled the history of the punk aesthetic in popular culture in a book called *Ranters & Crowd Pleasers: Punk in Pop Music, 1977–92*. Last night we discussed the end of the utopian '60s with the release of the Rolling Stones' album *Let It Bleed* and how by the late '70s punk's emergence had forced even mainstream bands like Fleetwood Mac to attempt to shrug off the mantle of respectability. Tonight, Greil joins me to talk about the 1980s and how the punk aesthetic continued to survive, and about some of the artists who helped define that aesthetic. Greil Marcus joins me from our studio in Berkeley. Hi, Greil.

GM: It's good to be with you again.

GP: Well, it's a pleasure to have you back again tonight. Greil, the era that I've just described, the '80s, was a pretty harsh decade and decidedly pretty conservative, too. Now how did punk survive the conservatism of the '80s?

GM: One of its first responses was to become conservative itself. After punk was declared dead and the funeral services were held, one of the first new things to pop up was the ska revival in England, the 2-Tone groups, particularly the Specials. And this music was instantly sold to the world as a sort of mature smile replacing the adolescent frown of punk. You had blacks and whites in bands together and they were singing music of hope; they were singing music about using condoms, and not using drugs, and living a good life. And I had nothing against all of this until I started listening to the music, which was god-awful, which was pallid, and imitative, third-hand, lacking in imagination or any spirit. And listening to the Specials, listening to Selecter, listening to Madness—these groups weren't any good, and that always makes me suspicious as a listener; I figure maybe there's something wrong with the ideas, too.

The one group that came out of the so-called ska revival that was different was the Beat, from England, from Birmingham, and what they announced was, "We're not 'ska,' we're punks! Just because there's black people in the band, you know, we're punks! And this is our kind of punk, what do you mean punk's dead?" They responded along with UB40 with some really hilarious anti-Thatcher songs: "Stand Down Margaret" and "Madame Medusa."

But in essence, people believed the headlines; people believed that punk was dead. People began to crawl back into holes, and it was only really very slowly, as bands like the Delta Five quickly appeared and disappeared, as groups like the Gang of Four struggled on for a few years but really seemed to have lost their reason for being, and just petered out in the most pathetic and unhappy sort of way, it was a number of years before people began to come out of their holes, out of their caves, and say, "No, we're not going anywhere."

GP: It seems to me too that something that went on in the early '80s was that after the demise of the Sex Pistols, the mantle of working-class punk purity seemed to be passed down by the music establishment—by the critical establishment—to the Clash. What role, then, did the Clash play in the early '80s, and I guess they were gone by about 1985.
GM: Well, the Clash's career is wonderfully paradoxical. Yes, the role of working-class tribunes was passed down to the *very* middle-class Clash, although Joe Strummer had worked *very* hard to learn a Cockney accent, and learned it quite well, and also because his teeth were so awful—

GP: Yes! [laughs]
GM: —his words came out garbled. The Clash were the great rebel rockers, were the great guerrilla fighters, and that's really how they presented themselves, and those poses would have been completely ludicrous if their

music wasn't so powerful. The Clash were the kind of group that could take everything second-hand, could read interviews with the Sex Pistols to figure out what they were supposed to say to *their* interviewer, say the same things, and then think about those answers and say, "Maybe the world really is corrupt" and begin to look at the world in a new way and write marvelous songs, and produce powerful music about these second-hand ideas that now seemed new and utterly authentic. And they really reached their limit with *London Calling*, a great, big, sprawling album about politics, and movie stars, about sex, drugs, and alcohol, about fear and wanting everything out of the world, about the end of the world and the chance to start it over, a funny album, an album that made fun of itself, that was stirring, that was exciting. It was everything you want a two-record album to be. And after that, they got hits, touring the United States again and again and again. They finally topped the charts, they finally made it with *Combat Rock* and "Rock the Casbah," a wonderful hit single, a great novelty record. Still fighting authority, this one taking on the Ayatollah Khomeini.

And then when they'd finally achieved success—and again this is what we've been talking about with Nirvana—they'd finally made it, Joe Strummer, the guy who's made himself into a punk, a middle-class son of a diplomat who had to learn how to talk working-class, thought, *Oh my god, if everybody likes what we're saying, we must not be saying anything.* He had what in essence was a nervous breakdown. He shaved his head. He kicked Mick Jones, the guitarist and the singer on most of the Clash's hits, on their love songs, kicked him out of the band, recruited new players, kids much younger than Joe Strummer or Paul Simonon, the bass player by now, kids in their early twenties with Joe Strummer crossing the line into thirty now by '85. And they said, "We're gonna be a punk band again; we're gonna go back to where we went wrong; we're gonna start over again from the beginning." What a strange thing to say right after your hit. And so they played a show in San Francisco I went to see in late '84, early '85; they had one new song: "We Are the Clash." It was like "Hey, Hey, We're the Monkees."

GP: Right.

GM: It was so awful, and so embarrassing to stand there and listen to them sing it. And then they put out a last album; it wasn't supposed to be the last album. The "new" Clash. And the album was called *Cut the Crap*. And that's what the reviews in England all said about the album: "*You* should talk about cutting the crap, you know? What do you think *this* is?" And there were these funny liner notes about rebellion in the streets, and old men and young kids getting together to overthrow the established order, all this boilerplate.

And a lot of the songs really no better, except, except, one song, the song that was released as a single, the song that has never been included on any of the Clash retrospectives or box sets or whatever, a song called "This Is England." And it's a song about the hopes that were alive in England in the days of Swingin' London, and for a brief time in '77/'78, and those hopes are very simple: the hopes that people could make their own lives, that they could reinvent themselves, that there really was an arena of freedom in culture and in politics where new things were possible. And at the end of the '60s that collapsed; by the end of the '80s nobody even wanted to *talk* about this anymore. They were so ashamed by their naiveté. And "This Is England" is a song about what happens when you accept the notion that novelty in your life has passed, that tomorrow's going to be like the day before, and that you can't change anything, and if you want to live a decent life you better not try. It's a portrait of a country that lives on lies, where violence increases and has no purpose and meaning, where no one is safe, and yet there's nothing really to be afraid of, there's nothing to be scared of because there's nothing that makes any demands. It's as corrosive a picture of a society without convictions as you'll ever hear. People said punk was nihilistic; this song was a picture of everyday, commonplace nihilism.

GP: Greil, I'd like to talk a bit about Elvis Costello. Costello was someone who sort of emerged from the punk era but someone who is not often considered in stricter, pure terms, a punk, and someone who's had a wide-ranging career that's involved him in everything from string quartets, most recently, to country music. How much punk is in Elvis Costello?

GM: Well, a whole lot of punk is in Elvis Costello. Elvis Costello never would have been heard, never would have been seen, were it not for punk. One of the things that punk did immediately in England, in London, was to destroy all rules and all restrictions on what rock and roll was and who could sing it, who could play it, who could appear in public pretending to be a musician. No one as geeky looking as Elvis Costello would have had a chance before the Sex Pistols. He was, in a sense, just another freak. And just because his first album *My Aim Is True* was very melodic and he was actually backed up by a band from Marin County called Clover, was really beyond the point. The point was that Elvis Costello was looking for an edge, was looking for a harshness that he had heard in the Sex Pistols and that he had heard in the Clash, and he found that on "Watching the Detectives," and his second album, *This Year's Model*, which is a punk album as played through Bob Dylan's *Highway 61 Revisited*.

From that point on, Elvis Costello was someone who you'd better not cross; he was someone who was, as he said in his first interview—and I really do believe this is the key to his career—he said the only emotions he understood were revenge and guilt. People took that as a really great line, which it is, but I think people tended to miss how deep it is. There are few emotions in life as bottomless as revenge and guilt; they lead in both cases to acts of violence, perhaps against yourself, perhaps against others. They have consequences, and those consequences can't be stopped or controlled. And Elvis Costello set out across the decade singing his songs of revenge and guilt, his guilt at being unable to change a world he hated, his desire to take revenge on that world for not changing according to his desires and his wishes. And I think that's the key to his career; I think it's been from then to now. Whether or not he's recording with the Brodsky Quartet, as he did on *The Juliet Letters*, or whether he's simply standing up and singing "Tramp the Dirt Down" which is a song about how he wants to dance on Margaret Thatcher's grave, and I'm not interpreting it. [laughs] *He uses her name!* I think he has always looked for the most effective way to make trouble.

Now, he made an album called *King of America*, I believe in 1986, and this was an album that was in some ways very much like Bruce Springsteen's *Nebraska*: it was quiet, it was almost folky. Even though there were accompanying instruments it was really like a solo record; it was a record certainly that he could have played standing on stage all by himself with just a piano or a guitar. And yet, it was probably more bitter, and more detailed in terms of social inequity, than any record he had made. It was a crueler record, it was more painful to hear. And somebody said to him, "So this is your 'folk' record, huh Elvis?" And he said, "No, no, no, you don't understand; this is my punk record." And that was a way of saying sometimes in the noise, in the sturm and drang, in the terrible clamor of punk, you can hear a silence, you can hear a void, and maybe the truest punk music is to get as close to that void, as close to that silence as possible. Force the listeners, lead the listeners to fill in the blanks, to fill in the noise and the cries and the screams for themselves, because that's what punk's about; punk is about making the listener as full a participant in the creative act as possible. It really is saying, *You can speak this language, too, and if you're not, why aren't you?*

GP: In this context, Greil, what struck you in particular about a track from the *King of America* album called "Sleep of the Just?"

GM: Well one of the things that I think Elvis Costello's fury, his sense of revenge and guilt, ultimately led to was a very, an almost extreme sense of craft, of honing words and manner of singing so that you heard details, so that nothing was trivial, so that the smallest things in life whether it was an itch in your palm, or a knife wound in your side, would be felt, would be sensed with equal power.

And it's on "Sleep of the Just" where I think this really comes to bear. There is a care in the writing and the singing; there is a sense of contingency and doubt, of all things being put into doubt, and into jeopardy, which is ultimately a sense of danger that in this very peaceful song I guess I hear more intensely than anywhere else. It's also a song that *is* a real judgment, that's a real condemnation; he talks about "the sleep of the just," and you listen to this song and you know at the end that nobody deserves it.

GP: There were a number of female voices who, of course, became associated with punk: Laura Logic from Essential Logic; the Slits; Laurie Anderson in a rather odd way. Was the punk perspective different when it was being articulated by women?

GM: I don't know that it was different. It was different in the sense that women spoke in different ways than men, and they often spoke about different things, but in essence I don't know that it was different. I think there is a greater charge in general in punk music made by women than there is in punk music made by men, because a woman taking the stage was not as obvious a thing as it was for a man. Until punk, until really the Raincoats, a London band, a woman standing on stage singing rock and roll was a novelty before she was anything else, and certainly playing an instrument, take that double, take that triple. A new kind of naturalism was introduced to music made by women through punk; it simply ceased to be a big deal, it ceased to be a selling point, it ceased to be a point of attraction. There were now people on stage doing various things and, as when you walk down the street, when you sit down in a classroom, when you get on a bus, some of them were male and some of them were female, and punk was the first kind of popular music that was able to demystify gender. So, I don't think that Klau Schiff of Kleenex and Lilliput, one of my favorite bands, was exactly speaking a different language than Jon King or Andy Gill of the Gang of Four, but there was a kind of glee, a kind of release, and a kind of eagerness, and a kind of anger and bitterness, a kind of pent-up resentment, that was stronger in the voices of so many women—not different, just more of it, I guess.

GP: And what does Cyndi Lauper's cover version of the Brains' "Money Changes Everything" have to do with punk?

GM: A number of things. Cyndi Lauper is another weirdo who never would have really had a chance to be heard was it not for punk. With that squeaky, Betty Boop voice and those funny gypsy clothes and the ludicrous interviews she gave, she stepped into the open arena that punk had created. And it looked like at first she was just another pop warbler, and "Girls Just Want to Have Fun" is a great record, but nothing threatening, nothing strange. And you thought, "Well, you know, I guess this person will go on to make a lot more pop hits." She didn't, as it happened.

Well, one of the things that she revealed on that first album called *She's So Unusual* is that Cyndi Lauper was a real fan; she liked records, she liked listening to the radio, and she wanted to sing the songs that had moved her. And one of the songs that she chose was called "Money Changes Everything," which originally had been done by a punk band from Atlanta called the Brains. And as Tom Gray, the leader of the Brains—his publishing company was called Gray Matter. Get it? Brains? The Brains?—

GP: Got it. [laughs]

GM: —as he sang the song, he is an aggrieved man who's been thrown over by his girlfriend for a guy with more money. And this is what evil women do; I mean there is this sort of old pop shibboleth floating through the song as he does it.

Cyndi Lauper when she sang that song, doubled, tripled, quadrupled the power and the intensity of the recording; she speeded it up, she screamed instead of sang, the song exploded—again and again and again—and this is what made it punk. Instead of simply changing the gender of the song and making herself, Cyndi Lauper the singer, the aggrieved party thrown over by her boyfriend for a woman with lots of money, she sang as the woman who's throwing her boyfriend over for money. And she sang out of hatred for the boyfriend's poverty, self-hatred for her own lack of faithfulness, hatred for the world that was forcing her to make this kind of choice; it was a maelstrom, it was a hurricane, and this was the kind of liberty, the kind of free speech that punk gave to so many people who purists would never permit to be called punk. Cyndi Lauper is a punk; "Money Changed Everything" is a punk recording.

GP: Greil, in 1977 you wrote a review of Margaret Drabble's novel *The Ice Age*. In that—and I may be paraphrasing incorrectly here—but in that you said that the sense of community that was shared at the time was sense of community that had kind of gathered around a sort of sordidness of the period, and that each person was finding a way to kind of turn away from it, and that you felt that punk, the Sex Pistols, as well as Margaret Drabble's book, were trying to get us to face the sordidness within the culture. Is that something punk still attempts to do?

GM: I don't know. I think there is still an impulse in punk to go toward the forbidden, toward the ugly to see what might happen there. And over the years, that punk impulse to go to the forbidden has led to a fetishism of Charles Manson, and a celebration of serial killers, and punk magazines illustrated with gruesome photographs from medical dictionaries of hacked-off limbs and stuff like that. There are a couple of hacked-off limbs in *Lipstick Traces* among the illustrations. I don't know that punk has a point of view to the degree that it did when it started; punk now belongs to millions and millions of people scattered all over the world, in many different cultures, people who make their own use of it. And simply turning our faces back upon the sordidness was perhaps the most important thing that punk could do in 1976 and '77, but it's only one aspect of the story punk is telling today.

That was that time, let's put it that way. That was a time when Labour was still governing England, when everything in England seemed to be slowing down, when there seemed to be no purpose to anything anymore, where, in a way, IRA bombings in London captured the spirit of the city more than anything Londoners could do themselves. And people turned away; people began to hide, people stopped coming out of their apartments, and both Johnny Rotten and Margaret Drabble were saying, "No, there has to be a public life, there has to be something we talk about with each other for there to be any worthwhile life at all." That was a moment when punk came together and it was whole, and it shattered like anything else, and yet those pieces spread out all over the world wherever they might be all seemed to replicate the whole story in each of them; they're not just fragments.

GP: If making us face the sordidness is no longer part of the primary *raison d'être* of punk, does it have one?

GM: I think it will always be an insistence that's carried out mostly in the negative, mostly by taking something that's unacceptable and pretending to embrace it. I think punk will always be the insistence that things don't have to be as they seem, that the game is still up for grabs, that the game is not yet caught. And that's why it's not just a musical style, and that's why the punk language can be spoken in so many languages.

GP: I have been speaking to pop critic Greil Marcus. His books include *Mystery Train, Lipstick Traces, Dead Elvis*. His new book is *Ranters & Crowd Pleasers*. Greil, thank you very much.

GM: Thanks so much. It was just great to be talking with you again.

Greil Marcus

Nick Pemberton/1994

From *Closed Volumes* (U.K.), 1994.

It is perhaps worth remembering that the cultural landscape of 1975—the year that Greil Marcus's first book *Mystery Train* appeared—was very different from today's. Punk was still no more than a rumbling noise up around the bend, most rock writers wrote sycophantically about superstars, and books about rock and roll were not published by Penguin. If you wanted to read *Mystery Train* in 1975 you had to get hold of an American import.

I mention this because nowadays—when all you need to do is wave a chequebook and any number of tame media intellectuals will gather in a TV studio at midnight just to peel the cellophane wrapper from a collection of soft porn photographs of Madonna, and then solemnly pronounce on what they find within—it is hard to imagine a time when things were otherwise. Pop culture has not always been the subject of such endless and solemn exegesis as it is today. Far from it. In fact, in 1975, Elvis Presley—who had just begun his bloated and serious decline—was not a figure that people took seriously as an artist. Consequently, to read someone prepared to write about him and, more importantly, about his music with the wit, intelligence, and generosity that Marcus brought to *Mystery Train* was wonderful.

In the ensuing years I read his books when they came out, or when I could afford them. I enjoyed the rambling, quirky mystery story that he made of *Lipstick Traces*—a tale of punks and heretics, Dada and rock and roll, anarchy and fascism, of simple ideas taken to extremes—and, later, *Dead Elvis*, a retrospective collection of essays gathered together round a premise that was comical, bizarre, macabre, and irresistible.

Last year, an editor asked me to review *In the Fascist Bathroom*—a collection of Marcus's music reviews, which also managed to provide an oblique take on the increasingly conformist and corrupted times which they have appeared across. Along with the review copy came a publicity flyer with details of the dates on which Marcus would be in England to promote the book. So I phoned up, and in June last year, in a small conference room on the fifth floor of his publishers' building, he was kind enough to give me an hour of his time.

Nick Pemberton: In *Mystery Train* you refer to Melville saying, in essence, only the man who says no is truly free. Is this the idea that attracted you to punk?

Greil Marcus: I was looking at that line this morning, correcting some galley proofs for a reprint of *Mystery Train*. I go on and say we don't expect that sort of thing in pop culture, and we'd be foolish to. That's not what pop culture's about. Pop culture's about acceptance, about saying yes; there has to be a no somewhere, a possibility of saying no, but really pop culture's about acceptance—that seems to be what I was saying in *Mystery Train*. And then *boom*, a couple of years later there's this whole kind of music that's completely about saying no. Melville had this phrase about saying no in thunder—*whram!*—and that's certainly what was going on in punk, and this shocked me as it seemed to break all the rules about how pop culture worked.

NP: So you feel that punk is apart, that it's somehow "other" than the rest of pop music?

GM: You can argue a case that traces punk guitar styles back to Chuck Berry, or the way X-Ray Spex is really inspired by Roxy Music. You can make all those kinds of connections, but the spirit of the thing, the way people were talking, and the way that the music kept driving itself to extremes, that really didn't seem to me to be in the rock and roll tradition. *Lipstick Traces* was about the traditions it was in, but that its parentage wasn't a simple matter.

NP: I felt that in *Lipstick Traces* you were discovering these things yourself. That punk brought you to Tristan Tzara, Dada, and so on.

GM: That's right. I mean, suddenly, here's punk—it's exciting, disturbing, every time you turn around there's something new yelling at you in a way that's both attractive and repellent at the same time. I started to ask where does this come from, what's this about? I would read things that other people had said—"Punk is like Dada"—and I didn't know anything about Dada, and I thought, if punk is like Dada then maybe I should learn something about Dada, then maybe this will all make more sense. I began to read about Dada, and I became fascinated with that in its own right. Forget about punk—I spent two years just investigating Dada! The same with the Situationists. Those things became obsessions for me on their own terms, and then they began to link up into a grand story. Not a chronological progression, Dada-Situationist-Punk, but really all of those people speaking with the same voice, and trying to say the same thing. But I didn't know anything about Tristan Tzara. I'd never heard of Richard Huelsenbeck, who's now one of my great heroes.

NP: Is he the guy who became a therapist?
GM: That's right.

NP: And you say somewhere God knows what it must have been like for his patients.
GM: Yeah. And I tried to find out. I really wanted to know, but I wasn't able to. But he seemed like such a cool bastard, and that's what he was always about.

NP: I read *Psychotic Reactions and Carburetor Dung*, the book of Lester Bangs's essays you edited, and I thought what a lovely and infuriating man he must have been. His prose is always on the edge of collapse.
GM: Dissolution. Yeah.

NP: And he seems to seethe against the mainstream, as if he wanted more from the music than was there.
GM: Maybe. Lester was always against the mainstream wherever and whatever it was. In other words, if you were his best friend and you suddenly became the mainstream then he would attack you. Not in any personal sense, but he'd let you have it. He'd tell you, you're in the wrong place, you're not doing what you ought to be doing. When I first met him in 1969 he was a mad Velvet Underground fan when in California at the time there might have been about five Velvet Underground fans. Most people thought of them as a complete waste of time, a bunch of junkies involved with Andy Warhol—and he was a complete waste of time. So Lester was always looking for something that no one else was interested in, and by doing that he ended up stumbling on all kinds of wonderful things. When he came here in 1977 and went on the road with the Clash and wrote about them for *New Music Express*, he's almost fighting with them about where they're going. He wants to be their spiritual saviour.

NP: He seemed to have the same thing with Lou Reed.

GM: I know. He wrote about him again and again. But I don't think Lester was very predictable. I mean if he was alive today and the Velvet Underground, as they are, were playing dates, I think I know what his reaction would have been. He would be furious, he would be disgusted, he would be repelled at this corny old reunion tour, but he would go. And if it was good he would be completely transported, and he would acknowledge it, and he would write something that would make you curse your very existence that you weren't there. But if it was bad he'd say that too.

NP: Your own particular favourites, or maybe obsessions, seem to be the Mekons and the Gang of Four.

GM: When I came here in 1978 the Gang of Four were graduate students. They talked and acted like graduate students had done when I was in graduate school in Berkeley in the 1960s. I mean I just knew their culture. It wasn't other to me, but it was other to rock and roll. There had never been this kind of talk in pop music before; in the way that they put it onto their records. The same with Laura Logic: her music was not made the way pop music had been made before, or for the same kind of motives.

NP: Do you think it was a purer motive?

GM: No. I think one of the great things about pop music is that it's completely corrupt. Purity doesn't come into it. Let's say we're in the middle of punk—it's 1977. Somebody jumps in because this is the hot new trend, and they want to make some money, meet some girls, or whatever. Now they don't care about the Queen, the nature of life, or whatever. They just want to make it. So they jump on the bandwagon. And they can make the phoniest punk record of all time and it can sound like the most pure one. That's one of the great things about pop music. So it's not about purity of motive. People never went into pop music before because they wanted to see how far they could push it. And that, in a way, is a lot of what I think punk was about. I know people had been into pop music before because they wanted to say, for instance, that they were against the Vietnam War or something like that, but that's different. Punk was never so limiting as to say war is bad. Punks would say "War is good; take that!" It's the summer of hate instead of the summer of love.

NP: But then, if punk works shouldn't it destroy pop music?

GM: The Sex Pistols, through Johnny Rotten, said, "We come to destroy pop music." Well that's an old, old line. It's like Dada saying it was anti-art but we're going to make art anyway. Who would even think that pop music was worth destroying, except someone who wanted to be a pop star? A really serious political person who wanted to ask what was the true danger to a better way of life would not immediately focus on pop music. That's why I tend not to believe in the folk in the United States who are always trying to ban this record or that record. What they're really trying to do is raise money from gullible people for their propaganda campaign. I don't think they care one way or the other about whether Judas Priest is making people kill themselves, or whether 2 Live Crew is corrupting the morals of innocent white kids—which is what they say they're upset about. No, if Johnny Rotten really wanted to destroy pop music, then when the Sex Pistols ended he would not have continued to make records. He would have written novels, or become a serial killer, or something else.

NP: In all of your writing you seem to communicate the enthusiasm of a fan.
GM: I think if I ever stopped being a fan it would be completely fraudulent for me to write about this stuff. I mean the other day I was driving along in my car and the first notes of Tom Petty's "Out in the Cold" came on. It's a hit he had about a year and a half ago—not much of a hit actually, and it's the most explosive piece of music he ever made. The beginning of it is just these drums taking off like a guitar solo, and it's fast, and it's thrilling, and I'm driving along and I heard that and my hand went to the dial, and in that split second I turned up the volume my foot went down on the pedal, and I was gone. And I was in the middle of doing this when I thought, God! Thank God I can still respond this way because, if I couldn't, then there'd be nothing left but pedantry. I try to stay away from the kind of "You can only get this on a Japanese import which is actually out of print so you'll never hear it ha ha ha" sort of attitude, because one sort of obsession which I feel is really tiresome is the collector, which comes down to I have it, you don't. Sometimes, though, it is the only place you can find a certain track, and I still want people to know about it.

NP: In the latest British Telecom shares advert, the Inspector Morse character says, "You never saw the Rubettes live, did you Johnson? What an aching void your life must be."
GM: I just hate that. One of the last pieces in *In the Fascist Bathroom*, which is about Bikini Kill, starts out about that very thing, about people saying, "You weren't there, I was." And it's mainly about sixties people sneering at

younger people, and saying, "Well, I was at Woodstock and you weren't, and therefore your life is like an aching void that will never close up." It's disgusting, that attitude, and everybody falls into it at some time, and when I do I hate myself for it.

NP: So you still find things to love in pop music?

GM: Well, one of the things that punk did was to break so many rules, and destroy so many preconceptions about what pop music was, or what it had to sound like, or what kind of people made it, that suddenly nobody really knew what it was any more; it could be everything and nothing. Now there are so many thousands and thousands of performers and records that nobody can possibly keep up any more. I mean, it used to be, some years back, very easy to keep up with every new release, and know what it was, but now it's impossible, absolutely impossible. Ninety percent or so of what's put out on the market I don't even know about. Now, I'm not saying that any rock critic is as ignorant as I am—some people keep up better than I do—but I'm always looking for something that moves me, and I tend to focus on it. For instance, I've never been a big Pere Ubu fan—I thought their album *Dub Housing* was just great, but big deal, that was fifteen years ago. And then they put an album out this year called *Story of My Life*, and it completely seduced me. I didn't want to listen to anything else, and I didn't listen to anything else for weeks. I began to listen to all their old records, and go out and try to find the ones I didn't have in record stores; and now I know there's all kinds of stuff there I never really caught, I never really heard. Well, I'd rather spend three or four weeks listening to Pere Ubu, and missing being knowledgeable about a whole load of stuff that wouldn't matter to me. It would mean eventually I'd be able to write something interesting about Pere Ubu, rather than something that is ultimately meaningless about a whole lot of other stuff.

NP: You seem to write about music that's made for high stakes, like the Sex Pistols, or Elvis's comeback on his TV programme?

GM: I think that what you're saying points out my own limits. I like to write about stuff that seems to be about high stakes, or maybe I'm able to write about stuff that seems to be for high stakes. But a lot of the music, the movies, the books that I love are not about high stakes, but I'm not very good at writing about that. For instance, one of my favourite records is "You're the One That I Want" by John Travolta and Olivia Newton John. A lot of people think I'm putting them on when I tell them this, but I'm not. But I don't know how to write about that record, and why I think it's so wonderful. I don't know, maybe some day I'll be able to. My favourite records in the world when I'm in a certain mood are girl group records Darlene Love, the Crystals, the Ronettes, all those mid '60s Phil Spector groups—and I'm not real good at writing about that. That is for high stakes, it's about love and death, love and tragedy, and all in the most direct and simple manner. So I don't write as well, or as freely, about all the stuff I like. I wish I could. So I think I sort of tend to give a false picture. One of the pieces in the new book that I'm most happy with is on the Go-Go's, which in a way is just fluff, and yet it was so great. It was like one big smile, and I wanted desperately to find a way to talk about that. So you could say that I was attracted to music that was made for high stakes, but I'm also attracted to music that's completely meaningless.

NP: Do you think that popular music can survive all the critical freight that goes along with it nowadays?

GM: A lot of rock criticism is incredibly dumb-headed. But I don't think there's any way—and this is really what I believe—I don't think that any number of people, I don't care how smart or how stupid they are, can exhaust the meaning in the way Little Richard sings "Ready Teddy." I think that song can support all the critical junk piled on top of it. It will still sound like what it sounds like, and people will still encounter it years from now and say what the hell was that? So I don't think it really hurts. So much of the academic writing I read on pop music is so terrible. It's so patently fraudulent. What I mean by that is that the people who are writing don't care about the music. They don't like it. They aren't interested. They might pretend to be, but they aren't. They see something that might get them tenure, or get them published, or maybe seems like a trendy thing to do, or maybe their students will think they're hip, but that sense of "If I wasn't listening to this music my life would be poorer," that isn't there. You don't feel that.

NP: In *Mystery Train* you talk about Mark Twain, Robert Johnson, Jonathan Edwards, Harmonica Frank, and Herman Melville as if they were part of the same tradition. You don't seem to have much truck with what is generally cranked out over here as the Keats v. Dylan debate.

GM: I think these people would have had a lot to say to each other, let's put it that way. I think what I said in *Mystery Train* was that when I play Robert Johnson I think of Jonathan Edwards, the great Puritan preacher of the eighteenth century in Massachusetts, and sometimes I fantasise about

Jonathan Edwards sitting down and listening to a Robert Johnson album, or Robert Johnson being in church listening to one of Jonathan Edwards's fire and brimstone sermons, and that it's too bad those connections couldn't be made—but in a way they are made. The fact is that the kind of religion Robert Johnson grew up in, the whole sense of sin that drives his music is a Puritan sense of sin that came to the South during the Great Awakening in the 1700s and 1800s, through Georgia, and then on down, and you can actually make history out of this. Robert Johnson is living out what Jonathan Edwards started, and he is a true heir of Jonathan Edwards. So to make divisions between them is silly. Bob Dylan is a true heir of Keats not because he writes in the same tradition, or because his lyrics are as good or similar or anything, but because Keats is one of the reasons that Bob Dylan is a singer. Have you read Michael Gray's book *Song and Dance Man: The Art of Bob Dylan*? It's about the literary sources of Bob Dylan's songs, and it was written about twenty years ago, and it's just great. It's completely unpretentious. It's a very cheeky book in a way. Full of ideas and knowledge and stuff, and it will make the songs sound different. It really will. And he doesn't recognise this difference, and neither do I. It's just as tiresome doing it in the other direction as well. Somebody once said "If Keats was alive today he'd play the electric guitar," and my response was "what a waste."

NP: You argue, rightly I'm sure, that the question of race—its paradoxes, tensions, mysteries, and injustices—is central to what rock and roll is about. Quite a few times you talk about Huck, Jim, and the raft in relation to rock and roll. But there's a last third to Twain's book where everything that has been lived through and learned by the two of them is forgotten.
GM: Yes. The first two thirds of the book are like a nightmare and dream, with Huck finding his dead father in the cabin, and then the nightmare turns into this beautiful dream, and everything is fine in the book until they get to land again, when Jim gets enslaved again, and Tom Sawyer becomes this sadistic little twerp who's running the show, and Huck loses his voice and doesn't know what to do, and everything sort of goes back to normal.

NP: But this normality is horrible, isn't it?
GM: Yeah, except what's really going on there? I think in some ways that's supposed to be just that horrible. But I think it's Twain saying, "No, there is no escape, there is no way out." A man called Richard Middleton, I think, a number of years ago, wrote a novel called *Huck Finn for the Critics*, where he rewrote the book and left out that ending because everybody has said

that the book just goes to hell there—well, maybe it does. On the other hand Leslie Fielder, who's a great American literary critic who was a tremendous inspiration to me, argues that in almost any great American book you can always see the writer plotting to betray himself or herself, that the writer goes to a certain point of saying what he thinks the world's really about, of telling the truth, and then says, "Oh my God, they're gonna lynch me, so I better clean this up and back off." I think Fiedler would say that's what's going on in *Huckleberry Finn*. There's that backing off.

One of the most remarkable things about punk, not to change the subject, is that it seemed to me—in certain groups—that as they went on they got more extreme, they got more desperate, they began to discover even more dangerous subject matter, and more thrilling ways to talk about it. That's certainly what happened with the Sex Pistols, there was no pulling back. I mean, songs like "Bodies" and "Holidays in the Sun" are in some ways so much more extreme than "Anarchy in the U.K." and "God Save the Queen," maybe not as great, but you can't listen to that song where, in the middle, Johnny Rotten starts losing his mind without wondering why you're doing this and what you're opening yourself up to. I think the same thing happened with X-Ray Spex, and a few other groups. The normal pop progression is to arrive with something startling—unique and special, and then within a couple of years sound like everybody else, and just completely lose whatever was special that you brought to the conversation in the first place. And in punk that wasn't the case. That self-betrayal, or whatever you want to call it, didn't happen. One of the reasons that didn't happen was that they cracked up, they quit, or they disappeared. Poly Styrene had a breakdown. She didn't go on to become a club singer. She just went crack.

NP: I feel that a similar kind of closing up of possibilities has happened since punk, as happens to Huck and Jim in Twain's novel. Everything lived through and learned from life is suddenly unlearned again and denied.
GM: I'll tell you, not to sound totally pompous, but one of the things I've learned over the last twenty years with what's going on in politics—with Ronald Reagan as president, and with the enormous power and resurgence of the religious right in the United States, and the entry of evangelical Christianity into politics and all this sort of thing—is (1) people can forget anything, and (2) it doesn't matter how completely something is forgotten, it never goes away. In the 1950s and 1960s it was believed by everybody that religion was on the way out, and that science was triumphant, yet in the U.S. polls show again and again and again that fifty percent of the people believe

in the biblical account of creation, and twenty-five percent aren't sure, and only twenty-five percent believe the scientific view of the universe and life, and all that. And that's horrifying. I once asked an anthropologist—Don Johansen, one of the most eminent anthropologists in the world—how can you do your work when the whole country believes that it's complete nonsense, and he said, "Well, it's very scary." Not that people are trying to kill him or anything, but he's working in a nonscientific context. What I'm trying to say by this is that, even if it seems that everything has closed up, and that what happened with punk has been completely forgotten, even if it really has been completely forgotten, it's still there like an evil seed, and it will sprout at some other time, in some other form, and maybe not even until it is even more forgotten than it is today.

NP: Punk played with images and symbols a lot, and one of them it played with was the swastika. In *The Great Rock and Roll Swindle* film we see Sid Vicious, who looks completely out of his mind, wandering around the Jewish Quarter in Paris and I thought, *This is horrible.*
GM: It is. When punk began playing with the swastika, first here, and then picked up as an imitation in the United States, the first explanation of it that I read was that these kids were too young to know what the swastika really meant, and they just knew it was a sort of bad symbol, and so they used it to show they were bad, and that they didn't respect the pieties of society and art. I didn't believe that for a minute. Everybody knows what the swastika is. It means Hitler, it means extermination, it means mass murder. There's no secret about what the swastika means, and no one is too young to know that. I don't think Johnny Rotten ever played around with the swastika: it was a stupid thing to do. Yet there are times when a certain kind of self-loathing brings you to a point where you can use no other symbol. Lou Reed once shaved an Iron Cross into his hair. Now Lou Reed is Jewish, right? That was as close as he could come. He couldn't quite bring himself to shave a swastika into his hair, but he did everything but. And what was he saying with that? Well, who knows exactly? I don't know. I don't presume to say. There's a way in which the only person who could have carried off wearing a swastika is Elvis Costello. Elvis Costello is the premier anti-fascist of pop music, the one who's most obsessed with fascism as something we've inherited, as something we'll never escape; a seed that was planted within all of us in the West by what happened fifty or sixty years ago, that we will never escape; that we will always be part fascist. You know the part in *Lipstick Traces* about the movie *Quatermass and the Pit* where there's this whole

business that we're part Martian and that some of us are more Martian than others, and that this is an inheritance that we've completely forgotten and that we don't know anything about—but suddenly it breaks out? Well, I think we're all part fascist because of what happened. Once something happens in the world it's much more likely that it will happen again than it ever would have been before it happened for the first time. Once mass murder as a legitimate, moral, necessary, holy act is put on the world stage, then it makes sense in a way that it never has before. It doesn't matter how we revile it. That's why it makes sense in Bosnia for instance. It makes sense. It is part of their inheritance, and everybody knows that. I think Sid Vicious was really stupid. I think Sid Vicious was a lump of clay. I really do. I'm not one of these persons who worships him and thinks, "Wow, he was so bad." I mean, walking around a Jewish neighbourhood in Paris with a swastika is disgusting. He should be beaten up for doing something like that. However, standing on a stage in front of a bunch of gullible people who think you're really great wearing a swastika on your jacket might be something different. Or it might not be.

NP: The title of your book *In the Fascist Bathroom* comes from an essay in which you say, "The bathroom in the fascist utopia is made of plaster and ceramic tile, not rubber and leather; it contains pills and soap, just like any other bathroom, not arcane sexual aids."
GM: It looks like any other bathroom. Yeah.

NP: But punks are as likely to be fascists as anybody—it's not a matter of bathrooms and haircuts, it's something, as you say, that's in everybody.
GM: One of the things that punk said was that you should now give vent to all of your hatred, to all of your angers, and all of your resentments. Well, a lot of people aren't necessarily angry, a lot of people—if they are angry—don't know what they're angry about, a lot of people don't have the nerve to identify their real enemies or the people they're really angry with, and so they turn on ordinary scapegoats: black people, women, homosexuals, whatever. I don't know if this was true in England, but in the United States, in the early days of punk, it was almost required that you go round saying words like "nigger," "chink," "faggot," "kike"—that showed how cool you were, because it showed you had total contempt for anyone who wasn't like you. I remember I was working as a DJ at a punk club one night—I got to be a DJ for a few hours and play whatever I liked—and I had a wonderful time playing all this great stuff, and people were dancing and it was really fun, and

then this woman comes up to me and says, "Hey, play some nigger music," and she's dressed total punk, and I hadn't heard that word used in a casual manner since I don't know when—since forever—and I was too shocked to just say, "Go fuck yourself," which is what I should have said to her. But that was ordinary punk talk. Let's say we're all living under a rock, we all feel oppressed, and punk or something else lifts the rock up, and suddenly we're free—well, a lot of other things live under the rocks, worms, scorpions, slugs, and they come out too.

NP: Do you see the Oi bands and all this "Strength through Oi" stuff as a direct line from punk?

GM: Sure it is. One of the things that happened after about '78 was that punk split into all of these parts. Oi over here, Rough Trade bands over there, very experimental and very self-consciously avant garde, and then a strain that meets up with heavy metal pretty quickly. All these different areas. There was no longer punk as a whole social phenomenon as well as a musical event. So it was broken into parts, and those parts could be pretty easily sold. The whole Oi business was an attempt to create a market and sell records. And so what if it meant some Asian had to be beaten up? Big deal. That's how I saw it. I thought what Garry Bushnell . . . is that how you say his name?

NP: Bushell. He writes in *The Sun* now.

GM: Yeah, he was supporting the whole Oi thing, right? He was supporting it because he wanted a trend he could jump on, he could identify with, and he could own. So he could say, "Look, I've created a scene."

NP: He now writes a column in *The Sun* promoting similar kinds of racial and nationalistic stuff.

GM: Well then, maybe he wasn't just being cynical about it. Maybe he was just a fucking racist to begin with. Maybe that was just his first stab at the whole thing.

NP: My younger brother was a punk, and he used to rant and rave at me for being a tedious and boring old hippie. Now all he'll say about punk is that it was wonderful, that you could do anything. And he speaks about this with a kind of wonder now he's an adult, and he's discovered that this is not possible in a way.

GM: Yeah, but to have experienced a moment like that, of total possibilities, is something that never leaves you. And in some ways it's a terrible thing, because you'll always be dissatisfied by ordinary life once you've been through an experience like that.

NP: You said the same thing about the Dadaists. That though they might have lived lives of achievement and so forth, nothing compared to this strange, brief moment of destruction back in 1916 or whatever.

GM: Right, and I'm not making that up. That's what they all said, and you have to respect that. You have to take that seriously. And I think that on the one hand that's really pathetic, and on the other there's something really noble about being able to fess up. You know what it means, that expression?

NP: I'm not sure.

GM: To confess. To say something that's embarrassing, or that doesn't reflect well on you. To say, "Yes, my life reached its height back then, and nothing I've done compares to it, and nothing ever will, and what's really terrible is that I still don't know what happened. I still don't understand it." It's much better to say, "Ah yes, as I grow older I achieve more wisdom" and stuff that.

NP: In both *Lipstick Traces* and *In the Fascist Bathroom* you write movingly about failure. You have the line, "Maybe all success is simple and all failure complex." You describe going to see the Mekons—of whom you say, "They barely had a career at all"—playing at an almost empty nightclub in San Francisco, and they're older, and wearing Stetsons, and it sounds like there's hardly anyone there. Similarly, when you go to see Alexander Trocchi in *Lipstick Traces.*

GM: Going to see Alexander Trocchi was not like anything I've ever done. Here I go and see this legendary figure . . .

NP: Did you come to him through punk?

GM: Oh yeah. All part of finding out about the Situationists. Trocchi had been a member of the Situationists, and vaguely knowing his name, but not knowing anything about him and then reading all his books, I thought maybe he was someone who could tell me some things, who could maybe answer some questions. I got hold of his assistant—a man named Denis Brown, who had been involved with the Sex Pistols, and who knew my work (so the punk connection was right there)—and he told Trocchi he should speak with me. But here I am in this horrible place filled with needles all over the place, the classic junkie pad that nobody ever cleans up—and this is where a man who once believed he could change the world has ended up. And yet there was something totally honest about that. The guy had given up nothing. Well, he'd given up everything in a way: he'd given up everything for junk. But, on the other hand, he was still saying, "No, this is still what I believe in, this is still what I care about."

Now, the stuff about the Mekons I wrote, I have to tell you, during a period when I was in such despair over what was going on in the United States that I didn't know if I was going to see anything look any different. And I wanted to follow that despair as far as I could, and I didn't want to let go of it. We had reached a point in the United States where not only was evil running the show, but we had reached a point where it was almost impossible to talk about anything else, that anything else could be real. In '84, '85, '86, that was the worst of it. It wasn't until the Iran Contra scandal that the spell was broken a little bit, the spell of Reagan as the definition of everything good in life that had taken over the country. I saw the Mekons' failure, and their bravery, and their persistence, as a metaphor for a life I would probably lead for the foreseeable future. Which is crying out in an ever more feeble voice from a wilderness that no one cared about. That's what that's about. I don't mean to be pompous about it, I mean to be pathetic about it. Because the Mekons were pathetic then. They were also wonderful. But that song "King Arthur"—"people hiding / people like bees / divided and lonely / too weak and too late"—I knew who they were talking about. They were talking about me, and all the people I cared about. Left behind by a history made by people far older than we were. And there were other people who were in tune with that. You know that Mike Leigh movie *Life Is Sweet*? That's about people like that. They're just going to be rolled over. A steam roller's going to crush them, and they don't care.

NP: In the playlist of the CD you hope to put out to coincide with the reissue of *Lipstick Traces* it says that one of the tracks is Marie Osmond reading Hugo Ball's sound poetry. Is this a Dada joke?
GM: No, this is completely real.

NP: That's astonishing!
GM: I'll tell you what happened. In *Lipstick Traces* I talk about this episode of *Ripley's Believe It or Not!*, a TV show, and one of the things they have on is a film of an actor playing Hugo Ball doing his sound poetry. "Can you believe it? Someone got up and he recited poems that didn't have any words. Wow! And now, a three-headed monkey. . . ." Well, it turns out that the little

snippet I'd written about was from an earlier episode of *Believe It or Not!* which was all about sound poetry. A whole half hour, and it was about sound poetry from all over the world today, and it began with Marie Osmond, who was the hostess of the show, reciting a little bit about how sound poetry began, and she, in a sort of simpering voice says—the camera comes in and picks her up—I didn't know anything about this when I wrote *Lipstick Traces*, I found out about this because of the book; the guy who produced the show gave me a tape of it, and said, "I bet you've never seen this"—well, the camera comes in on Marie Osmond, and she's sitting at her dressing table putting on her make up, and she says, "Today we're going to talk about sound poetry. You probably don't know what that is." And then she goes on to say, "Well, a long time ago there was someone called Mr. Ball, and Mr. Ball liked to write poems that didn't have any words." It's just horrible. And then she says, "And one of his poems went like this." Well, what she was supposed to do next was recite one line of the poem: "Karawani, jolophanto, babbalaboo." Well, she knew they all thought she was a bimbo. They knew they all thought she was stupid. And she was pissed off. So she memorized the whole poem, and these poems are hard to memorize because they don't have any words, they're hard to hang onto, and she delivered this absolutely passionate, brilliant reading that was saying, "Fuck you, I'm not as stupid as you think I am." When I was putting together the soundtrack to accompany the book, I said, "Well, this has got to be included." Wait till you hear it, if it comes out—you'll maybe say, "No, that's not Marie Osmond," but you'll know it's no joke.

In October, the *Lipstick Traces* CD was released and, despite the attention paid to them in the book, there was no Sex Pistols or Clash on the album. This absence was due to matters of money rather than the conceptual reasons claimed in the sleeve notes, but so what? As Marcus was only too happy to acknowledge elsewhere, their music's pretty easy to get hold of, whereas work by, for instance, Raoul Vaneigem is—to say the least—a little harder to track down. What we do get, amongst other things, is Jonathan Richman's "Roadrunner" rubbing shoulders with Richard Huelsenbeck, Marie Osmond reciting (as promised) "Karawani," Bascam Lamar Lunsford wishing he was a mole . . . all kinds of interesting and unexpected stuff. As with the book, the juxtapositions and connections make their own noise, their own harmonies, their own cacophonies. We get conversation and the silence that surrounds it or, to turn the image inside out, we get the fury of punk and the silence at its heart. These are sounds full of laughter, surprise, shock, recognition, bewilderment, fear, boredom, amazement, rage, whatever. They were made by human beings and they strike a strange chord that still resonates. We get something unfinished. If you don't believe me then turn on the radio or the TV. Breathe in and out. Walk around. Go for a bus ride. Or think of the empty, aggressive rictus of Whitney Houston's smile, and then think of Little Richard singing "Ready Teddy." Which is *really* the more demented?

Greil Marcus: Do Politics Rock?

Jason Gross/1997

From *Perfect Sound Forever*, June 1997. Used by permission of the author.

Anyone who has done any reading about music knows about the person responsible for *Mystery Train, Lipstick Traces, Dead Elvis, The Dustbin of History, Ranters and Crowd Pleasers* and most recently *Invisible Republic.* He's also edited a great collection of Lester Bangs writings (*Psychotic Reactions*) and the original collection of desert-island discs (*Stranded*). Above all else, Greil Marcus's writing is compelling—a lot of times I've found his descriptions of a song he loves better than the song itself. Another striking quality about his work is his sense (and knowledge) of history that he brings to his writing. In the space of a sentence, he can jump back and forth between a "simple" rock song, French Situationists, media theorists, and an old ad and make the connections all make sense.

One interesting thread that's been in his work has been the connections he's found between popular music/culture and revolutionaries/incendiaries. Though this aspect was touched on in his earlier works, it came out clearly in *Lipstick Traces* and *Ranters.* So, what is the connection here? Do politics and rock mix or are they just weird, distant bed-fellows? How have they affected each other? (By the way, Marcus describes his own political leanings as: "From a left, New-Deal tradition: no one in my family has ever voted Republican.")

Perfect Sound Forever: Before the first wave of rock and roll, do you find that there were any rebellious youth movements around connected to music?

Greil Marcus: Albert Goldman, in his twisted neurotic way, made the argument that there was nothing new about rock and roll. In his words, it was "a regurgitation of the swing era." He was saying that *everything* in rock and roll had been done before, as culture and as music. He was talking about the swing period where he grew up. He could have just as well been talking about the ragtime era or the jazz era in the '20s. He was saying that these were times when young people focused their energies and their aspirations and got much of their identity from popular singers and popular songs. It was a language between people. He said that the point wasn't to act like a kid, the point was to act like a sophisticated adult in New York. His argument was that this was good. He thought that teenagers wanting to act like teenagers was something worse. People who were older than teenagers were still maintaining the attributes of people who were younger and he thought this was disgusting.

It was the years after the War in the late '40s and the early '50s when there was so much money floating around the American economy. In England, there was so little money that there was such a sense of betrayal and disappointment that they had won the War yet they had been ruined and impoverished that (for also different reasons in Germany and France) youth cults began to spring up. Sometimes they were organized around gangs or motorcycle clubs or schools. A culture where the notion that being young was a blessed state that you should affirm as being good in itself and you should try to hold on to because of its goodness for as long as you could began to emerge before there was anything identifiable as rock and roll, like Bill Haley or Elvis Presley. It was unformed, spectral. When rock and roll arrived and when you had two absolute symbolic teenagers suddenly appear in front of a nation (James Dean and Elvis Presley), everything fell into place. Then people had an image to connect to, to try to live up to, to imitate. That's when that connection was made. There wasn't at this time any sort of political rebellion unless you're looking at something like the Lettrist International, which started in '52 and which was definitely a political movement, a cultural movement, and a youth movement.

One of the popular novels in the '50s was a book called *Auntie Mame* by Patrick Dennis. It was about a guy growing up in the '20s and '30s. There's a wonderful chapter where he talks about how he and his friends are in college and they all worship Fred Astaire just like people would later worship Elvis Presley. They want to dress like him, talk like him, light cigarettes like him. They all walk around in this absolutely hilarious, unknowing parody of sophistication and adulthood. That's exactly what people in the '40s and particularly the '50s were not doing. They were not in any way imitating or acting out adulthood. They weren't like little girls putting on their mother's dresses, high heels, and lipstick. The rebelliousness that was everywhere perceived and what has today become a cliché wasn't about politics.

It wasn't about changing society or addressing injustices. The rebelliousness was the insistence of young people of all kinds on autonomy, on being able to act as they wished for no particular reason and engage in play or delinquent activities that weren't going to lead into adulthood or jobs or family or responsibility. This was people living in a self-contained and seemingly autonomous realm of being. That was really something new. You could go back to find precursors like the zoot suit riots of the '40s. But as a whole culture, with movies, music, novels (to a lesser degree), modes of behavior, and private languages, it really was something new.

The Beats don't figure into this—they don't really matter until the late '50s/'60s. They came at a later youth culture from the side. The Beats were adults acting like adults but they were living according to a different code of values. There was nothing teenage, nothing juvenile, nothing naive or innocent about them, at least in terms of their intentions and their self-conscious position.

PSF: Is it a contradiction that some of the main figures in rock and roll movement came from conservative, religious backgrounds?

GM: That's true except you have to see it in terms of mainstream (northern, urban) America and the rural South. The people in the rural South didn't see themselves and weren't seen as the rest of the country as part of mainstream America. They were always considered (and they considered themselves) scorned outsiders—if they wanted to be in they would have to fight their way there. The great emblematic song of Pentecostalism is "The Great Speckled Bird." In the song, the bird is this weird, almost beautiful creature that everybody looks at like, "Look at that freak, what is this?" They all turn away from it in disgust. The great speckled bird is the true believer, the Pentecostal Christian. So these people would say, "The world may consider us ugly and insane but we're on the true path." So, to call these people conservative is to miss the point. They were outside. Any attempt by these people who didn't belong and weren't invited in to make a claim on the attention of the nation is going to be seen as a violation.

Plus you've got the fact that Little Richard may have come from a very conservative church background but he was a raving queen. He was desperately trying to find an outlet for his homosexuality and his sense of style and his wish to strut in public. The great figures in the community for these people were the great politicians (like Huey Long) and the Pentecostal preacher, which was closer to home for them. He was the man who gets up before the congregation and sings at the top of his lung, stalks to and fro behind and in front of the altar and shakes his fist and makes a complete spectacle of himself. That's where people got a sense of feeling odd.

PSF: Do you find that this youth movement that grew up around rock and roll faltered after the late '50s?

GM: There was always an element of rock and roll that did want to grow up, go to nightclubs and get married and make their parents happy. Frankie Avalon was that sort. You also had people like Dion who came from a very lower-class Italian background and got himself into a gang and into heroin. When his rock and roll career collapsed, he found his way into Greenwich Village and the folk scene and followed a real twisting road.

It wasn't just the big guns being silenced (Presley, Chuck Berry, Buddy Holly, Jerry Lee Lewis, Little Richard) but it had more to do with the audience. People like me and all the people I knew got a taste of something dangerous when rock and roll first really exploded. A lot of people thought, "Now the world has changed, now it's different, we're different, we're different from our parents." But by '58 or '59, the number one song was "Tammy" by Debbie Reynolds. I remember at the time thinking this was all a trick that we played on ourselves. We only pretended that we were rebellious, that we were different, that we wanted something different. In fact, deep down, what we really wanted was a lullaby. We wanted "Tammy." There's no question that the people who bought "Tammy" were the same teenagers who were buying "Hound Dog." I remember at the time being very disappointed with that. I think that the great proportion of the audience was just in high school. When they graduated from high school, they put aside childish things to grow up.

So, it was a big shock to a lot of people when in '63 and '64, the story started up again. I don't think that most people ever expected that, in any fundamental way, rock and roll (music that affirmed meaninglessness and in that affirmation contained every conceivable kind of meaning) would ever be a part of their lives again. That's one of the reasons that people dove headlong into the Beatles. It wasn't just thirteen- or fourteen-year-old girls that were part of the audience—it was also college students and other people.

PSF: How do think their cultural impact was different from the first wave of rock and roll?

GM: One thing was that the original figureheads weren't supposed to act very smart. They were supposed to be extraordinarily polite, as both Jerry Lee Lewis and Elvis were, or they were supposed to be extremely circumspect, as Chuck Berry was. If Berry, as a black man, said *half* of what he was thinking at any given moment, he might have been lynched. He probably should have been a hell of lot more careful than he was because the cops were always on him. He had already been in prison long before he had become a musician. He was arrested and held in jail overnight in Mississippi in the '50s. He supposedly looked at a white woman "the wrong way" after a concert—he might have winked at her, and she became hysterical and called the police. Chuck Berry was a handsome, smart, cool black man who, for white cops, was nothing but trouble.

The only person of that first generation who could have started to act hip was Buddy Holly. He had married a Puerto Rican woman and moved to Greenwich Village and God knows what would have happened if Buddy Holly had lived.

The Beatles were the first group of people to come along who didn't pretend to be stupid. They acted and talked as intelligently as they actually were. They allowed the Rolling Stones to come along and then be as cool, as obnoxious, as bohemian, as "fuck you," as in-your-face as they wanted to be. It suddenly turned out that that you could act this way and not suddenly burst into flames. You could just get away with it.

Here's where the Beats come in—they had already infiltrated contemporary culture and made themselves felt. The British are people who read *On the Road*, an utterly romantic piece of shit as far as I'm concerned though it influenced many people. That's the difference there. This difference leads to a perception of rebellion and ultimately to a real affirmation and acting out of rebellion. That line was pretty easy to trace and pretty direct.

PSF: As the '60s progressed and the bands and political movements around it got more radical, did you think that their politics were sincere or meaningful at all? You've said that you thought that Jerry Rubin and Abbie Hoffman were phonies.

GM: I always thought of Jerry Rubin and Abbie Hoffman as careerists and people who wanted to be pop stars. They wanted attention. They wanted people to admire them, to look up to them and get lots of pretty girls to fuck. I'm not putting down those things as motives, but when you say "I'm only here to change the world," then you have a right to be criticized. The Beatles, the Rolling Stones, and Bob Dylan didn't say, "I'm here to change the world and if I get benefits on the side, I won't turn them down." I also thought that Rubin and Hoffman had the most puerile ideas—they weren't interesting and they weren't good at what they did. If I had liked them as people or found their ideas inspiring, I might think differently.

When the bands became "political," they never did become political. Instead, individuals in certain groups began acting as whole people. Whole people have political dimensions. They can get outraged at things and they're moved by other things. They talk with their friends about these things and if they have a public forum, they speak publicly about these things. That doesn't make that the whole of their lives but any real person who's living in the real world is going to be energized by a political situation or disgusted with those same things. They're going to react with a sense of confirmation or exclusion at that political event.

That's what people began to do. They were doing this within the protection of a culture that seemed autonomous. It gave them the permission and the strength to do that. When everyone around you is taking drugs, having sex, and espousing extreme political opinions, then it seems like the natural way to live. So just as you say, "Why shouldn't I take this LSD?" you also say, "Why shouldn't I say what I think of the Vietnam War?" That was something absolutely new. People didn't do that before.

In 1956, Elvis Presley didn't exactly endorse a presidential candidate but bizarrely, when he was asked who he was going to vote for, he said he was going to vote for Adlai Stevenson. They shut him up really quickly. They didn't want to alienate anybody plus this is a good American boy who's supposed to sing songs and NOT have opinions. You might think that it's odd that Elvis Presley would vote for the egghead governor of Illinois but (white) people in Mississippi didn't vote for Republicans then—it wouldn't have occurred to them. Stevenson carried Georgia, Alabama, South Carolina, and that was about it.

PSF: How do you see that the radical movement, along with the music, changing once the Nixon administration came into power?

GM: The Nixon administration saw as one of its missions to wipe out and destroy dissent in whatever form it occurred. It affected music in two ways. First, it made some people more combative (i.e., the Jefferson Airplane, the Byrds, David Crosby). Ultimately, the world of pop music responded like the rest of the world, which is to say that after Jackson State and Kent State, people got really scared. They found out that you could really get killed by doing this stuff at any time. They began to back off and they began to shut up. What broke the anti-war movement was that. That was a self-betrayal analogous (in my mind) to teenagers waking up one day and saying, "We really do like 'Tammy' better than Arlene Smith [the Chantels]." When people found out that you could die from this, they backed off. It was a lack of a sense of history, intelligence, and nerve for people to go into a battle against their own government with the illusion that nobody was going to get hurt.

PSF: A few years after this disillusion, the punk movement came along. What do you see as its legacy and how it also became a unique youth movement?

GM: I don't know how to put it or position it. I don't know if punk started out as a rejection of pop music or life in the U.K. at that time. Certainly, as soon as it started, as soon as the Sex Pistols began to perform as a public outrage and even before they released their first record, a whole conflict of symbolism immediately gathered and was drawn to what they were doing. None of this was accidental because Malcolm McLaren and Jamie Reid, who were the real college-educated Col. Parkers of this movement, had a Situationist background and were schooled in a haphazard way in nihilist European art politics going all the way back to the nineteenth century. They believed that architecture could be as repressive as a law [that would] put people in jail for criticizing the government. They believed that the music that people heard every day had as much of an effect on how people thought of themselves as anything people learned in school. They saw records as a way to disrupt the assumptions that people didn't question, that people used to hold themselves together. This is to say that these were the assumptions that held society together. I don't think they saw records, performances, and songs as a way to change the world as such. It was more of a theft—"Let's set off a bomb and see what happens."

Within that perspective, everything was a target. Pink Floyd are no more or no less the enemy than the government. That's the mindset here. This was utterly true for Johnny Rotten as someone who really schooled himself on James Joyce and Graham Greene and his sense of being an outsider because he was Irish and being just astonishingly smart and vehement and impatient. For the other people in the band, I don't think it was ever anything more than a chance to be in a band in the beginning and later what an absolute thrill it was to tell society to go fuck itself. By the time the band was really making records, they were all understanding (except maybe Sid Vicious) what it's about and what it's for. It was a chance, if not to change society, to live a life that you would never expect to live within society. That's not a life of money and fame and girls. That's a life of feeling free and complete and alive. From that, anything can flow.

From that, you get the Clash, an ideological band which really did have political positions. They went out and named the villains and wore political slogans on their clothes (which I think is hilarious in a way but they were great looking costumes). The funny thing about the Clash is that they turned lines that Johnny Rotten threw out in interviews into songs. They worked with received ideas and they were authentically changed by those second-hand ideas. Joe Strummer might have started out mouthing ideological slo-gans because it seemed like a good idea. But he began to think about the things he was singing and I think he actually decided they were true and they actually got him thinking.

Then of course by the time you get to the mid '70s in England, the Beats are really a pervasive influence, William Burroughs and Kerouac in partic-ular. That sense of autonomy and nihilist rebellion, saying, "the dominant society is a bunch of boring old shits and we are true and virile," is really strong. The angelization of the heroin addict is very strong. There's a lot of parallel with that scene.

PSF: How did the U.K. punk scene compare with the one that was going on in the States? Didn't it have any significance itself as a movement?
GM: With the exception of Pere Ubu, I never found the U.S. punk move-ment all that interesting. I think X was a great band but if they came out of any tradition at all, if they tell a story, it's an L.A. story. In a way, it's a story that's already been told. You find all of X in film noir and Raymond Chan-dler.

Pere Ubu was in essence a bunch of European aesthetes who happened to find themselves in Cleveland and said, "My God, what the fuck are we doing here?" It's like they suddenly woke up and said, "Toto, I don't think we're in Paris anymore. We're in Cleveland. Holy shit!" So they created their own bohemian community and their own bohemian traditions and heroes, among them Alfred Jarry, and went on from there. They were a great band in '75 and they're a great band today. David Thomas said an interesting thing a few years ago. When they put out *Story of My Life*, there were quotes from the band members and he said, "People always ask why we're doing this." He had a wonderful analogy. He said "It's kind of like people who became Com-munists in the '30s. Even when you find out that the theory is wrong, that the victory will never come, you don't give up on it. It's changed you. You're stuck. You really have nothing left to do with your life. You still believe in it and you have no choice." I thought that was both wonderfully humorous and incredibly moving.

Charlotte Pressler was Peter Laughner's wife. He was the mad fool of the Cleveland punk movement—the person that everyone knew was the true genius and the person that nobody could stand to be around. She wrote a wonderful memoir about the beginning of the Cleveland scene, which was very much an art scene. People were putting together their own bohemia out of second- and third- and fourth-hand fragments, picked up from weirdo high school teachers and local libraries and *Mad* magazine. She said that these people were very self-conscious. They were intentionally trying to find a way to get outside of society.

They all had to make the decision not to go to college because they knew that if they went, the world would open up to them. The temptation to follow a career that had already cut its path would be irresistible. The chance of doing the work that you realize at the age of sixteen that you had to do would be lost forever. So these middle-class people whose parents could easily send them to college and were smart enough to go there just said, "No, I can't do this." That's very moving too because that's very different from the English punk movement or the Beatles or Rolling Stones, all of whom had the chance to go to art college—this is where you put people who are real smart, sensitive juvenile delinquents in England. That's where you expose them to the whole tradition of the avant-garde in the hopes that maybe they'll become decent commercial designers. Art college has always been the great spawning ground for British rock and roll bands, except for Mick Jagger who went to the London School of Economics, a real college.

PSF: So you don't see the New York punk scene as having any significance then?

GM: I don't think there's any question that for over twenty years the Ramones have inspired countless people to do all kinds of things. They inspired the Sex Pistols and the Clash. I didn't like them. I always thought they were a bunch of twits. As one of the guys in Gang of Four put it, "These guys must be really thick." Gang of Four *loved* the Ramones. They just actually believed that you get past the parody/stupidity and find the real stupidity. Television was an arty version of the Grateful Dead. To me, it was just a new form of rock and roll. It was all just a downtown New York bohemian scene. It was a local story. I still believe that. This was local music as far as I was concerned. I don't believe that the reason that punk came to life again and again all over the world is due to anything that happened in New York.

It was because of the glimpse of possibility that people got out of the Sex Pistols or the Adverts or X-Ray Spex. These were bands where the most unlikely people suddenly appeared in public and said, "I can say anything I want," which is the most liberating thing in the world to do. I don't think you ever saw that in New York. What New York said was, "You can become a heroin addict and become cooler than anybody else and you can play guitar and be a real poet, and we obviously know that being a poet is the best thing in the world to be."

PSF: After the first wave of punk died out, did you find that there were other political movements building up around music or rock in particular?

GM: I don't see literal connections between bands and youth movements or songs and political activity. Both are forms of discourse, both are different forms of conversation. They inform each other but in ways that are not obvious and in ways that can only be teased out or imagined or churned into stories. I don't have anything to say about, for instance, the connection between the Gang of Four or the Mekons and what they were doing and their effect on what people might be doing politically. If anything, the effect is the other way around because these bands came out of a tremendously politicized milieu where feminism, gay rights, skinheads beating up and killing non-whites was their frame of reference, their everyday life. To make music that in some way didn't incorporate that would be to deny your own experience and knowledge and the things that got you excited, angry, or happy or allowed you to make friends. The lines between what you could say in a song and what you said to people you cared about had long since been smashed by Bob Dylan. If you look at the most politicized music that the Mekons made, like *Fear and Whiskey* or *Edge of the World*, the music is a lament for a battle that's been lost. This is not rallying troops or defining good. This is the kind of art that's often been made after the defeat of a revolt or a rebellion. This is music made as the Mekons understood it in the shadow of fascism. The same with Elvis Costello's music.

Now if that music goes out into the world and hits peoples' hearts or makes people think the political situation that they perceive isn't as locked in as it appears to be, or if it just makes them think more deeply, the consequences of that can lead in any direction. The Weathermen actually used pop songs as part of their metaphors (they named themselves after a Dylan song). They went underground and set off bombs in strategic places to make sure people wouldn't get killed and they got publicity and made people see that the government is really not in control. Then a few of them got killed making bombs and they thought that maybe their strategy wasn't good after all because "Gosh, you can get hurt making bombs." This is the same with "Tammy" and Kent State—this is the naiveté that beggars all understanding. It had nothing to do with the validity of the strategy—it was "Golly, we can get hurt. Better change our strategy." Their manifesto announcing their new strategy was called NEW MORNING, after a Dylan album. One of the songs in their songbook was an adaptation of "Bad Moon Rising"—the only change was "Better get your shit together" instead of "Better get your things together." You can say that there's a connection between the Weathermen and pop music but I don't think there's a connection at all. I think the connection is utterly meaningless, trivial, and exploitive on the part of the Weathermen. It was just a way to look with it. It's a direct connection but, I think, a meaningless one. The connections among Elvis Presley, Jim Jones, and David Koresh are much more interesting.

PSF: Do you see that a lot of rock has lost its rebellious nature as it's been used so much in commercials and elsewhere?

GM: That depends on your point of view. I think in those places where real rock and roll persists, it might be just as much a threat as it ever was in a way that's mysterious and hard to track. Sleater-Kinney is as inspiring, dangerous, and troublesome as any band we've ever seen. What the consequences of their music are going to be is impossible to say.

You're talking about a perception where you say, "This doesn't seem like a threat—it's part of mainstream culture." Bill Clinton gets inaugurated and Bob Dylan and Aretha Franklin show up to perform. Every old rock and roll song is turned into a commercial and rewritten. It's everywhere you look. I don't believe that for a minute. I don't believe that any bite has gone out of "Gimmie Shelter" or "Ready Teddy." I don't believe that "Whole Lotta Shakin' Goin' On" has any less power to change anyone who's heard it for the first time today than it did in 1957.

PSF: Do you find that songs with implicit or explicit political statements make a stronger case or point? For instance, how would you compare Elvis Costello's music with Woody Guthrie's in this context?

GM: Woody Guthrie had a sign on his guitar that said, "This machine kills fascists." That's just the kind of connection between music and politics that I'm arguing against. It wasn't a machine and it didn't kill fascists. It made Woody Guthrie and the people who listened to him feel noble. I'm not say-

ing that he wasn't against fascism but to say that you could defeat it by singing songs is not helpful in the war against fascism.

The original title of *Armed Forces* was *Emotional Fascism*. Elvis Costello
was making a very, very complex and sophisticated argument with that record in the words that he wrote and in the way that he sang them. He was
saying fascism is the dominant mode of political behavior in the West today
and it has seeped down to our everyday lives. If fascism now pervades our
everyday lives and our interactions with each other, our whole understanding of social intercourse supports and ultimately affirms fascism. This makes
it a more interesting and less fixed statement.

Woody Guthrie says, "Sing my songs and defeat fascism." Elvis Costello
says, "Fascism exists—look around you." Is that a stronger political statement? I don't know. It doesn't tell you what to do or promise any results. It's
a stronger *statement* but I don't know if it's a stronger political statement.

All These Inches Away Where Greil Marcus Began

Dave Weich/2001

From Powells.com, 2001. Used by permission.

"Greil Marcus," Nick Hornby has written, "is simply peerless. Not only as a rock writer but as a cultural historian."

Wondering how Bob Dylan resurrected his career in the nineties or what Elvis Presley and Bill Clinton have in common? Curious which novel's unabridged audio cassettes Marcus calls 2000's Album of the Year—"Nothing came close," he insists—or what made Lester Bangs one of rock music's most eloquent critics? Greil Marcus recently spent an afternoon at Powell's, browsing the shelves for hard-to-find titles and answering as many questions as I could squeeze into an hour.

Dave Weich: In the introduction to *Mystery Train*, you explain that you meant to address rock and roll not as youth culture or counterculture, but as American culture. People tend to think of you as a rock critic—that's where we shelve your books—but it seems like you write about America and contemporary culture as much as anything.

Greil Marcus: That's true, but most of the time music is where I start. I start with a song, or maybe just a riff or even a whole body of somebody's work. I start with some kind of musical interruption. Something musical makes a breach, opens up questions that I wind up pursuing.

At the least music is a jumping-off point, and at the most it's an organizing principle. It's a shadow cast over anything I might write.

Lipstick Traces starts off being about the Sex Pistols and it ends up being about the Sex Pistols, but in between there's four hundred pages of other stuff covering hundreds and hundreds of years. The Sex Pistols aren't an excuse. They're the bad conscience of the whole book and of all the other people who emerge in its convoluted story.

A lot of people were confused or upset by *Invisible Republic*, which is about Bob Dylan's Basement Tapes. They said, "Only half the book is about the Basement Tapes!" and "You only write about six or seven songs in any detail!" Well, yeah, that's the point. The Basement Tapes is such a mysterious piece of work, and they're so shrouded, the songs are so disguised, that they open up into all different directions. Were you to write about that music and only that music I think you'd be defrauding it. The whole point is where it can take you, not whether you can stick to the subject.

DW: When Dylan's live 1966 album was officially released a couple years ago, I'd seen *Don't Look Back*, but it was the first time I'd heard extended live performances from that tour, when he went electric for the first time. And it blew me away, it really did. The first disk, the acoustic portion, is gorgeous.
GM: It is.

DW: It was so much more beautiful than I'd expected. Then you put on the second disk when he plugs in with The Band, and it's an incredible rock and roll band playing.

On the disk, you can hear people shouting from the audience. The crowd felt as if it had been betrayed. You wrote in *Invisible Republic*, "Dylan's performance now seemed to mean that he had never truly been where he had appeared to be only a year before, reaching for that democratic oasis of the heart. It was as if it had all been a trick—a trick he had played on them."

Simply the fact that this musician could stand in front of them playing an electric guitar, suddenly they felt alone and alienated and deceived.
GM: That was the hardest thing for me to write about in *Invisible Republic*, to get at why and how people were so upset and outraged and betrayed at Dylan's move into rock and roll, playing with a band. In California, myself and everybody I knew, we thought Dylan was late! Why did it take so long? We didn't understand remotely what all this fuss was back east, what people were upset about. We had no clue. The Beatles were as natural as breathing to us and the Rolling Stones as natural as dirt. The question of corruption or betrayal involved with these songs and this sort of music, it didn't make any sense to me.

So I thought a lot, listened differently than I ever had before. I had to go back almost thirty years to try and recapture what this felt like. I spent a lot of time trying to bring it to life for other people once I'd made sense of it myself because I think in fact it was something really deep, really profound.

People had committed themselves to living in another country, which is the name of the first chapter of *Invisible Republic*, "Another Country." Bob Dylan was in some ways the president of that country, and he committed treason by saying, "This country isn't real," or, "You don't really live in this country; you live in a bigger, more dangerous world in which the idea of purity has no meaning." That was not something people wanted to hear. They felt tricked. They felt fooled.

Not having been there, I had trouble imagining that people actually meant it when they booed, that they weren't just going through an act of what they thought they were supposed to do. But I've talked enough with Robbie Robertson and other people in The Band to know that it was ugly; it was hateful. Just to get the music across on a given night, particularly in England at the end of that tour, was a real struggle. It was dispiriting. They would say over and over again, "We've played the best we can play. We've made music that we know is great, and people are acting as if we've thrown warm shit in their faces. What are we doing wrong?" It wasn't a question of history will absolve us. They were thinking, *What do we have to do to get across to people how good this is?* And the answer is that there was nothing they could do.

DW: Bob Dylan resurrected his career in the nineties. He hadn't been taken seriously as a contemporary performer, at least in the mainstream, for quite a few years. Now in the last seven or eight years he's on top of the world again. What happened?

GM: A couple things, I think. I have no idea about his personal life, but leaving that out, in terms of his professional life and in terms of the music he was making, he had made one poor album after another, and every time one of these records would come out, whether it was *Under the Red Sky* or *Empire Burlesque* or *Knocked Out Loaded* or *Oh Mercy* or *Infidels*, any of these, really, quite bad records that made no sense, didn't hang together, had no point, and did not need to exist, every single time *Rolling Stone* and many other publications said, "He's back! He's done it! He's really broken through! This is the best record he's made in ten . . . in twenty years! Since *Blood on the Tracks*! Since *Blonde on Blonde*!" Whatever. It got to the point where somebody wrote a hilarious parody of all these "The real Dylan has reemerged" records.

So imagine if you're a serious person, an artist who knows that art is out there in the world, but you've somehow reached a point where you can't touch it. You can't really get there. And every time you do something that you know is a compromise, a fraud, something you just dashed off, people rush to it and celebrate it as if it's the best thing you can do. How do you feel? It's the opposite of what I was talking about before, when your best work is rejected. That's one thing. When your poor work is celebrated, it says that people don't care. They can't tell the difference.

So for whatever reason, in 1992, he sat down with a guitar and a harmonica, and he made a record of old blues and folk songs, stuff that in his own repertoire predated his first albums, songs he was singing at the Ten O'Clock Scholar in Minneapolis, in Dinkytown, in 1961. The stuff he was singing when he first discovered this music and was able to absorb it and find its voice more quickly and more deeply than other people.

There's a bootleg live album [from the late '80s and early '90s], a compilation of old ballads and folk songs. It's a wonderful record. But every time Bob Dylan comes out by himself in the middle of some concert and sings one of these old songs, you can hear that people in the crowd are drunk, and people are screaming, "Bring back The Band!" It's just the opposite of what had happened so many years before. Nobody's listening. Nobody's paying any attention.

So he makes this quiet record, *Good As I Been to You*, this funny, sexy, distant, odd record. He releases it, for whatever reason, on Election Day 1992. The previous year, he'd put together a new band with John Jackson and Tony Garnier and a couple of others, the band he used when he accepted his Lifetime Achievement Award on the Grammys in 1991 and played "Masters of War" in the middle of the Gulf War. The most electrifying, fast, indecipherable, furious, threatening version of that song imaginable. It took me a minute to realize what the song was and I only realized from the melody, not the words, but it was so exciting. It was the kind of music you don't hear on TV.

Right about that time, he's rediscovering the oldest music that he can touch, that he can transform, that's his. And he's also decided—something most people would not do at his age, at fifty-one—he decides to become a lead guitar player. He begins playing lead guitar in his own band.

In the shows he was giving in 1994 and '95, any given song would be two-thirds instrumental. The songs were an excuse for him to stretch out and play in a way that he'd never played before. With that impetus, discovering his old music, discovering abilities that he didn't know he had or had never dared present to the public, he finds his way into *Time out of Mind*, which is a set of new songs that all have the feeling they could have been written a hundred or two hundred years ago. They're written out of the old songs he'd been clearing his throat with on *Good As I Been to You* and *World Gone Wrong* in '92 and '93.

He established a new plateau, and that's where he lives, on this wide, flat expanse, overlooking his whole career. He's done something as good as anything he's ever done and different from anything he's ever done. For the time being, that's all he needs to do. He's at the top of his career.

DW: *Double Trouble*, which discusses that 1992 election, among other things, collects your essays and articles about Elvis and Bill Clinton, yet many of the pieces aren't about either one. They're more about the cultural atmosphere during those times.

Now that Bill's out of the White House is he going to get fat, sit on his couch, and shoot the TV? What does Clinton do now that he's out of the spotlight?

GM: I wrote a piece last fall about Clinton's future. The *Guardian* in London had asked me to do a piece, another Elvis and Clinton piece. I thought, I did that. But it struck me that Clinton's life would be very, very different were Gore to win or were Bush to win. It would really make a difference. So I imagined a life for him under Bush and under Gore.

In one case, under Bush, he goes through a slough of despondency where his life is utterly ruined, then reemerges and makes an Elvis-like comeback. Under Gore, though, his life is a complete tragedy. He's not needed or wanted. He ends up, in essence, disappearing. What I didn't imagine was that Gore would win and Bush would be given the presidency or that Clinton would disgrace himself upon leaving the White House.

The only thing factually that I got right was that the Republicans would retain control of the House and the Senate and Hillary would be elected—I needed Hillary to be elected because I needed Bill to be peripheral even in his own marriage. That worked.

I don't know what he's going to do. He's too smart and he's too stupid, he's too vain and he's too scared to live an ordinary, straight, and narrow life. He's fifty-four years old and he could have done anything if he had not been, with some help from the media, utterly smeared upon leaving the White House. He now has to reinvent himself or become a complete sleaze. I don't know which it will be.

DW: Why is Elvis such a bedrock of American popular culture? Is Elvis American popular culture, period? Is he at the heart of everything?

GM: He really is, for a whole lot of different reasons.

If you go back into his genealogy, you find out there's a very high probability that he's part Jewish. You find out that even before he became famous there were many, many people who believed he was part black, or as the phrase went, "There was Negro blood in the Presleys." Their background was pretty typical rural, very, very poor Southern. There's polygamy. There's polyandry. There's a complete confusion of genealogy and antecedents going back to the period before and after the Civil War, so it's very hard to pinpoint exactly what the line is. There are many people who tell the story that in fact Vernon Presley is not Elvis's father, that Gladys had an affair with a black man. I don't believe any of this, but it's not impossible.

The point is that people tell these stories because they made sense to them. There's something about Elvis that a single ethnic or racial identity cannot contain. So you have a figure who is, at least in the common imagination, Christian and not Christian; part Pagan, because of the nature of his music, but devout; black and white; and in terms of the way he looks and moves, male and female, masculine and feminine. You have a figure who breaks down if you fix him narrowly.

Then you add to that the way he looked, how gorgeous he was, and the way he sounded, with a seductiveness, a thrill that threatened to break out at any time that really no singer had ever had before, and you have a mystery that nobody can solve. But you also have a figure that everybody can recognize, everybody can relate to, maybe with hate and fear, maybe with love and envy and desire. No one can be indifferent. This is not the sort of person who comes along very often.

Albert Murray, the great jazz critic, was once writing about how the notion of genius is denied to black people, that black artists are always seen as exemplars of sociological principles. He said he didn't know how many times he's read that what made Bessie Smith Bessie Smith could be ascribed to the fact that her people had suffered and bled for hundreds of years on American soil, and it was the pain and suffering of African Americans as a whole that found a voice in hers. He said, "Isn't it interesting that four hundred years of black pain and suffering have only produced one Bessie Smith?"

That's the point. This is not sociology. This is someone who comes along and becomes a mirror for all of our desires and our fears, someone to whom we can all connect on very basic levels, whether negatively or positively. Elvis is a fulcrum of American culture, regardless of how cheesy, tiresome, redundant, and repetitious the idea or the reality of Elvis Presley becomes. He will always reemerge as a way to talk about who we are and how we got here. He'll always be around.

DW: You mention Peter Guralnick's biography as being "the only reliable biography of Elvis." Those books have been huge sellers around here for a long time.

GM: They're real books, different from the other books about Elvis, but I do have problems with what Peter did. When Peter started to work, to him Elvis Presley was no longer real in the world at large. That was what fascinated me, but it appalled Peter. He went in a different direction.

In the first volume, he leaves out completely whatever he can't absolutely document. That's extraordinarily responsible, but it also leaves entire areas of Elvis's story as others have told it blank. For instance, there are any number of people who talk about the shows Elvis played on Beale Street when he was nineteen years old, the only white guy who would perform on Beale Street. There are lots of people who speak in great detail about those shows. Peter believes they never really happened. It seems to me that if they never happened, you have to explore why these various individuals—and they're notable people—why they want us to believe that. What's going on there?

In the second volume, which is the story of someone losing his life as he continues to live it, Peter has a certain argument to make that not everyone would agree with, but it becomes airless, it seems to me. There's no room even for the humor that had to be there over the years. And in fact the explosion of vitality that comes in 1968 with Elvis doesn't make sense to me in the book.

But what Peter accomplished that no one else did—I don't think anyone else even tried—was to tell Elvis's story as if it was ordinary, as if it was down to earth, as if it was everyday life. You could walk down the street and here was this guy walking down the street beside you and he just dressed a little differently than you did, because he had more nerve or he wanted something—who knows?—but you could walk down the street with him and have a real conversation. He wouldn't know what was going to happen to him in the future. You wouldn't know, either. That kind of naturalism is what makes certainly the first volume of the book so alive and so real.

DW: You anointed *The Human Stain* audio cassettes the Album of the Year in one of your Top Ten lists on Salon.com. Do you listen to a lot of audio books?

GM: That's the first one I've ever listened to all the way through. I'd read the book twice and written about it. My wife and I were going to Hawaii for ten days, and she said, "Why don't we get the audio book of *The Human Stain*?" So I got it, and it was fourteen and a half hours! It's uncut, unabridged. We rented a car in Hawaii and we started playing these cassettes. Very, very quickly, we were spending a lot more time driving than we'd ever imagined we would.

Arliss Howard is the actor who did the reading, except for a small part by Debra Winger, his wife. And he was phenomenal. He not only has different voices for each character, he has different voices for the same characters at different points in their lives. And yet he makes sense. You can follow the physical growth or the aging of a character. It was completely real. One day we drove an extra hundred and fifty miles; we kept driving and driving because we didn't want to stop listening.

Ultimately, we made it last for the whole trip. And when we reached the end, we were both shattered, both because it was a shattering book and also because it was over! A whole dimension of life, of being in a play.

Imagine being seated on the stage and all the actors are moving around you, they don't notice you but you're right next to them and you feel their physical presence. Everything that's happening is as threatening to you or as full of promise to you as it is to them, that's what listening to this audio book was like. I was shocked that anyone could produce something on this level.

Nothing came close in terms of Album of the Year. Nothing.

DW: What else have you read or listened to lately that's really excited you?

GM: The new Daft Punk album, *Discovery*. They're two French guys who never show their faces—they don't paint their faces like Kiss; they wear this bizarre, futuristic headgear. They're a techno group, but what they're really doing is making eighties dance music with a glamorousness and an emotional depth that's quite overwhelming. It's funny and it's cheap and tinny, and it's beautiful, and it's uplifting. It's amazing stuff.

With books, I haven't had much time to read lately beyond what I'm reading for stuff that I'm writing about, so I've read a lot of lousy books that I'm reviewing.

DW: Do you generally choose the books you're reviewing?

GM: Someone might call up and say, "Would you like to review this book?" and I'll say yes or no. I've never worked in a situation where I've had to write anything that I didn't want to.

DW: Is it less interesting to write about a book that you didn't enjoy as much?

GM: It's a lot easier to write about something that you hate, to pick it apart and show why the author is a cretin or why his or her whole approach is misguided and twisted and all of that. It's more difficult to make a case for a book that you desperately want other people to read. To do that, you have to avoid proselytizing and get to what makes the book or record or movie different, what makes it strange, what makes it not like everything else out there, and that's hard to do. But I don't like one better than the other.

DW: Whether it's music or books or movies, is there a quality that differentiates good from bad for you? What do you look for? What excites you? Reading through a few decades of your reviews and criticism, it seems that you like everything, at least in bits and pieces. There's no genre or style, for example, of which you say, "Oh, that's not worth my time," or, "That doesn't do anything for me." On the other hand, you're more than willing to say when you think something is bad.

GM: I try not to walk through the world with preconceptions and rules, that something is good if it fits certain categories in certain ways. I just don't understand that stance. It's just so sterile, the idea that, let's say, poetry has to have a certain level of ambiguity before it can affect you emotionally. Well, if you've got to let it through several locked doors before it can affect you emotionally, then it's never going to affect you.

I watch movies, I listen to political speeches, I read the newspaper, I listen to records, I go to shows, I read books, and I'm always hoping that something will trouble me—it might be in a way that's truly pleasurable, it might be in a way that's scary, but it will move me an inch or a mile away from where I began. Once that happens, then I might begin to think, Why did this happen? What qualities in the work had this effect on me? Or, What did I bring to the work that brought it to life and allowed it to affect me? What's going on?

I remember when I first saw *Reservoir Dogs*. It's one of those works that gets meaner and meaner and meaner, and keeps pushing its own boundaries until it's gone too far so many times that at last I was utterly helpless before it. I was defenseless. It was like a nightmare I couldn't wake up from. And when I think back on that movie, which I do often, it's scenes that take place in the middle of it that I can't get over. They're still shocking and hideously ugly. But I couldn't even afford to quite register them as they were shooting by. To make sense of what made that movie special, what made it harder than anyone had any right to expect, that's interesting to me. But to say, "Well, it really can't be very good because in fact it's kind of a rip off of this Hong Kong movie," that's not the point at all.

For me, it always begins with the event, with the artifact. It doesn't begin with ideas that are brought to bear on the artifact to see whether the artifact will measure up to them.

If you look at art criticism from the forties on and the whole notion of flatness as a value in painting, certain critics decided that painting should be this way, so they went looking for artists who either exemplified what they were looking for or who were reading what these critics were saying and were doing what they were told to do because they knew they'd get good reviews and their paintings would sell. It's corrupt intellectually and it's corrupt commercially. None of this makes sense to me. I really have never understood it.

While I can make an argument for the value of "Anarchy in the U.K." by the Sex Pistols—that it's valuable because it crystallizes hundreds of years of cultural aspirations in a form they'd never taken before, that it acts out something culture had been trying to do for a long time—that's not why it's valuable. It's valuable because it's like a volcano exploded, it seems to me.

DW: By coincidence, the day I called your publicist to set up this interview, a friend of mine here had the Lester Bangs book you edited on his desk. He was really excited. He said, "It's the first time in years I've felt this excited about music." And he listens to music all the time.
GM: Reading Lester's book?

DW: Right.
GM: He could do that. Lester was very, very good at not censoring himself. That's one of the hardest things for a writer: to figure out what you really want to say, then to say it—not to say what will sound good and will reflect well on you. Often that happens unconsciously, but Lester was able to remove his censor a lot of the time. Not all the time, but a lot of the time, and to do it more completely than most writers ever do.

In that sense, he's a great inspiration to other writers. I can read Lester, and I can become aware of my own compromises or cowardice or hesitations, and I can say, "No, it doesn't have to be that way. You can make a fool of yourself."

That's what a writer has to do. I learned this from John Irving, though when he said it to me I didn't really understand what he meant. Years later I did. He was talking about Neil Young and Bob Dylan and why they were heroes of his. He said, "Because they're not afraid to make fools of themselves, and you have to be able to do that." I didn't quite get it then, in '78 or whenever it was, but for a critic or any person who does his or her work in public, to take the stance of You can't fool me and to always be careful not to be fooled, to always be one step ahead, to always be a figure of good judgment and probity, is absolute death. It's the worst thing you can do.

DW: How did you start writing the "Real Life Top 10" columns for Salon. com? Are those a major focus for you or something to keep you busy between larger projects?

GM: I started a column in *New West* magazine in 1978 called "Real Life Rock." At the end of each essay, I'd include a little list called "Real Life Top 10." The point was not to just be a list of records, but anything that remotely had to do with music, a dress Bette Midler wore at an awards show or a great guitar solo in the middle of a song that otherwise wasn't very interesting. At some point, Doug Simmons, the music editor at the *Village Voice*, said, "What if you made that into a real column, annotated each item?" I'd never thought of that. So I made it a monthly column for the *Village Voice* in around '86.

When the *Voice* got a new music editor who didn't like the column, I moved it to *Artforum*, and I did it there for quite some time.

It's the kind of column that really needs a general interest magazine to work. It wouldn't work in a music magazine—everybody else would be covering at least half the things I'd be covering, and it wouldn't make sense to go as far afield as I like to go, into books or movies or advertisements. I'd been reading Salon with more and more enthusiasm during the impeachment year, when they were at their absolute best, both in terms of reporting and critical writing, so I asked if they were interested, and they were.

They said that because people have a shorter attention span on the web the column should appear every two weeks, and in fact it's much easier to do it that way. I'm always thinking about it; I'm always looking for items. I can't afford to let it pile up till the end of the month. Also, with *Artforum*, I had a two-month lead time. With Salon, I can have a two-day lead time if I want. It's much more current in that way.

It's not a central focus, but it's a kind of organizing principle. I do it for fun. It keeps me looking, keeps me listening, keeps me alert. I'll do it as long as someone will publish it for me.

Online Exchange with Greil Marcus

RockCritics.com/2002

From RockCritics.com, 2002. Used by permission.

Readers of this site were invited to submit questions to music critic Greil Marcus, who sent his responses by e-mail. Thanks to everyone who took part in this exchange.

From: Tonya
Subject: Question for Greil
Date: Tue, 12 Mar 2002 09:15:38
I have two questions:

    A) Do you have any research (published or otherwise) or notable quotes regarding the Portland, OR hardcore/punk band Poison Idea or their singer Jerry A? This band never seems to get its due . . . it always just gets "mentioned" in the same breath as The Wipers . . . and nobody wants to dig any deeper than to state the obvious about them.

    B) With all the books/articles you've written on the subject of punk, why have these leviathans of the genre gone relatively unsung?
Greil Marcus: No idea.

From: Steven Rubio
Subject: Question for Greil
Date: Tue, 12 Mar 2002 09:18:43
Hey Greil. My question is pretty obvious, but maybe no one else asked it: what do you think of the canonization of rock critics that a site like Rock-Critics.com represents? Why does rock criticism lend itself to this kind of, for lack of a better word, idolatry? Film critics never got or get this particular kind of attention . . . someone like James Agee was famous, but not really for his criticism as much as his other work, and others from that era,

say Manny Farber or Robert Warshow, weren't quite the "stars" that writers such as yourself have become amongst a certain population. Even Pauline was more important as an inspiration to future critics and as a conscience to filmmakers than she was a key popular figure (although I guess Roger Ebert might be the one to give the lie to my argument). Cameron Crowe might have gotten it wrong in *Almost Famous*, but the fact that Lester Bangs is an important character in a popular, highly-regarded movie is telling, I think; I can't recall anything similar featuring a film critic, or a book critic, or a cultural critic of any type.

GM: Dear Steve, I wasn't aware rock critics were being canonized, but now that you mention it, be sure to address me properly the next time we run into each other—and by the way, what is the proper form of address to a saint? I don't think it's "St. So and So," because you have to be dead to be a saint. "He who is sure to rise above me" might do, but it's a mouthful. I think perhaps just backing off several feet before speaking might be ok. But in fact I don't see it, not remotely. Lester, when he was alive, was certainly a magnet for certain kinds of scenesters, and Lester played a role, he both loved and hated his scene-making as a Falstaff—as a clown, a fool, a crazy, a madman, and so on. Dead, he can be a hero, a mentor, a presence, a conscience—but it seems to me he appears in Cameron Crowe's *Almost Famous* not because of his larger-than-life role in pop culture and his status as a wise man, but because he was personally important to Cameron. He made a difference in Cameron's life. He appears in the movie, and for all I know played the same role in Cameron's career, as Cameron's ideal audience—someone who could tell the difference between truth and lie, on the artist's own terms. There was a lot I didn't like about that movie, but the portrayal of Lester (along with everyone singing "Tiny Dancer" on the plane, and Billy Crudup tossing out a line of "Peggy Sue" just as the plane seems about to crash) was just fine.

Who follows writers of any sort around? Or, rather, what writers get followed around? Writers who make an effort to cultivate a mystique, who combine imperiousness with noblesse oblige, who work to be stars, and whose publications promote them as stars—*Rolling Stone* with Hunter Thompson, *Vanity Fair* with Christopher Hitchens.

What you're referring to isn't part of my frame of reference. I imagine there are people out there who having nothing better to do, or nothing else they can imagine doing, than to wonder what this or that writer, music critic, film critic, novelist, TV news reader, is really like, how fabulous it would be to just hang out with the person, to bask in their presence, to be them. (Which brings up the question: what is "hanging out"? Is it different from "hanging around," one of the most boring activities of all time?) Edmund Wilson once wrote than anyone who has spent a year working for a magazine knows there is no piece so good that its publication will not bring forth letters from people canceling their subscriptions, and no piece so bad that it won't bring forth letters from people claiming it has changed their life. I think it begins and ends there.

From: Astral Weeks
Subject: Questions for Greil
Date: Tue, 12 Mar 2002 10:10:51
What is your opinion of the lashing that Richard Meltzer gave you in his essay "Vinyl Reckoning"? I ask because it didn't seem to irk Christgau that much and I wondered if you were as good a sport as he.
GM: While the question is posed in classic "Have you stopped beating your wife?" terms—be a good sport or burn in hell—I've always thought there was no reason to respond to attacks, unless I've been accused of making a factual error I didn't make. I figure that I've had my turn in print; now it's someone else's turn. I've always been embarrassed, just as a reader, by all those *New York Review of Books* or *Village Voice* exchanges where someone writes in complaining about something that's been published (usually, "So and So must not have actually read my book, where I clearly state . . .") and the author replies in words drooling with condescension (especially when the complaining writer turns out to have been right). Plus, in every case I've come across so far, I've written far more awful things about various people than anyone has written about me. With that in mind, my only response to Meltzer's article has to do with his charge that I somehow seized, and refused to give up, the plum of writing an introduction to the Da Capo reissue of his *Aesthetics of Rock*, as against Meltzer's preference for Billy Altman. I was asked by an editor at Da Capo to write an introduction to the book. I said I'd be honored but would only do it if Richard approved, and if Richard felt comfortable with what I ended up writing. I never communicated with Richard (or Billy Altman) about this, but was told by the editor that, first, Richard was happy with the idea of my writing an introduction to his book, and, later, that he was happy with what I wrote. Beyond that it's simply a matter of two people seeing things differently. Richard evidently has a reason to discuss the matter in public; I don't.

AW: How do you feel about John Morthland's upcoming new anthology of Lester Bangs work?

GM: Along with Billy Altman, John Morthland is Lester's literary executor, and the two of them exercise any rights to Lester's work: licensing pieces for reprint, publishing unpublished material, and producing books. I never had any legal or financial position regarding Lester's work, including the book I edited, and I don't now: I took no fee, was paid no royalties, and had no approval over the publication of the book, beyond the original Knopf edition. I edited *Psychotic Reactions* because Lester and I had long talked of my editing a book of his work—editing it while he was still alive, that is.

In that sense, for John to be taking up the project himself is absolutely the right thing for him to be doing. John knew Lester far better than I did, and Lester relied on John far more than he relied on me. John's book, I'm sure, will be very different from the one I edited, and like many others I can't wait to see it.

From: Clayton Grisso
Subject: Question for Greil
Date: Tue, 12 Mar 2002 12:00:23
I recently had the pleasure of seeing the *Lipstick Traces* theatrical production. I thought it was quite amazing. My question is this: How does it feel to have one of your works adapted for the stage? And also, what was your initial reaction after being asked by the Rude Mechanicals to let them adapt it? It seems some disbelief would be in order, since the very idea of a rock book on stage was kinda audacious.

GM: I heard about the Rude Mechanicals' idea of turning *Lipstick Traces* into a theatrical production through my agent. Her assistant, it turned out, had gone to college with Kirk Lynn, who was the company's resident playwright; she vouched for him. Knowing nothing about theater, I had no idea what the group would be doing, but figured they did. I told them to go ahead and make of the book what they might; to use it for raw material; that I wanted no approval of anything, did not want to see drafts, hear about rehearsals, etc. I wanted to see what they came up with. I sent them a copy of the soundtrack album for the book that Rough Trade put out a couple of years after the book was first published, as I've always done whenever a new publisher took up the book; that was it. In Austin one weekend, I met Shawn Sides, the director; we got along. But we didn't discuss the production.

A first version of the play was presented at the Fringe Festival in New York; my friend John Rockwell, to whom *Lipstick Traces* was dedicated, called me from backstage following the first performance. "It's not good," he said, "it's great. It's to die for." That was more than encouraging, but I still couldn't imagine what it was. My wife and I went to Austin later in the year to see the play at the end of its run there, in its full, complete version. I was astonished. I hope the book is not devoid of humor, but I couldn't have imagined turning it into a comedy, even if I wrote the whole thing while listening over and over to Monty Python and Firesign Theatre records, for nine years, until they were all grey and cracked. The simultaneity I'd aimed for in the book was present in a physical, factual way that had escaped me. The greatest revelation of all, though, was the Cabaret Voltaire sequence. I understood the Cabaret Voltaire in terms of its effects, just as physicists can deduce the presence of an otherwise undetectable particle by its gravitational pull on other particles, but I'd never understood directly what happened in the Cabaret Voltaire in Zurich in 1916 until I saw the Rude Mechanicals' performances of what they imagined might have taken place there. I've since seen the play eight or nine times—every time that scene comes up, it's happening for the first time. I can't anticipate it; I can barely remember it, it's so much an event, not a representation.

The New York performances last spring were different—the cast was different. It gave me a sense of the play as something that might have room for all sorts of people in it.

When I first saw the play, in Austin, I told Shawn that she'd staged the book I'd wanted to write. There was a spirit of play, of nihilism, of anything-can-happen, that I'd tried to get into the book; I only understood how much I'd failed when I saw how others succeeded.

What a writer wants from a review, I think, is for the reviewer to tell the writer, with a sense of empathy but also distance, something about one's book one didn't know—to read the book for the writer. In that sense, the Rude Mechanicals' version of *Lipstick Traces* is the best review I've ever gotten.

From: Graham Coleman
Subject: Question for Greil
Date: Tuesday, March 12, 2002 3:45 PM
You've written countless words about Gang of Four, Wire and the Mekons but I've yet to find a single reference in your mighty oeuvre to another seminal U.K. post-punk band—the Fall. Why the ominous silence on the greatest of them all?
GM: They never did a thing for me.

From: Sterling Clover
Subject: Questions For Greil
Date: Tue, 12 Mar 2002 16:28:59
Ja Rule or Mystikal, and why?
GM: Anything is better than Ja Rule.

SC: What makes for bad "classic" blues?
GM: If by classic blues you mean recordings from the '20s and '30s, it's hard
to think of anything that doesn't have at least the smell of the unlikely on it,
which is to say I'm not sure I've ever heard a bad classic blues. I know "classic blues" generically refers to urban women singers of the '20s, but so much
of that doesn't sound like blues to me, which is my parochialism, not theirs.

SC: Does socialized art production result in good art (WPA) or bad art (Canadian Rock)?
GM: The fruit of socialized art production depends on who's doing it and
why. So much of the art produced under the aegis of the WPA—including
theater as well as murals in public buildings, or the photographic projects
of the FSA—was done by people animated by their sense of a world to be
changed by exposing its existence to people unaware of it. It was a chance
for artists to make a living, and make a difference. Merely subsidized art,
as through the NEA, is a completely different story. It's about artists who
believe the government has a responsibility to support their work, because
it has intrinsic value, and the impulse of government to censor and protect
itself from censure. It's naive to think this won't result in conflict. People
who act outraged when it does—Karen Finley, who once wrote that the First
Amendment had ceased to exist when "her" grant was rescinded—aren't
to be trusted. People who trust government agencies to support free and
autonomous art are fools.

SC: Punk or Post-Punk, and why?
GM: "Punk or post-punk, and—" What?

SC: More important: social backdrop or individual genius?
GM: "Nature or nurture?" Maybe the question can be answered by saying
that genius is a word that probably should never be used in any discussion
of pop culture. People who are not the same do their work, pursue their de-

mons or angels, on a field of action that tends to make people appear more like each other than they actually are, and this is not necessarily a bad thing.

From: InMyEyes
Subject: question for greil
Date: Tuesday, March 12, 2002 5:19 PM
One of the things I like about your criticism is how you approach each song as if it were a mystery you're trying to investigate. Unlike most rock critics, you avoid journalistic completism and stylistic range—particularly in your "Real Life Rock" column—in favor of picking and choosing specific songs or albums that baffle and excite you. This reminds me of the way certain literary critics will meditate upon a few stanzas of a poem to draw everything out of it that they can. My question is, do you have a background in poetic interpretation, and if so, how has that influenced the way you write about rock? And what, in your opinion, are the chief differences between poetry and rock lyricism?
GM: You're right about my approach, which is a matter of affinities—what I'm drawn to—and learning to follow affinities where they lead—in other words, to trust your affinities. I have no background in poetics. The difference between poetry and "Rock lyricism"—if by that you mean song lyrics—is obvious and complete: except for people who think they are poets, like Paul Simon, lyrics are meant to be sung, come to life when they are performed, take their weight and muscle and ability to move from music, and true songwriters understand this. They understand that the most intricate allusive subtleties will be lost in performance, superseded by another quality altogether, and that the most impenetrable banalities can reveal infinite possibilities of thought and emotion when sung. In this sense I think the best songwriters are less afraid of words than poets can afford to be.

From: Bromley, Charles
Subject: Questions for Greil
Date: Wed, 13 Mar 2002 10:15:29
You're a critic whose tastes range from country to rock to folk to blues. From Rabbit Brown to Daft Punk. From the twenties to whatever-the-hell the name of this decade is. Yet you've never written much about jazz. How come?
GM: Jazz is a foreign language to me, and while I can read French and pick my way through a German-language newspaper—at least in Germany—I've

never been any good at speaking either. I can make my way through some jazz—Miles Davis's *Birth of the Cool* sessions, say—but I don't think I'm hearing what's there.

CB: On the face of it, the "Images of America" in *Mystery Train* and *Invisible Republic* are very different from the European, Dadaist, art-centric ideas in *Lipstick Traces*. But a pervasive idea in all your writing on punk is the ability it gives people with limited musical technique and even a limited access to the normal forms of discourse to "find a voice" and make a mark on society. I think the real theme of all your writing is democracy. Care to comment?

GM: As far as a guiding—or, really, governing or impelling—theme being democracy, as a matter of finding a voice and making a mark, you've said it as well as I could.

From: justyn dillingham
Subject: A question for Greil
Date: Wednesday, March 13, 2002 12:49 AM
I was really happy to see you mention the Manic Street Preachers recently in your *Salon* column. They're my favorite band, and I rarely see them mentioned in any U.S. publication. I was wondering, what do you think of their earlier records, esp. the Richey Edwards-era material?

GM: This was the first Manic Street Preachers album to reach me. Obviously it's time for me to go back and start from the beginning, as if I'd never heard them. I've been going through something similar with David Thomas and Pere Ubu over the last seven years or so, after letting most of their music from *Dub Housing* on go right past me.

From: Phil Dellio
Subject: Questions for Greil
Date: Wednesday, March 13, 2002 2:08 PM
Early in your "Real Life" column's run, in the mid '80s, you wrote about Top 40 on a fairly regular basis—hits from Timex Social Club, Billy Ocean, Electric Light Orchestra, the Moody Blues, Eddie Money, Bryan Adams, and others, one or two per column for a while. Sometime in the early '90s, you seemed to stop writing about popular hits altogether. Was this prompted by a deterioration in the quality of hit radio (I don't think many people would point to '86–'88 as a noteworthy high point in the history of Top 40), by Nirvana's impact, or did you lose interest for other reasons? (Or have you lost interest?)

GM: The last Top 40 hit (not that there has really been a Top 40 for years) that got me—still gets me—is the Corrs' "Breathless." I've always heard that music on the radio; where I live you don't hear much of that radio, mostly oldies and MOR album cuts. Pink's "Don't Let Me Get Me" is a big exception.

PD: Do you have any thoughts on the way pop music is used in *Boogie Nights, Rushmore,* or *The Virgin Suicides*? I think they're as musically rich in their way as *Mean Streets* or *GoodFellas.*

GM: *The Virgin Suicides* was such a strong movie the music seemed peripheral; music as such is part of the story, what's playing didn't seem that important. I never saw *Rushmore.* The use of music in *Boogie Nights* was expert, as is everything Paul Thomas Anderson does, and soulless, like everything he does. The music in *GoodFellas* seems there to plug the holes in the characters and the story, to distract you from the complete hollowness of the picture; the music in *Mean Streets* is part of the streets, the air, the clothes, the walk, the talk, but maybe not quite so completely as in *Who's That Knockin' at My Door.*

PD: Just about anyone who writes about pop music lapses into unchecked ridicule, or glibness, or sarcasm, or meanness on occasion. I think you're good on calling people who cross a line in that direction, be it Albert Goldman, or Public Enemy, or the Stockhausen quote after the bombings. No one's going to put the Spin Doctors on a plane with the issues you were objecting to in those instances, but can you see where someone might feel you crossed a line yourself in your published comments a couple of years ago about that group's singer's medical problems? I know you hated the Spin Doctors, but what you wrote really threw me.

GM: No. Anyone who could sing "Little Miss Can't Be Wrong" the way Chris Barron did—"Things been a whole lot easier since the bitch is gone," he said, like someone throwing dirt out the window—deserves what he gets. Especially not being able to sing it anymore, if in fact he can't.

From: Colin Freebury
Subject: Questions for Greil
Date: Thursday, March 14, 2002 11:19 P
What does Mr. Marcus think about this: "Obsolete rock critics like Bill Flanagan, James Miller and Greil Marcus are proof that geezer rock stars aren't the only ones who've stayed too long at the party."

GM: I can't speak for Bill Flanagan or my friend Jim Miller, whose 1999 book *Flowers in the Dustbin*, as I read it, was pretty much his farewell to writing about pop music and to rock and roll as such, but I write about those subjects because they interest me, and because to some degree what I write seems to interest at least some other people. No one has an obligation to bother with what I have to say. Name calling usually sounds like the frustration of people who seem to think more people should be listening to them.

CF: Is Mr. Marcus really the publicist for the Kill Rock Stars and Mr. Lady labels whose artists are always featured in his column in *Salon*.com?

GM: Of course I'm the publicist for Kill Rock Stars and Mr. Lady. That Mr. Lady in particular has for the last two years been releasing the most surprising and moving music in the country is mere coincidence.

CF: Did Mr. Marcus really mean to say this: "Corin Tucker shuts her eyes—scrunches them shut—Carrie Brownstein starts moving her arms and legs, and instantly the noise they're making seems abstracted from their mouths, fingers, bodies, instruments. It seems much too big, too much in motion: On stage three people are drawing a diagram of the big bang, every particle of the universe flying away from every other, but in the audience a diagram is the last thing it feels like." How is a diagram of the big bang drawn?

GM: I assume you're asking if the sentence was a big typo, since otherwise, why would it have been published if I hadn't written it, and why would I have written it if I hadn't intended to do so? As for the diagram question, normally one would draw a diagram of the big bang with a hand, pencil, and paper. It's not very complicated; looks like the sort of drawings of bombs going off that eight year olds make when they're bored in class.

From: Scott Woods
Subject: Question for Greil
Date: Thursday, March 14, 2002 4:22
I know you're a big fan of Daft Punk's *Discovery* album from last year, and I was wondering if some of the more obvious reference points in the song "Digital Love"—the Supertramp piano break, the Frampton talk-box solo, the gauzy ambience of the whole thing, which strikes me as close in sound and feel to Gary Wright's "Dream Weaver"—hit you with: the thrill of recognition in an improved context? a new or vital sound all its own (in which "Reference points" are meaningless)? something different altogether? I ask this because, for someone like myself who grew up in the mid '70s listening

to pop radio, I no doubt have more of a soft spot for the likes of Supertramp and Frampton than you do (my guess is that you hate that music); I can't not hear these things in there. Does any of this register when you listen to "Digital Love"?

GM: Regarding Daft Punk's *Discovery*, I've loved them since I heard my first Daft Punk note. I like the name. But this album seemed like the most inside-out worship of '80s dance music imaginable—or rather not imaginable, imaginable only by these guys, but recognizable for anyone. A bath of sound. Because of the distancing, the sense of representation, what they've done sounds bigger, fuller, more conscious than its source—which it likely won't in a few years. What I really mean is that their version of this music was glamorous in a way that the original ("Rock Your Baby," etc.) was stylish. That's why a band can play "Rock Your Baby" for over an hour, as I witnessed a year ago, and Daft Punk probably couldn't sustain what they do longer than they do it. But who cares? It glows.

From: barbara flaska
Subject: Question for Greil Marcus
Date: Fri, 15 Mar 2002 08:54:09
To help explain the world as it was to future generations, what on earth inspired you to write your original review of The Masked Marauders?

GM: It was late, I was tired, and I'd been sitting around talking with my friend Bruce Miroff about how stupid all the then-so-called supersession albums were. Right at that moment Al Kooper, Mike Bloomfield, and Stephen Stills had all dead ended, but somehow people convinced themselves that if you put three threes together you'd get 47.

Today it's called "Featuring"—in 1969 it was rounding up famous people to sell junk by name. There was a story about several then-iconic performers, refugees from this band or that, walking off stage after "jamming" together for hours on end, infinite versions of this or that song by somebody else, and someone saying to one of the guys, "Not such a great night, huh?" and the person responding, "No, but we got a couple of albums out of it." So it was simple: if there were a real supersession, with John Lennon, and Bob Dylan, and Mick Jagger, and whoever else they'd deign to let into the club, what would they play? And it came out just like that. All oldies ("Duke of Earl," "Season of the Witch") or current beyond-criticism classics ("Will the Circle Be Unbroken," "A Little Help from My Friends," "Oh Happy Day"). A couple of originals which, when the joke was turning into a record, I had to write ("I Can't Get No Nookie," "Cow Pie"). I signed it T. M. Christian, after the prankster in Terry Southern's novel *The Magic Christian*—"Of course," I thought, but nobody got it. I remember showing the piece to Jann Wenner in the *Rolling Stone* offices the next morning. "Great," he said after reading it. "We should run lots of fake reviews." If we'd only known.

The Rhino reissue has it right.

From: Phil Dellio
Subject: Questions for Greil
Date: Saturday, March 16, 2002 2:17 PM
This may not be something you're able to or necessarily want to answer, but I think you'll understand the impulse behind it. Ever since Pauline Kael gave up her column in the early '90s, I'm sure the same question followed a lot of people out of movie theatres for the next decade: "I wonder what Kael would have thought about that?" I was able to piece together her reactions to *Pulp Fiction, American Beauty*, and a number of other prominent films released between her retirement and recent death through various interviews, but I still wonder about others. Did she ever share any thoughts with you on any of the following: *Reservoir Dogs, Coppola's Dracula, Boogie Nights, Casino, The Virgin Suicides, Smoke, Fargo, Crumb, Boyz 'N the Hood, Menace II Society, Big Night, Trees Lounge, Jackie Brown, The Straight Story*?
GM: I don't recall discussing any of those movies with Pauline. We did talk about *American Beauty*, but I think I went on so long about how much I hated it she didn't get a word in. I mean, I know what I think of the movies you mention, but—I've never known anything that people otherwise seemingly in sympathy disagree about more predictably than movies. That's what movies are for—for people who think they understand each other to disagree about.

PD: With the exception of a somewhat cryptic three-word "Real Life" entry on *Midnite Vultures*—"This is embarrassing" (I assume you meant that literally, but it was listed first, which is almost always reserved for something you like; maybe you meant embarrassingly good . . .)—I've never read anything by you concerning Beck. Does he at all interest you?
GM: I had one conversation with Beck about folk music, backstage at a benefit show where the Pretenders had just played. Chrissie Hynde was walking to her trailer like a queen; Beck was sitting in the dirt. After that, I worked hard to listen to everything, sure I was missing something. I found a hint of that something in *One Foot in the Grave*, but not elsewhere—except on his "Mexico," a fantastic rewrite of the folk song "Hills of Mexico," where he's

working at McDonald's, it gets robbed, he gets blamed, he gets fired, he decides to finance a trip to Mexico by robbing his old McDonald's, and ends up working for a McDonald's in Mexico. It's on the compilation *Rare on Air: Live Performances, Vol. 1* (Mammoth, 1994).

Online Exchange with Greil Marcus, Part Two

From: Scott Woods
Subject: Question for Greil
Date: Monday, March 18, 2002 1:07 AM
Your book jackets have only hinted at your career (or part-time profession) as a teacher—you've taught American Studies is all I know for sure. What and where have you taught? Is it something you've enjoyed doing? And did pop music ever enter into the curriculum?

GM: I taught an American Studies honors seminar for sophomores at Berkeley in 1971–72. I was still a graduate student. I was thrilled at the chance—when I took the same course in 1964–65, I found my subject matter, I discovered what it meant to be a student, I learned how good teachers could be, reading and writing became more than either had ever been. My teachers were the late Michael Rogin, who died last fall, and Larzer Ziff. I was arrogant and self-important enough in 1971 to think I could follow their examples, and I was wrong. I was utterly unsuited to be a teacher. I had no patience, and a teacher without patience is not a teacher. It was a year of misery and failure. Oddly, lasting friendships came out of it—there are two people who were my students who remain close friends, and one, David Ensor, who I keep up with by watching his work as a foreign correspondent for ABC News—but I had had enough bad teachers not to want to become one. I had always expected to get a Ph.D. and become a professor, but that year taught me I had to do something else. There was no point spending my life doing something I wasn't good at and didn't like doing. That was the effective end of my university career.

The curriculum was extremely traditional: the Puritans, the American Renaissance writers, the founding fathers, Lincoln, Twain, Hemingway. I had already finished my first go-round at *Rolling Stone*, and was beginning to write for *Creem*; students asked me to introduce rock and roll into the class, but I said I thought college was for finding out about stuff one wouldn't find out about otherwise. I still believe that.

I didn't teach again until 2000, when I was invited to apply for a teaching fellowship in American Studies at Princeton. I taught the course first at Berkeley, in the spring, and in the fall at Princeton: "Prophecy and the American Voice." That meant not prophecy in terms of predicting the future, but prophecy in the Old Testament sense, the prophet as one who delivers judgment on a society, and America itself as a society, or a nation, that, seeing itself blessed beyond all others, carries within itself the expectation that it will be judged more harshly than any other, even if it has to pass and carry out that judgment itself. Again the curriculum was traditional, beginning with John Winthrop, the original Puritan governor of Massachusetts, and his 1630 sermon "A Model of Christian Charity," and moving from there across three more texts on its level and following its example: Lincoln's Second Inaugural Address, Martin Luther King's 1963 March on Washington speech, and Allen Ginsberg's long poem "Wichita Vortex Sutra," both as it was written in 1966 and as Ginsberg performed it, with an orchestra of downtown New York musicians, in 1994. There were novels: Lee Smith's *The Devil's Dream* (read along with Nick Tosches' *Hellfire: The Jerry Lee Lewis Story*), Philip Roth's *American Pastoral*, Ishmael Reed's *Mumbo Jumbo*. There were movies, watched in class (it was a three-hour seminar, so we could see a movie and discuss it immediately after): *The Manchurian Candidate* and three versions of *Invasion of the Body Snatchers*: the 1956 Don Siegel original, the 1978 Phil Kaufman remake, and *Pleasantville*, which to me is precisely the same story, except here the humans take over the pods. There was Taylor Branch's Martin Luther King biography *Parting the Waters*, read in its entirety; an essay on Lincoln by Edmund Wilson; JFK's Inaugural Address; and the most intense and unforgiving of all prophecies, *The Book of Amos*. There was music: the Revenant collection *Raw Pre-War Gospel*, Bob Dylan's 1990s albums—*Good As I Been to You, World Gone Wrong*, and *Time Out of Mind*, along with the complete text of *Saved!* gospel speeches Dylan delivered from the stage from 1978–81—and a CD of Martin Luther King speeches (Revenant and CBS provided 20 copies of each of their titles for free, which allowed me to give the CDs to students at the beginning of the term so they could listen to them casually, over time, rather than studying them for a week).

The classes at Berkeley and Princeton were completely different. At Cal there were 16 students, and for the first half of the semester usually 3 or 4 would be absent. There were two women about 40, one 30, the rest about 20, only three men, one African American, one Hispanic American, one French person, and no Jews. At Princeton all 19 students were about 20. There was one African-American and one Chinese American, and no Jews, and more men. Until the very end no one was ever absent. At Berkeley people dove into the material with a sense that it was about them, that they were part of its drama. While the classes on Winthrop and "Invasion" #1 and Lincoln and gospel music fell flat at both Cal and Princeton, and the Roth and Ginsberg classes were fantastic at both places, otherwise there were no parallels. At Princeton, students who were direct and passionate outside of class were reticent and analytical in class. There was no sense of complicity with the material, no sense that it had anything to do with their lives. I remember one very sophisticated discussion of *The Devil's Dream* and saying, after a break, that while I had learned a tremendous amount about the book from the discussion (which was true for most classes in both places), I couldn't tell from anything anyone said if anyone had actually liked it. The students at Berkeley made noise in class. The Princeton students made noise in their papers, which were imaginative, funny, daring, ambitious, while papers at Cal were more narrowly framed and less intellectually alive.

I talked a lot to other teachers at Princeton about my feeling that the classes were airless. With one exception, every professor said, in effect, "That's Princeton." I heard again and again that it was the student culture: "Princeton students find out very quickly that it's considered uncool to display passion about an intellectual subject in front of one's peers." But when the class was over, I went out drinking with a few of the students and raised the question again: "We find out very quickly," they said, "that professors here aren't interested in our responses or opinions. They want stuff analyzed, from a distance."

My approach was to keep quiet. My ideal class, which didn't happen, would have been one in which I didn't say a word. I discovered that as a discussion developed, and it seemed to me absolutely essential that a certain point be raised or example be given, if I kept my mouth shut, within minutes that point would be made, that example, or a better one, would surface. Within a few weeks, I had one or two students begin each class discussion, according to his or her choice of an approach: a whole agenda, one provocative question, followed through, whatever people could come up with. This worked.

I also found, at Cal, that bringing someone whose work was being discussed into the class made a huge difference in terms of the students committing themselves to the class. I invited Phil Kaufman to come to class just after we'd finished watching his *Invasion of the Body Snatchers*. I assumed that at some point someone would ask him, "Why did you do this picture?" and he'd say something like, "Well, my first two movies had been commercial and critical flops, and I was offered this project, and it was a chance to keep directing and pay my mortgage, so I took it." That turned out to be the first question asked, and his answer was, "It was 1978, the beginning of the New Age movement, and I was living in San Francisco, and everywhere I looked, all I saw were pods." He began the discussion on a philosophical level and it stayed there. I never had another absence. At Princeton, students are not absent, but I still needed that kind of visit to power the class, and for one reason or another it didn't work out (Phil Kaufman happened to be in New York the week we were seeing his movie, promoting *Quills*, but wasn't able to take off a day and come to Princeton).

I could go on for thousands upon thousands of words more. I could talk about my culture shock over Princeton as such—the place, the town (or lack of it), the people, vs. Berkeley, which is where I went and where I live. I could discuss students individually, and the difference between grades at Cal and Princeton, and the effect of the election on the class, and much more, but this is enough for now. What it comes down to is this: I learned to keep my mouth shut, and I'll be back at Princeton this fall, teaching an American Studies seminar called "Practical Criticism."

One highlight: on the train back from Princeton to New York one evening, I saw a thin blond man get up from his seat in front of me just as we were pulling into Penn Station. It took me a split second to recognize him: David Ensor, from my American Studies class 29 years before. By the time I got up to follow him the aisle of the full car was jammed and I never caught up with him, to say, "You'll never guess what I'm doing now. . . ."

SW: What's the most valuable thing you've learned about your own writing from an editor you've worked with?
GM: I can't answer the question. I have had good relationships with editors, especially Lindsay Waters at Harvard University Press and Jon Riley, now at Faber & Faber, over very long periods of time. I'm not sure what I've learned from them. They are friends, and I trust their judgment. I have had extraordinarily good editing from countless people—Robert Christgau, Jim Miller, Kit Rachlis, M. Mark, David Frankel, Doug Simmons, Ingrid Sischy, and many more. I'm sure I could have learned a lot from them if I'd paid more attention. But what I mostly remember is again and again thinking, Thank God, he/she saved me from ruin! Again!

From: Brian O'Neill
Subject: Question for Greil
Date: Monday, March 18, 2002 7:55 PM

Lipstick Traces came out at the last moment it was possible for nay-sayers to write off the Sex Pistols and punk in general as a fad due to the lack of commercial acceptance. Does the subsequent success of the movement the Pistols started add further validity to their legacy? Or on the other hand, doesn't it now make comparing punk to any "counterculture" movements such as Dada kind of erroneous since punk is no longer counterculture at all?

GM: Someone—maybe Malcolm McLaren, maybe Jamie Reid, maybe Johnny Rotten, maybe someone else—said "the Sex Pistols were a one-band movement." Meaning that everyone and everything that circled around them, that was pulled into their black hole, that was inspired by their example, was something else—on another plane of seriousness, intensity, and we-don't-care. I think this is right, and that while the commercial success of Nirvana says a lot about punk, it may not say anything about the Sex Pistols.

I've said this before, but I'm always amazed to find out, by happenstance, how true it is: whether or not punk is counterculture, or ever was—in a sense it was elsewhereculture, maybe—the Sex Pistols were on the other side of whatever line you might want to draw, and they have not been absorbed, recuperated, brought back into the fold, their disease made into a cure. They have not been able to absorb themselves, to bring what they did back into the fold of who they were before and who they are now. Not that I begrudge them a penny of all they can collect from every reunion tour from now to doomsday. But the reason Sex Pistols records are almost never played on the radio—not by mainstream FM stations focusing on the '70s and '80s, college stations, pirate stations, Pacifica stations—is that once a Sex Pistols record appears on the air, everything around it, anything played just before or after, sounds stupid and compromised. The idea that "Marilyn Manson [or whoever] makes the Sex Pistols sound like the Chipmunks" has always been a joke on whoever tells it—the demands in that music—"Anarchy in the U.K.," "God Save the Queen," "Pretty Vacant," "Bodies," "Holidays in the Sun," "Belsen"—are irreducible, and no one has gotten to the bottom of them yet.

From: Daniel Villalobos
Subject: Question for Greil
Date: Tue, 19 Mar 2002 12:38:18
What do you think about *Almost Famous*? I really hate that movie, but all my friends just loved it. All right, it's just a movie, but for me it was also a sign. A sign of hard times. How do you point to the enemy, when the enemy is listening to your music? And putting it on his soundtrack?

GM: Some of my problems with *Almost Famous* come from being at least tangentially part of its milieu. I had left *Rolling Stone* [in 1970] before Cameron Crowe became a presence there, and when I came back [1975] he wasn't around. We've never met. But the picture of the place makes no sense—like so much of the film. It starts with the hero's idiot mother, who by the end of the movie will become a fount of wisdom no one can resist, just because. The portraits of *Rolling Stone* editor Ben Fong-Torres, writer David Felton, and editor Jann Wenner are just as other-worldly: the idea that Ben was a dope who could be fooled by a kid's earnestness, or that Jann would hold the cover of his magazine for an unwritten story on an unknown band by an untried writer is—by the time the movie is set—absurd (in the early days of the magazine anything went). The denouement of the movie—the young writer turning in a warts and all piece—is ridiculous. Cameron Crowe made his reputation by writing expert, convincing pieces that showed musicians as decent, interesting, conflicted, real people, to the point that soon enough many refused to be interviewed by *Rolling Stone* unless Crowe had the assignment, knowing how well they'd come off in his hands. Cameron had a lot to do—I don't mean intentionally—with turning *Rolling Stone* from an independent voice into a publicity machine (the economy in general had a lot more to do with it). And I didn't like Kate Hudson.

I did like Billy Crudup—he's perfect riffing on "Peggy Sue" when the plane seems about to crash. He's always good, because on camera he projects modesty. I liked Phillip Seymour Hoffman as Lester Bangs. "He's not much like the Lester we knew," my wife said, and that's true, but to a degree I played an older-brother role for Lester, which is the role he's playing for the Cameron Crowe character in the movie. Whenever Hoffman was onscreen I felt real heart, Crowe trying to live up to his story and succeeding. Here, Lester Bangs seemed as unforced as everyone picking up "Tiny Dancer" in the plane.

I haven't seen *Say Anything*, which people love, or more than a few scenes of *Jerry McGuire* on an airplane. I thought *Couples* was OK and *Vanilla Sky* an abomination, even as a recruiting ad for Scientology. *Fast Times at Ridgemont High* remains a miracle—funny, honest, imaginative, unbelievable cast, fine direction, not a false note, and many brave ones, especially because the book Crowe wrote, on which he based his wonderful screenplay (not that I know how much of his screenplay is actually on the screen), is so unconvincing.

When we saw the movie, in New York, in a theater now ruined by the terrorist attacks on the city, there were six people in the seats.

From: Brent Sanders

Subject: Questions for Greil

Date: Wednesday, March 20, 2002 10:54 PM

In Jim DeRogatis's excellent biography of Lester Bangs, the valid point is made that Bangs' legacy was ill-served by the editor's choice of material. Said editor would be Mr. Marcus. The theory is that since Lester's free-wheeling, hooligan-in-print style was the polar opposite of the rather dry, scholarly style of pseudo-bohemian hucksters like Marcus, Christgau, etc., the idea of letting his work be anthologized by the like would leave it open to A) a complete misrepresentation of his work, and/or B) a subconscious desire to show Bangs' work as mere buffoonery without illustrating or presenting the genuinely solid philosophy behind his writings. A solid point that Mr. Marcus should address.

The second question (well, hell . . . they may not really be questions, so much as points for Mr. Marcus to expound deep upon . . . let's appeal to the ego, here) was that while Marcus's writing in articles I have read does seem to enhance and enlighten, his books seem just pompous, long-winded exercises in semantic gymnastics. I read an interview with him a few years ago, in which he was asked about his book on Dylan's Basement Tapes. His answer went something like, "Well, I wanted to write a book, so. . . ." Whoa, such inspiration. Pick a subject, showcase my intelligence, pick up an award, badda bing, badda boom. I mean, was he really inspired by this music, or just wanting to give his thesaurus a workout? As one of the few people who has actually seen Mr. Marcus perform (as part of the Critic's Chorus with the Rock Bottom Remainders), I can honestly say he does indeed love the music he writes about; the sheer joy on his face was obvious. But his book-length writing seems to strip away all the transcendence and bog it down into mere dissertation. Even his much lauded, highly overrated *Mystery Train* is a lugubrious trail that doesn't illuminate or inspire so much as it plods along in it's quest to illustrate what we already know: this music can change your life, Sparky. And the high-handed tone is so blatant as to scream out it's desire to teach us unwashed heathens a thing or two. Quite frankly, his book-length work seems damn anti-Rock and Roll. Do I just not get it?

GM: Sorry—as I've said elsewhere in this conversation, it's not up to me to convince people my writing is wonderful/essential/decent/tolerable if the writing itself doesn't convince/interest/intrigue/provoke whoever might read it. The questioner already knows what he thinks.

From: Tom Sawyer
Subject: Questions for Greil
Date: Thursday, March 21, 2002 10:17 PM
My questions are about the discography in *Stranded* (I've never come across the reprinted edition, so my apologies if you've touched on the first two of these):
1) Are there any entries on that list that you would drop today?
2) Is there anything from that time period (pre-1979) that you now wish you'd included?
3) Name 20 records—albums or singles—from the past 23 years that rank with those on your *Stranded* list.

GM: The second edition of *Stranded* was published in 1996 by Da Capo; it is itself out of print now, as Da Capo recently dropped many of their music titles. There was a new introduction by Robert Christgau, a new preface I wrote about the tortured publishing history of the thing the first time around, and updated contributors' bios.

I've rarely had as much fun writing as I did in the couple of weeks I took to write the original *Stranded* Discography. As soon as the book was published in 1979, I started marking up a copy with stuff I'd forgotten or stuff that had come out afterward—and almost immediately quit. With hip-hop, the continuing flood of punk singles and albums, the more obscure corners of Jamaican music—I never made the connection to African music—and then the true explosion of the revision of the history of popular music by means of CDs—the kind of discography I'd played with would have required a whole book, updated every few years at that.

In the margins of that 1979 edition there is, from 1979 or 1980, the Beat, "Twist and Crawl" and "Stand Down Margaret," the Brains' "Money Changes Everything" (of course I'd add Cyndi Lauper's version, along with "Girls Just Want to Have Fun"), *London Calling* by the Clash, Sam Cooke's *One Night Stand: Live at the Harlem Square Club*, 1963, Essential Logic's *Wake Up, Broken English* by Marianne Faithfull, Fleetwood Mac's *Tusk, Entertainment!* by the Gang of Four, Jefferson Airplane's 1966 already included "Runnin' Round This World" crossed out, Shorty Long's missed 1964 "Devil with a Blue Dress On," the Mekons' "Never Been in a Riot" (now I'd add *Fear and Whiskey, The Edge of the World, The Mekons Story,* and *The Curse of the Mekons* at the very least), the Melodians' profound *Pre-meditation,* a 1979 collection of releases from 1965–72, the Raindrops' missed 1964 "Let's

Go Together," the Prince Buster's Judge Dread series, Sam & Dave's missed "Hold On I'm Comin'" (dropped and not caught originally, not omitted).

What I'd really missed: most of the Velvet Underground, which didn't come across for me, perhaps because of West Coast snobbery, until punk had opened it up. Most of Pere Ubu before *Stranded* came out and certainly afterward, until the 1990s, when to me the band made its best music, still continuing through *Raygun Suitcase, Story of My Life, Pennsylvania*, and last year's *Surf's Up*, plus David Thomas's live *Meadville*. Much Southern soul that barely got out of the south in the late '60s or early '70s (now collected on *Down and Out: The Sad Soul of the Deep South*). Also much early commercial folk: I'd add the Kingston Trio's "Tom Dooley" and Peter Paul & Mary's "Don't Think Twice" and "Too Much of Nothing"—I was much too cool to mention them the first time around.

What I'd add, now, just off the top of my head, ignoring the hundreds or thousands of discs that CD reissue projects would mandate: Grandmaster Flash, "Adventures of Grandmaster Flash on the Wheels of Steel" and "The Message," the Geto Boys' "Mind Playing Tricks on Me," Alphaville's "Big in Japan" and "Forever Young," Foreigner's "Urgent" and the transcendent "I Want to Know What Love Is," most of the Peter Green Fleetwood Mac's early music, Heaven's to Betsy's singles, Sleater-Kinney's *Call the Doctor* and *All Hands on the Bad One*, Nirvana's *Bleach, Nevermind*, and *Unplugged in New York*, Bob Dylan's *Unplugged* and *Time Out of Mind*, Billy Ocean's "Slow Train Coming," "Tenderness" by General Public," Bruce Springsteen's *Nebraska*, Elvis Costello's *King of America* plus the singles "Let Them All Talk," "Everyday I Write the Book" and "All This Useless Beauty," the Slits' 1977 demos collected on the 1980 *Once Upon a Time in a Living Room*, the soundtrack album to my book *Lipstick Traces*, Counting Crows' "Mr. Jones," Eleventh Dream Day's *Lived to Tell*, Madonna's "Live to Tell," "Holiday," and especially "Like a Prayer," Eminem's *The Marshall Mathers LP*, PJ Harvey's *To Bring You My Love*, everything by the Handsome Family, Lou Reed's *Ecstasy* (among many great solo albums), Big Sandy's L.A. doo wop tribute *Dedicated to You*, Come's *Don't Ask Don't Tell*, DJ Shadow's *Endtroducing*, Van Morrison's *The Healing Game*, Daft Punk's *Homework*, Hooverphonic's *A New Stereophonic Sound Spectacular* (now I'm looking through old notes), the box of Costello & Nieve 1998 live shows—see what I mean? I could keep this going all day and not come close.

From: Tom Sawyer
Subject: more questions for Greil
Date: Saturday, March 23, 2002 11:00 AM
I'm interested in your thoughts/impressions on any or all of the following:
Eminem
GM: The best New Dylan in years, because he's also the New Prince—in love with words, and he swings, he knows a beat from a bleat, he can keep up with Dr. Dre and Snoop Dog, he's as funny as Pete Townshend. Scary, because he gets down under anyone's skin, can make anyone uncomfortable, including, quite obviously, himself. Not a clue where he might go, what he might do.

TS: Ryan Adams
GM: Zero.

TS: Lucinda Williams
GM: As great an emotional fraud as Destiny's Child—wins the prize over them as the most mannered singer in pop music because she's been fooling people with it longer. A monster of self-praise, of the poor-mouth, to her own self be true, but I love one of her comments in the current *Esquire*: "Some of my best friends are music critics." What a shock.

TS: The White Stripes
GM: I'd have more to say if I could find their earlier records. Their sister/ brother wife/husband mystique is about as interesting as the debate over how Jeff Kent broke his wrist, though.

TS: Jay-Z
GM: Talent.

TS: Alanis Morissette
GM: Does not know a beat from a bleat. I still think "You Oughta Know" is the whiniest record ever made. She's better in movies.

TS: Aimee Mann
GM: Up there with Lucinda Williams, but a much more obnoxious whiner

than Alanis Morissette—there's a difference between making a horrible hit record based on an irritating emotion and basing your whole life on it. The sense of entitlement, of condescension, comes off of her in waves. Given that a whole movie was based on her wisdom, though—who can forget every character, dead or alive, mouthing along to, "Wise Up," I think, in *Magnolia*? And then, lo and behold, everybody did wise up. Gosh.

TS: Gorillaz
GM: Nothing to say.

TS: *O Brother, Where Art Thou*
GM: It's not *Fargo*, but I liked the movie. I'm a sucker for George Clooney. His miming of Dan Tyminski's "Man of Constant Sorrow" was fabulous, as was the singing and arrangement. The pure-Coens' notion of having an a cappella "Oh Death" come out of the mouth of the Grand Klavern of the Ku Klux Klan, offering a philosophy lesson to the blues singer who's about to be lynched, was astonishing. The album is not as good—Gillian Welch, the Whites, and the Cox Family are very dull, and after a while you realize the best thing there is the 1927 Harry McClintock version of "Big Rock Candy Mountain," which should have been on *Anthology of American Folk Music*. Still, it's no surprise the album reached so many people so strongly—if you don't know this music, it's like doors in a mountain opening, and you can't help but want to go inside. It's an old-timey version of *The Harder They Come* soundtrack, and there's as much to discover in a more-where-this-came-from sense as there was there.

TS: Peer-to-peer file sharing (Napster, Morpheus, Gnutella, etc.)
GM: Haven't done it.

TS: Michael Jackson's *Invincible*
GM: He lives. As in *They Live*. Doesn't anyone remember that he's a child molester?

TS: The Beatles *Anthology* project (discs and/or videos)
GM: The good stuff is on their albums.

TS: Bob Dylan seems to have held your regard as a critic longer than anybody in rock and roll, so I'm wondering how you'd respond to the following debating proposition: Dylan is the towering figure of the rock and roll era. And, if so, why is it that the public, by and large, doesn't get it? (It seems to me that the inverse ratio of critical esteem to public acceptance—i.e., sales— is unmatched in the music, and he's forever the butt of easy jokes.) And one other thing: I don't think I've ever seen any criticism that comments on the huge changes in the quality of Dylan's voice over the years. Unlike almost any of his contemporaries, his voice has changed so much from his earliest recordings that, set side to side, you'd never recognize him as the same guy. Yet critics never really acknowledge this. Any thoughts?

GM: I don't think he's the towering figure of the rock and roll era. For one moment, from roughly the time *Highway 61 Revisited* was released in the fall of 1965 to the end of his tour in the U.K. in May 1966 he truly did tower over everything around him—everything, not just other musicians, but other artists, other politicians, other philosophers, other evangelists. He knew it, and you could hear the fact and the knowledge in his sound, and you can hear it now. But if anyone has to tower over an era, it was the Beatles and the Rolling Stones.

Dylan is a strange, dubious character. He has more to do with the Lone Ranger than John Wayne—"Who was that masked man?" He keeps his distance. He is from somewhere else. He not only speaks in riddles, he lives in them. For more than ten years, he has had more in common with a dead blues singer or old-time ballad singer than with any contemporary.

I think the reason the changes in his voice have not much been commented on—and I think this because your question made me realize how completely I'd ignored the question myself—is that, despite changes in tone, pitch, clarity, etc.—any formal description—the attack, the point of view, the way in which the voice enters a piece of music, what it does there, how it gets out, or how the music gets away, if it does—has not changed. That is: it remains unpredictable. It's music as a game of three-card monte. This hasn't always been true. It wasn't true for *Slow Train, Saved, Shot of Love, Infidels*. But the way in which the singer works on "The Drifter's Escape," "Like a Rolling Stone," "The Lonesome Death of Hattie Carroll," and "High Water" defines Dylan as a singer, and defines his voice, in the greatest sense. As long as Dylan can draw breath, I imagine this will matter more than the actual sound he makes—because the twisting and turning that goes on in performances like these, the ability to bring a whole world into focus with the dramatization of a single syllable—the first "care" in "High Water" say— is the actual sound he makes.

From: William Altreuter

Subject: Question for Greil

Date: Sunday, March 24, 2002 9:13 AM

Rock music seems very atomized at the moment, a category which contains a number of very specific sub-genres. Is it meaningful to talk about "Rock music" as anything more than part of the trinity of blues based American popular music forms? Was it ever?

GM: For Noisefest in San Francisco a few weeks ago, I was on a panel with other writers. One, Gina Arnold, author of *Route 666* and *Kiss This*, also teaches swimming and diving to younger students. She had mentioned the panel she was going to be part of, and her students asked what it was about. "'Is Rock Dead?'" she said (it wasn't, but the theme was so vague I can't even remember what it actually was). None of her students knew what "Rock" was. That seemed to answer the question.

I stopped using the term "rock and roll" to apply to anything contemporary years ago, because it seemed to have been completely emptied of meaning. If anything, by 1993 or so the term seemed to refer only to a certain style of playing, i.e., rockabilly. In other words, "rock and roll" had been reduced to the same level of meaning, or un-meaning, as it had long had in the U.K. In my frame of reference, though, "rock and roll" meant a way of being in the world, of talking about that manner of being, of separating yourself from all the assumptions that seemed to govern the world, of affirming that anything could be said at any time. It was a sound of surprise, both in terms of form, genre, style, but also of the individual voice, word, melody, note, riff, an interruption of the ordinary, the obvious, that could come at any time. It seemed to me that all of these things came together as a single standard of value, and it was that value that defined rock and roll, and made it different from any of its antecedents. It was not blues. It was not country, swing, mainstream pop, or anything else. The music itself, as an idea, an impulse, asked Carl Perkins, "What would it mean to have fun?" and Perkins, who had never asked himself that question, because the limits of his life as he had been raised to respect them proscribed the question, answered with "Blue Suede Shoes." With the sound, the words, the will, the idea.

I think it was Robert Christgau who called "Blue Suede Shoes" a protest song. In 1992 I could still hear the Geto Boys' "Mind Playing Tricks with Me" as part of the same culture, deriving from the same sense of value. In the 1950s and 1960s it made sense to consider all popular music that derived from and sought to extend and deepen that value as "Rock and roll"—doo wop no less than rockabilly, Chicago soul no less than Motown, later Philly soul no less than LA country rock or the San Francisco sound, the Rolling Stones and reggae speaking the same language. I recall a conversation with Richard Meltzer one night, it might have been about "The T.A.M.I. Show," but he said, with great vehemence, as if a huge amount was at stake, something like, "The point is, it was ALL ROCK." Rock and roll contained multitudes, could absorb and transform anything without it itself losing its value, its purpose.

This is clearly not true any more. When I stopped using the term "rock and roll" I used "pop music" instead—that is, I went with something that was not simply functionally meaningless, but which was obviously and aggressively meaningless. Now, at times, I can still hear that Public Enemy and Sleater-Kinney, Eminem and the Corrs, the Noonday Underground and Low all could and ought to travel under the same name. But it would be useless to write or speak as if they did, if one had any interest in getting something across to someone else.

Why is this? There are a lot of reasons. Ethnic/identity politics. The historical fact that "rock and roll," which once signified music made by black musicians for black listeners—younger listeners who responded to the kind of stuff Alan Freed was playing in Cleveland in 1953 under the name "rock and roll" as if it was something new, not blues, jump-blues, swing, not like anything, too crude, too fast, too silly, for older listeners—had come, by the 1970s, to signify music almost exclusively made by white musicians for white listeners. The fact that with the appearance of reggae, punk, and hip-hop, not to mention music from Africa, Mexico, South America, and the Far East, the number of people vying for the attention of listeners expanded far more rapidly and to a much greater extent than the audience did, even though it was expanding too. Marketers, in order to somehow rationalize this situation, insisted on identifiable labels and pushed musicians to remain with genres. Listeners, in order to identify themselves to others and to themselves, did the same. Certainly there were times when "a rock and roll fan" could maintain an awareness of what was happening in "rock and roll," even if rock and roll meant, as with "The T.A.M.I. Show," Motown, James Brown, the Rolling Stones, the Liverpool groups, Jan & Dean, Lesley Gore, and more, more, more—"ALL ROCK." Now it is impossible. Can anyone be completely on top of Northwest female rock and roll, New York hip-hop, San Francisco turntablism, Chicago British country, and several hundred other not meaningless groupings, at the same time?

I long ago decided I couldn't, and didn't want to. I write about what reaches me, as someone who is simply present in culture. Whether that's good enough is for others to judge.

From: Patrick McAvoy
Subject: Question for Greil
Date: Wednesday, March 27, 2002 7:33 PM
I know you have done a fair amount of research on Harry Smith and his life in the Berkeley area in the 1950s. I know he had connections with the San Francisco art scene. Did he know Pauline Kael at the time? I assume that they knew many of the same people, so I was curious if they were familiar with each other's work. Thanks.

GM: I walk past the apartment where Harry Smith lived in the 1940s every day. It's at the foot of Panoramic Way in Berkeley, just above the football stadium, a basement apartment in a woodsy part of town. Certainly Pauline Kael and he knew each other. A few years ago, right when my fascination with Smith's work was reaching the point of obsession—the point where, for me, real work starts—I was talking to Pauline, and I said, "When I started looking into all this, I knew nothing about Harry Smith. I didn't know if he was from Seattle or if he was from Mars." "Oh, he was from Mars," she said. She hadn't hesitated a second.

Greil Marcus: Interview

Oliver Hall/2005

From *Perfect Sound Forever*, March 2005. Used by permission of the author.

Perfect Sound Forever: *The Rose & the Briar* (W. W. Norton & Co., 2004) has come out during an election year, a year in which not only have there been no good protest songs, but hardly anything on the radio could make you think twice about the way you live. Do you see this book in any way as an appeal to the memory of the country, or to the soul of the country?

Greil Marcus: No; I think if anything is under that umbrella, it's more an argument that the country has changed, or changes, less than it might seem. Certain themes and obsessions have been part of the country always, and there's no reason to think that they won't be. And those obsessions have to do with murder as a solution to all problems, and with people continually putting their trust in people who mean them nothing but harm. There is a strain of real sadism in the country that we're deeply attracted to, both as entertainment and something more psychotic than that.

We thought about this book—we thought it up two years ago—and we weren't thinking in terms of when it would be finished, when it would come out, what kind of milieu it would enter when it was published. So, maybe it's a naive bet that regardless of the enormous transformations that the country may be in store for, it may be a kind of bet that they won't be as significant as they appear to be.

PSF: Then the question is, why is Bush so distressing to you and to so many other people? I haven't read Philip Roth's new book [*The Plot against America*, which Marcus reviewed for the *Los Angeles Times*], but my impression is that one of the things the book's about is how much an election can really transform a nation, and how much can really be at stake in the identity of the president.

157

GM: Well, Roth's book is funny that way, in that it's questionable whether Lindbergh becoming president transforms the nation, or whether he simply is able to draw on aspects of the national identity that had never really been exploited before—or exploited on such a mass scale—essentially turning the entire country in the early 1940s into what the Klan was able to turn states like Indiana into in the 1920s. So it's not as if the country's being remade out of whole cloth—hardly. And it's also quite odd that at the end of the book, Franklin Roosevelt rides in over the Hill with the cavalry and puts everything to right again, and the country goes on as if nothing had happened, as if this strange interregnum had been some kind of fantasy. So that's very tricky.

The thing about Bush is that he's an extraordinarily effective demagogue. So was his father. They know how to play on people's fears, and even more than that, on their bigotries. Both of them—George W. Bush more so than his father, I think—are in essence bullies. They take pleasure in lording it over other people, pushing other people around, in stomping people in the face metaphorically, and by going to war, not metaphorically at all. These are very small-minded people with large talent, and they're frightening because certainly Bush—more than his father—understands how to use power.

One thing that Ronald Reagan should have taught everybody is that this whole idea of political capital . . . if that phrase has any meaning, then it is capital. And when you spend capital, if you spend it wisely—or if you spend it with verve, and take chances that other people are afraid to take—then you don't expend your capital, you don't use it up; you make more.

The way you amass political capital is by spending it, by using it, and Bush understands that very, very well. If you're timid, then you have a limited amount of capital to work with, and you spend it slowly, sooner or later it's all gone. And that's not the way Bush works. So, he's a frightening figure because he's very, very good at what he does, and he is very clear on what he wants—on what kind of country he wants to live in. And it's a country very similar to the one he grew up in, which is to say a world of privilege, where you never meet anybody unlike yourself and you never have to think about anybody other than yourself, and where straight white males have all the power, and all the legitimacy, and all the rights.

PSF: Do you think the Democratic Party has any chance of becoming as ruthless and seductive as the Republicans have become?

GM: Well, certainly not as ruthless. It's not in the nature of what the Democrats are about, and the Democratic philosophy of government, and the

Democratic Party's vision of what the country is and what it's for. You can't combine ruthlessness with fairness, sadism with therapy [laughs]. It's self-contradictory. No, certainly not.

PSF: The two essays I find really scary in *The Rose & the Briar* are the ones about "Delia's Gone," and the one about "Frankie and Albert," or "Frankie and Johnny." There's something about the idea that these stories were based on real crimes that's so much scarier than anything the songs could say. Does that make any sense to you?
GM: Well, it's not the way I would see it, but it makes sense that somebody could see it that way.

PSF: How do you see it?
GM: I think what goes on in "Delia" is much more appalling and disgusting, much more of a waste, than what goes on in "Frankie and Albert." Yes, these are songs based on real incidents that we can document. There were trials; there are records of what happened, and there's testimony. And then there's the song, which transforms the event as it happened into something that can travel, that's portable, that holds its shape.

And what happens with "Delia" is, you're really talking about a couple of kids, and one guy's going around bragging, saying, "I fucked you from here to Wednesday," and the girl's saying, "No, you didn't," and keeps going on, and she's saying, "You're nothing but a son-of-a-bitch," and he pulls out a gun and shoots her. The waste there, the squalor of it all, is horrible.

In "Frankie and Albert," you're dealing with a much more ambiguous situation. You've got a woman in her thirties who's a prostitute, and her pimp—who she's clearly madly in love with—is about sixteen years old, and he's this very glamorous character: he's good-looking, he's a ragtime piano player who has to beat the girls off with a stick (except he doesn't beat them off), and he's cheating on her. Not only is he cheating on her, after she finds out that he's been running around with Nellie Bly, he comes back to their place and slugs her, because she hasn't brought in enough money that night. He's her pimp, she's the prostitute, and she's not doing her job. So he beats her up, and she claims that he pulled a knife on her, so she shot him. In any case, she got off. The judge let her go, self-defense. That is less of a waste. That is a crime that the law makes an allowance for.

What's fascinating to me is the way one crime gets turned into a ballad and lasts, and how other crimes that might seem almost identical don't; either they don't get turned into ballads at all, or they do and it's stillborn, and nobody wants to sing it—it doesn't travel, it doesn't get made into sheet music or become a Broadway play, like Frankie & Johnny. It doesn't go anywhere. They just die. I don't understand that, I don't know how it happens. I think Cecil Brown, who wrote the "Frankie and Albert" essay, has a pretty good understanding of how it works.

PSF: Now, do you see that as a transformation? Do you think it was true at one point in America's history—that these crimes or incidents would grab hold of someone's imagination and spread—and that that no longer happens? Or is it something that can happen depending on the imagination of the songwriter, the singer, and the nature of the crime itself?

GM: No, I don't really understand how it works. It'd be easy enough to say, as Cecil Brown has said, that the Scott Peterson case is absolutely tailor-made for the ballad. David Thomas, in this book, in his piece on "Dead Man's Curve" and "Wreck of the Old '97," has this dictum: What the ballad wants, the ballad gets.

In other words, if the main character in the ballad has to be married—even if he wasn't, even if the ballad's based on a real event—well, he's going to be married. And if he has to be heroic instead of a drunk, well, he's going to be heroic. If he has to be a drunk instead of heroic, he'll be a drunk! Depending on what shape the ballad needs to take. It used to be that the ballads that were based on true crimes emerged almost right away, sometimes that very night, or the next night, but usually very, very quickly. Oftentimes the real-life characters in the ballads would live out their lives to the soundtrack of a song about themselves; that was true with Stagger Lee, and was true for all of Frankie Baker's quite long life: from 1899 into the 1950s she heard that song over and over and over again, countless versions—in the movies, on Broadway, on the radio, people walking down the street, when they would see her, singing it at her.

What Cecil Brown has said about the Scott Peterson case—it's not just that this guy murdered his wife because she was pregnant and he didn't want to be tied down, he had all these fantasies that he got from Jack Kerouac's *On the Road*, a book that has probably ruined more lives than it's saved—Cecil says, "Okay, fine, this kind of thing happens all the time. But he killed her on Christmas Eve." That's what the ballad wants; it wants a detail like that. It wants the bodies washing up at Easter-time; that's what the ballad needs.

I don't know. You could say today that all this stuff gets devoured by the public so completely and so quickly that there's no room for the kind of contemplation, or the kind of immediacy, that a ballad demands, so that the Scott Peterson case—there's already been a TV movie, it's been on the cover of *People* countless times, and God knows what forms it's going to take.

But look at Charley Starkweather and Caril Fugate. Now, here's a shocking, terrifying series of crimes that take place in Nebraska and Wyoming in 1958, where these two teenagers start off by killing the girl's parents and her baby sister, or baby brother, and then move through Lincoln, Nebraska, and are killing elderly people, killing other teenagers. And it's just absolutely horrifying. It gets turned into a number of movies before it ever becomes a song, and becomes a song only many years later, in 1982 I guess, when Bruce Springsteen picks it up and makes it into "Nebraska," and creates a much more poetic, much more metaphorical ballad. He doesn't name the victims, he doesn't tell you exactly who got killed when, doesn't even tell you how many people got killed, and yet he's basing the ballad on real things that Charley Starkweather actually said.

You know that incredible line—Charley Starkweather's imagining himself on the electric chair, and he says, "When they pull that switch and they snap my poor head back/ Make sure my pretty baby is sitting right there on my lap"? Bruce didn't even make that up! Charley Starkweather really said that, not quite so fluidly, but that's what he said. So this is a ballad that's following the poetic contours that existed inside the gore of the event very, very closely, and many, many years later, whereas according to Cecil Brown's research, the ballad of Frankie Baker, of Frankie and Albert, was written the night after the shooting. The same day it made the papers.

PSF: One of the things I like about your essay "Envoi" that finishes up the book is that you admit that folk music can be really embarrassing. I remember being dragged to see Burl Ives when I was seven years old and I thought I was going to die of boredom. If it's true that folk music has all this stuff in it, all this dark stuff about murder and sex and sadism, why is it boring to some people? What is it about folk music that makes people either obsessed—fans who have to know every version of a song that was ever performed—or just bored to tears?

GM: I think it depends on who you're exposed to. There are singers who can make the most thrilling material deadly dull. It just depends on who it is, and it depends on what mood you bring to a given performance—it depends on how it strikes you. When I first heard the Kingston Trio's "Tom Dooley" on the radio in 1958, it was absolutely shocking. This was a period of time when rock and roll had gone really soft, and there wasn't much to listen to on Top 40 radio that wasn't embarrassing in its own way. I think in 1958 the number one song of the year was "Tammy" by Debbie Reynolds—talk about embarrassing. Everything it seemed had become very clichéd and it was very, very hard to find the surprises that, a year or two before, just seemed to be everywhere. You couldn't wait to get up in the morning and turn on the radio and see what bizarre freak would be shouting in your ear, and who would follow him or her.

And so, you turn on the radio and here's this guy talking—Dave Guard of the Kingston Trio—and he's giving you a little spoken-word introduction to this song, "This is a song about the immortal triangle," *rrrrrr*, and you think "God, how did this get on the radio?" And then this song comes on, and it's so different from everything else on the radio—it so much doesn't belong— that people respond to it. They responded to it in the same way that people did when "Smells Like Teen Spirit" came on the radio. It was just so shockingly different it stopped you, made you ask what it was.

It's perfectly possible for someone to sing "Barbara Allen" and leave you turned to dust. And yet, it just depends. We had a show in New York a couple of weeks ago, a "Rose and the Briar Floorshow," it was called. It was produced by Hal Willner and Jeanine Nichols, who do extraordinary musical events—they have the ability to bring together all different sorts of people, to play for free, for some reason that may escape anyone's ability to explain it. In this case, they drew on all kinds of people, some quite famous, some not famous at all, to devote their time and their energy and their talent to an event organized around a book that a lot of them had probably never heard of, and certainly a book edited by two people none of them knew. So God knows how they were able to do it.

At the very end of this evening—the way it worked was that various of the writers from the book read from their pieces, and then the songs that they read about would be performed, and for the writers who weren't able to be there Sean Wilentz and I would read a little bit of their piece and then the song would be performed—at the very end Terre Roche of the Roches came out to do "Barbara Allen." She was playing acoustic guitar, and she was accompanied by a punk cellist from the Northwest named Madigan, who recently moved to New York—this very innocent-looking little blond woman who appeared to be about nineteen, and is quite a bit older than that, and just looks like she has no experience, like she just walked out of a convent or something.

So Terre Roche proceeds to sing "Barbara Allen," and I swear it was as if I had never heard the song before. It was as if the world had stopped turning.

I felt like I had never understood the song before. I had never understood what was so terrible about what Barbara Allen did, and this night, I understood it, and I thought, "Oh my God. She did that? Oh, I don't believe it."

So it depends on what you bring to a performance and what the performance brings to you. What I found so oppressive about folk music when I was a kid was the ideology behind it. This goes way back into the twenties and thirties, when the Communist Party in the United States seized on folk music as the music of the people, showing that the people were full of vitality and had their own true culture and were able to resist the depredations of mass culture.

And that was a large part of the Communist Party slogan in the thirties: "Communism is just 20th Century Americanism." And the ideology was that when people sit down to sing or stand up to sing, they are communicating universal values of love and community and fraternity, in a universal language. And so, even if you're singing a murder ballad, you're not singing about a real murder, you're not singing about blood on the forest floor, you're singing about the fact that we're all together, we're all alike, we're all one. So the ideology of the performance overrides any specific song, and it determines the nature of the performance, which is warm and open and smiling and friendly. And that's not really [laughs] what folk music is about, I don't think. That's what I found so awful at the Quaker school that I went to in Menlo Park in the 1950s.

PSF: I don't know if you want to talk about this, but there are little bits and pieces of your life that I can pick up from your books, yet there's no account of your childhood or your family or anything—do you want to talk about that?

GM: Not really. Unless there's a point to be made, unless somebody wants to make a point, I don't particularly find the details of other people's lives all that interesting; I mean people out there in the world, I don't mean the lives of my friends or something like that. To take someone who I'm fascinated with as a performer, I don't care about Bill Pullman's childhood, or Sheryl Lee's. I'm not interested. I don't think that the details of one's life really tell you very much about whom they are, or why they became what they became. I think the choices people make have a lot more to do with that than the circumstances of their lives. Also, I guess I just have a very strong sense of privacy. There are things about my family background that I find actually interesting, and sometimes I talk about them, but I don't think my life itself is very interesting.

PSF: I guess I was asking more about where in the country you grew up, and how those places shaped you, if they did.

GM: Well, I was born in San Francisco, I grew up on the Peninsula, I've lived in the Bay Area my entire life. I've been other places [laughs], but I'm a Californian, and I was very, very lucky to grow up in California when I did. I couldn't imagine having a better childhood. I don't mean in terms of my parents or my siblings, I mean growing up in a suburb with great weather where you could just get on your bike and go wherever you wanted to go, or a little bit later you could get in the car and cruise up and down the El Camino every night during high school, looking for fun or trouble, as the case may be.

I thought that was all wonderful, and I was aware of it at the time, that this was great. And I became aware of what a great time it was to grow up later, when I realized what a great education I got in public schools, how good the schools were then, not only in terms of what books you read, but inspiring teachers and a sense of your own competency, your own ability to do things. I went to public schools at a time when they were all being built.

When I went to Elizabeth Van Auken school in Palo Alto when I was in first, second grade—that was in the early fifties, and the school had been built a couple years before. It was named for a teacher who was still alive and still showed up every year on School Day. When I went to Menlo-Atherton High School in 1959, I think it was built in 1951. So these schools were new, and they had a sense of their own newness and a sense of being part of a new world. And it was also the fifties, when there was more money flowing through the economy than anybody knew what to do with, and it was a time when companies like General Motors and General Electric had come upon this incredible revelation that if they were actually going to sell the stuff they were making, then the people they wanted to buy it would have to have [laughs] the money to pay for it! Therefore, it made sense to pay workers more so they could spend what they earned! Wow, what an incredible idea, and it really worked.

You kind of wonder why the captains of industry don't see the wisdom in that; not the social nobility of it, but the practicalities of it. Not the way the economy works anymore. So it could be that the time I grew up had a lot more to do with my luck than the place, I don't know.

When I went to Cal in 1963, which was when I started, I can't imagine that anybody could have gotten a better education anywhere else in the world than I got, at a public university, where my tuition, which wasn't called that, was $62 a semester.

PSF: Did you have to do ROTC then?

GM: No. There was still ROTC at Cal, but it had ceased to be compulsory a few years before I got there.

PSF: As to the question of whether the details of public figures' lives are interesting: I see folk music, or what's called folk music now, having turned away from historical events and away from the world, and towards a kind of solipsism, confessional songwriting.

GM: Well, as Sean Wilentz said after he went to the 2002 Newport Folk Festival, "The whole thing was Shawn Colvin"—"self-indulgent adolescent angst," I think was the phrase he used.

It's a lot easier to write that kind of stuff than it is to take a real event, or to make up an event that could be real, and bring it to life with detail and cadence and the different voices you sometimes have to use for the different characters in a song. And I also think over the last thirty or forty years, people have really been brainwashed by certain aspects of progressive education, where the whole idea of what education is shifts from instruction, or opening people very specifically to their cultural legacies, to something that's much more therapeutic—giving people self-esteem, letting people know that they're important, that they have something to contribute, that they're special—and so, if you say something that's about your real feelings, then nobody can criticize you. Nobody can say, "Well, that's a load of shit."

"Well, how can you say that? This is how I feel!"

"Yeah, but how you feel is FUCKED!"

That's a healthy way of discussing things, I think. Maybe a little rough, but that's the way to go, as far as I'm concerned. So it's much easier to write a song about your feelings, and cloak it with that kind of invulnerability, than it is to live in the world, it seems to me. There are certain performers that have really gathered followings over the last ten, fifteen years, who completely baffle me, people like Jeff Buckley, Rufus Wainwright. I think Rufus Wainwright's father is [laughs] a thousand times more interesting than his son will ever be, writing these dumb, jokey songs about whatever strikes him. You can tell he dashes them off in five minutes, whether it's a song about he and his mother getting drunk together, in a really pathetic Alcoholics Anonymous way, or rather just alcoholics' way, or something about George Bush, or for that matter a dead skunk. He can just throw this stuff up against the wall and it almost always sticks. But pop music is a field where it gives you people to fall in love with, just as folk music is a field that gives you a thousand different variants of a song to track down, if that's what you want to do, and I can understand the appeal of that. I just do my best to resist it.

PSF: What really bothers me about a person like Rufus Wainwright, who for some reason I equate in my mind with Thom Yorke, is the voice he uses. I feel like I'm in *Invasion of the Body Snatchers* or something: "Why don't you people hear that this is totally false?"

GM: I agree. And when you hear passion, despair, and frustration, that creeps through, that it's only the artifice of the song that gives it its physicality, that makes it seem real; the artifice of the song is like a mask the singer can put on that allows him or her to actually communicate what otherwise he or she would never be able to say—willing to say, have the nerve to say— and when that comes through, it's really shocking. You put something like the Mendoza Line up against the plaints of Rufus Wainwright, or the cleverness of Rufus Wainwright, and the sorrow of Jeff Buckley, and, God, who would you rather meet?

Well, I know who I'd rather meet, but quite plainly, lots of other people would rather meet this sad, sensitive guy that they could save. The people in the Mendoza Line, they don't want to be saved. They just want the country to be saved, and that's very different. And they know that they can't save it. Their music, to me, is like the Mekons' of the eighties, it's a music of loneliness, alienation and a fantasy of comradeship. That's the dangerous stuff today; that's in their music, over the last several of their albums, and the last one, *Fortune.* They have a song on *Fortune,* "It's a Long Line, But It Moves Quickly"? It's a very, very funny, incredibly sarcastic song—really nasty. More and more I've been thinking of it as my anthem for the next four years. I hope they move quickly.

PSF: As a brief aside: you were speaking earlier about how certain performers could sing "Barbara Allen" and not even come close to what the song's about, not surprise you in any way. I don't know if you've seen the new *New Yorker,* but there's an article by Dave Eggers, who's probably my least favorite writer, about Monty Python, and it's boring! And I thought only he could make Monty Python boring.

GM: Well, I don't know. I love Monty Python—I love the records, I never liked the TV show. And a lot of the records are just the TV show, they're just the soundtrack, the dialogue with sound effects, and I like that much better. I think there's something about the TV show that's very obvious, where everything is telegraphed, and when you leave out the visual dimension it becomes much less likely. But I think it's very difficult to write about comedy. I think somebody could probably write well about Monty Python, but I bet it's very difficult.

With "Barbara Allen," it's not a question of people making it boring. The version of "Barbara Allen" that's used on the CD that accompanies *The Rose & the Briar*—same name, same cover, [but] they're not part of a package, you have to get them separately—is by Jean Ritchie, from 1961, and it's the classic performance of "Barbara Allen." It's done a cappella; it's extremely beautiful, it's clear the singer has lived this song all her life. And Bob Dylan's version, from a bootleg called *The Second Gaslight Tape*, it's very long, it's eight minutes long, and so passionate, and it really seems as if everything in life comes to bear and is at stake when he tells the story.

And I can appreciate that, but I guess I can appreciate it in a kind of aesthetic way, because it wasn't until I heard Terre Roche do that song that it hurt—that I had to surrender to it, that I had to admit my own ignorance and say, "There's something in this song that I don't understand. There's wisdom about life in this song that has escaped me all my life, and I'm just now beginning to get a glimpse of what that might be." See, that's my weakness; that's not the failure of other people in their performance of it.

Years and years ago, I wrote a very nasty piece about the Roches, on the occasion of their first album, which I found just unbearably cloying and precious and preening and self-congratulatory, and I also was getting sick of the fabulous reviews it was getting from every New York critic. They were a local band. They were a downtown Greenwich Village trio that everybody loved, and everybody in this case had access to national media, and managed to make a local band, which really deserved and needed no more than local success, into a national phenomenon. They were unable to live up to that status, because they really weren't that good. And then here's Terre Roche, all these years later, and we're on stage together, and I'm kind of hoping she doesn't remember the piece I wrote about her and her sisters all those years ago, and I'm also not expecting anything. Boy, was I wrong.

PSF: On the subject of criticism, do you think there are places in a song that criticism can't reach, that it just can't talk about? If so, what are they?
GM: No, I don't think so. It depends on the critic. It depends on what talents a person has to bring to bear on the object of criticism, and how much time, how much effort you're willing to spend to get it right, to stick with it.

PSF: Well, let me put it a different way. Are there things that you can't talk about? Are there particular songs or movies that you just fall mute before?
GM: Yeah! But then I tighten my belt and snap my suspenders and give it another try. Sure. There is stuff all through *The Manchurian Candidate* that just leaves me awestruck, and has since I first saw it in 1962, and I really wasn't able to write about that for many, many years. And certainly anybody who wants to read the little book I wrote about that movie may very well come away saying, "Yeah, and he still wasn't able to. He still wasn't able to get at what is so remarkable here, what is so uncanny, what's so frightening."

But you keep trying. That's what criticism is all about. It is the attempt to get inside the moment that is already speaking lucidly and translate it—not because the world needs you to do that, but because there's something appealing about it, if you have a certain sensibility. Let's say you can't sing. You can't carry a tune. You have no musical ability at all, and you hear a song, and you want nothing more in the world than to sing that song, or to feel the way the person who's singing it must feel, you imagine, to sing that fully, that completely, that well, whatever. But you don't have any musical ability. So in order to sing the song, if you're somebody like me, you write about it. You translate it. And in so doing, you end up with something different, and something that may tell a different story, that may be interesting to other people on some terms. It's part of a conversation.

There are certainly places in works of art that I can't reach, but it would be arrogant beyond my abilities to say that nobody else could reach them. Every good critic, every critic I've ever admired, whether it's Howard Hampton or Pauline Kael or Dara Moskowitz—who is the restaurant critic for *City Pages* in Minneapolis—or countless other people, I've admired them because they can do things I can't do! Because I read them, and I say, "Wow! How'd she do that? How does that happen? What's that about?"

One of the greatest moments of criticism in my entire life—one of the great experiences of criticism—took place in 1962 in June in Menlo Park at a theater which has just recently closed, but it was the big movie theater in Menlo Park (there was one theater for Hollywood movies, one theater for foreign movies or art movies). This was right after school was out in June, and everybody had gone to see some awful movie, and everybody was either drunk or wanting to be drunk, and the atmosphere was totally raucous. This movie was called *The Pirates of Blood River*; I've never forgotten about it. It takes place, I think, in Brazil, maybe the eighteenth century; it has to do with a religious war, Catholics versus Huguenots, just really ridiculous, and a lot of people getting shoved into Blood River where they're eaten by piranhas; that's why it's called Blood River, because you step in to this river and you'll get bitten. And at one point during the movie—everybody's just absolutely stupefied by the badness of this thing—this guy stood up, and he turned his back to the screen, raised his arms in the air, and said, "I NOMINATE THIS MOVIE SHIT FUCK OF THE YEAR 1962!" God! God, this is so brilliant. I wish I'd said that. So that's where criticism began for me.

PSF: I was having this late night drunken argument with my girlfriend the other night—we were talking about a particularly egregious piece of unpublished writing, and about the responsibilities of writers and writing. And she said, "Well, what if this thing gets published and goes out into the world?" And I said, "That's the role of criticism, there should be critics out there making a big stink about it, there should be a public response to it." And she said, "Yeah, well there is no public criticism in this country." I don't know how much that's true.
GM: What does that mean, "public criticism?"

PSF: I can't remember now if she said "public" or "popular." But I think what she meant by that was: that book might reach somebody who wouldn't hear any voices in the newspaper or on the radio or on TV saying that it was an immoral, bad piece of writing.
GM: I don't see criticism as playing any kind of gate-keeping role, or any kind of moral guardian role, or guarding the public health. Criticism is written by people who have to write. Writers write: that's what they do. It's not a choice. It's a way of being in the world; that's what defines a writer: he or she has to write. Critics have to criticize, and if they can't do it—if they can't wrestle with something that has inflamed them in one way or another, then they're less alive, or they're not alive at all, and they don't really have a choice with that.

Different people find different ways of handling that, and some critics become artists: some critics become performers, they become film directors, they become novelists. There are sorts of people who make that transition, and then there are people like me who don't. But I don't think there's any good critic who sees himself or herself as protecting the public or guiding the public, protecting the public from what's bad and guiding the public toward what's good. I think Pauline Kael was very messianic about certain works—something like *Bonnie and Clyde*, which was being reviled by every other critic in New York as mindless violence that was going to corrupt the soul of the nation and ruin the country's youth and God knows what else; she said, "No, this is alive, this is funny, this is new, this is powerful, this is about our life right now, and, my God, you ought to at least open yourself to it, give yourself a chance to see it, make up your own mind." So maybe there's some public good in that, there's some public role. But also, she wanted to wrestle with that movie.

There's a wonderful collage by Richard Hamilton, the British pop artist, I think it was done in 1956. It's really one of the founding works of Pop Art. It's called *Just What Is It That Makes Today's Home So Different, So Appealing?* It's this really savage satire of modern postwar living, set in a modern living room. There's a coffee table and there's a vacuum cleaner and there's all kinds of stuff like that. And that's really the critical question: just what is it that makes this something so different, so appealing, so appalling, so horrifying, so seductive? That's the question you're trying to ask, not, "Is this good, is this bad?" There are plenty of critics who do that; they're worthless. David Denby is the classic example. "Is this good for you?"

PSF: I don't think the argument we were having was about whether there should be somebody protecting people from things that might corrupt them. I think it was about, what if you're a person, especially an isolated person—I guess this also has to do with the question, what is culture and who has access to it—but what if you came across this thing and you didn't hear anybody shouting, "This sucks!" Not to say that if you're not a critic, you can't make up your own mind about something, but just in terms of what criticism is or what it ought to be, I feel like—especially music criticism now, at least in the major magazines—there's not a lot of strong opinion one way or another.

GM: Well, I think that's true. I'm not quite sure why that is. I think that is true, but what a critic wants is a reader who is himself or herself critically inclined, someone who asks questions, someone who questions what he or she responds to, however it's responded to. You don't want an empty vessel to pour your opinions into. What could be more dull? What could be less compelling than to convince somebody you're right? I remember once reading—this doesn't exactly address the question—but somebody saying that it's very important for critics to be right occasionally. Which struck me as really funny, and also wrong. I didn't understand why it was important to be right, or even exactly what that meant. There was an article written, oh . . . some time in the late seventies I think, and it mentioned a whole bunch of people the writer of the article thought were good rock critics, and it named maybe half a dozen, a dozen people. And one of the things it said was, "None of them were fooled by Jobriath."

Jobriath was a singer who was promoted I think in the late seventies, in the mid '70s maybe, as a "true queer." David Bowie was the phony queer, but this guy was the real queer, and somehow this was going to make him a star. And a huge amount of money was put behind this guy. I think he was on Elektra; it was a period when Elektra was going for every absurd shtick imaginable, and that's all they were buying and all they were selling, was shtick.

So, here comes Jobriath, and he puts out this one terrible record, and he's never heard from again, and I never gave him another thought, until I met a guy, about my age, from a Midwestern state, who knew from the time he was very young that he was gay, and in that Midwestern state, in his town, he had no way of expressing this, no one to talk to about it, no way of understanding who he was or what was going on with his whole being. And not only was it the fact that a homosexual would be promoted as a desirable object, like Jobriath, but this became of huge importance—this guy was a huge music fan, worshipped the Rolling Stones, still does. The Jobriath album was a record that he listened to obsessively, and I found out later that this was true for thousands of people.

On the level of shtick, the album was a matter of self-affirmation for a lot of people, but they delved into the music on that album as if it had to hold the keys to the kingdom, as if it had to mean more, say more, express more than maybe it appeared to do. So they were able to find meaning and life in that album, that somebody like me—I wouldn't necessarily say I could never have found that, but I would never have bothered to do the work to find what other people found. So, to say that a bunch of good rock critics weren't fooled by Jobriath was maybe to say that they were simply fooled by their own prejudices against what might lie behind marketing. When a marketing campaign is self-evidently phony, that doesn't mean that what's being marketed is phony, or a lie. Tricky.

PSF: You mentioned David Denby; you've written a couple—I think it's fair to say—attacks on his writing, and I agree with them, but is it fair to see this as a fight over Pauline Kael's legacy?

GM: No. Pauline can speak for herself, dead or alive. She doesn't need me or any of her other friends to do it for her. I have to admit that I found David Denby's piece "My Life as a Paulette" absolutely disgusting and reprehensible and immoral. I could probably think of worse things to say if you give me a minute. But the real killer in that piece is, he talks about how he wrote some stuff, and maybe he gets a phone call or a note from Pauline encouraging him, and they become friends, and they go to movies together, and this is an experience that many, many people had with Pauline—her reaching out to younger writers.

PSF: Because she was generous.

GM: And because that was a way that she stayed young, she stayed aware of things she might otherwise not be aware of. She was interested in what other people had to say, and she was interested in what they knew that she didn't know. She was interested in the world that way; she wasn't just Doing Good.

In any case, the day comes, according to David Denby in this piece of his, when she says to him, "You know, you're really not a writer. You should do something else, maybe you should become a director, but you're really not a writer." And I don't know if she really said that, I have no reason to think that Denby is making it up. I have difficulty imagining her saying that, being that cruel, because that's a cruel thing to say: even if it's cruel-to-be-kind, it's still cruel. I have difficulty seeing her say that. But let's assume she did, I don't have any reason to think she didn't.

Well, she was right! He's not a writer. He has no sense of words. It is quite clear that this is a person who writes for prestige, for self-affirmation, out of some neurotic self-importance that has nothing to do with love of words or the compulsion to translate an experience from one language into another. That's clearly not there. His writing has never been alive—it's not even alive to itself. The reason I find it so difficult to imagine Pauline saying that is she's become friendly with somebody, and she realizes the guy's really not very good—well, so what! There are a lot of writers out there who aren't so good, they're not doing all that great damage to the public good—you really don't have to call them off. So I don't know.

I think it is quite odd that the *New Yorker* has run a number of pieces over the past couple of years that have seemed to be there to take down or erase the reputation of their most celebrated, or notorious, critic of the last forty, fifty years. Very odd that a magazine needs to pile dirt on somebody's grave, to make sure that she's really dead. I wonder what they're worried about.

PSF: Can you tell me anything about the book you're working on?

GM: Well, I'm working on two books. One is, for lack of a real title, called *Prophecy and the American Voice*. It's a very tricky project that, in one way or another, I've been working on for a long time. It tries to get at the way in which the prophetic voice, and "prophet" or "prophetic" as understood in the Old Testament sense of someone who calls upon a society to judge itself, or says "God is about to judge you! Look at yourself, see where you have failed, see where you have betrayed the promises you've made." [It's about] how that's an integral part of what the United States, or America, has always been. And that there's this shift that takes place in the United States from a community that the prophet says will be judged by God for its betrayals—for the promises it's made to God—to a community that must judge itself for the betrayal of the promises it's made to itself. That's the theoretical frame of the book. [And the book argues] that in the present [the role of the prophet] is taken up almost solely by artists. And that this question remains alive, the question of our community betraying itself, betraying the promises that we've made to ourselves, is at the center of our most interesting art, which doesn't appear to have any sort of political dimensions. So that's that book, and a tricky project.

And the other book is a book about "Like a Rolling Stone," which was a publisher's idea. He called up and he said he wanted me to write a short book on "Like a Rolling Stone," and I originally said no, because I thought it was not a very good idea and I was writing this prophecy book anyway, couldn't do two books at once. And when I mentioned it to people, everybody said, "Wow, what a great idea!" And I'd say "It is? Tell me why it is." And I found that I couldn't stop thinking about it, so after a couple of days I said I would do it because I had come up with this brilliant idea that I could write this book that was supposed to be 45,000 words—I could write it, I could do the research, I could interview people, I could do whatever was necessary—in a month.

And I did, I wrote it last May, and it's coming out in April. Right now I'm just doing the second pages, making corrections and changes and stuff, and it didn't turn out to be 45,000 words, it's more like 65,000 words. And it was really fun, it was great fun. And I also thought, "Well, this is the way to write books—do 'em in a month! What a great idea!" I don't know that I have another subject I could write a book about in a month; people may say when they read this one that this wasn't something I could write a book about in a month either, but we'll see.

PSF: What did you think of the Fiery Furnaces' second album? I know you really liked the first one.

GM: I just could not connect with it at all, and I don't understand why. Formally I don't see what's so different about it, I don't see that the singing is so different, or the orchestration, but it just left me absolutely cold. And I love their first record, and I still think it's absolutely wonderful and not like anything else around. Very embarrassing: I wrote this rave review of this album and got the name wrong—I called it [*Gallowsbird's*] *Park* instead of *Bark*. But I just think it's fantastic and mysterious and unsolvable, and the second one I played many times, left it alone for a couple of months, played it in different moods, and I just can't connect with it. Don't know why.

PSF: How much time a day do you spend listening to records?
GM: It depends on what I'm doing. I can play records all day or I can go a whole day without playing one.

PSF: Do you listen to music when you write?
GM: Yeah. But . . . I listen to music when I'm working—proofreading and revising, stuff like that. But when I'm writing I mostly listen to comedy records. Just need that clatter and noise in the background.

PSF: I was watching a rerun of *Saturday Night Live* the other night that couldn't have been more than a year old, and in the Weekend Update part of it they had two Clinton jokes, and I think one of them was a Lewinsky joke. I thought it was amazing that he's still alive in some way; he could have completely disappeared. In some ways he has, you see him every once in a while on C-SPAN . . .
GM: I think he's kept a very low profile, aside from publishing his book and doing some appearances for that; before that I don't think he was in public very much at all. I think what's so disgusting, and this doesn't really have anything to do with Clinton, is the way people are pigeonholed. People become one-liners. Clinton is a sex joke, and that's all the people on *Saturday Night Live* can do with him. And Tina Fey is very, very sharp and imaginative and a terrific writer, but she can't come up with anything else about Clinton. Sex sex sex, fuck fuck fuck—that's just all there is to it. It's ridiculous.

PSF: Even to make the same old jokes about him, there's a kind of nostalgia for him.
GM: No, I don't think so. Just a dog you can keep kicking.

PSF: Speaking of people being reduced, have you heard the Nirvana box set?
GM: No, I haven't heard it yet.

PSF: I think it's pretty awful; it's one of those box sets where you hear eight alternate versions of the same song over and over.
GM: Well, it can't be worse than that garbage they stuck on *London Calling*.

PSF: Isn't that awful?
GM: Embarrassing. There comes a point when the bootlegger, whether it's official or not, has to exercise some judgment [laughs] as to what's worth putting out there. These are people just messing around—anyone who's ever spent time in a studio knows how boring it can be, and this is real proof of that. You can't even say, "Oh, look how this turned into that, isn't that fascinating," or even, "God, this doesn't sound like it ever could become anything, but it did"—no, you just can't listen to that crap. And it sounds so bad, it's so muffled. It's a real insult. Really, really terrible.

So, I don't know. I didn't get the Nirvana box set and I haven't gone out and spent the money for it yet.

PSF: I heard that Gang of Four is reuniting.
GM: Well, they were offered a lot of money to play some shows in Europe, and presumably they're going to do that.

PSF: What do you make, if anything, of the sort of resurrection of that sound, or at least that people think it's hip to own Gang of Four records.
GM: I don't know . . . Nothing. Nothing in particular. I think it's good that the music is available; I think it's wonderful that there's a Lora Logic collection [*Fanfare in the Garden* on Kill Rock Stars]. Someone once asked Ed Ward [writer and radio commenter] if he knew what I was working on, and I was working on *Lipstick Traces* at that time, and he said, "Yeah, Greil's writing a book that's going to try and prove that Lora Logic can sing," and that's a one-line review of that book I really treasure. It's good that stuff's available, and people can connect to it or not, if they're able to or choose to.

As far as the Gang of Four go, they didn't make much money when they were a band, they were remarkable, they deserve whatever they can make now as far as I'm concerned, and you have no idea what will happen when a band whose music is based in the whole notion of instability, of things falling apart and then recombining in unpredictable ways—you have no idea what will happen when they get on stage. It could surprise them more than anyone in the audience, who knows. If I were around, I'd be there.

Interview with Greil Marcus and Werner Sollors

Asbjørn Grønstad and Øyvind Vågnes/2010

From *Journal of American Studies*, 45: E16, 2011. Copyright © 2011 Cambridge University Press. Reprinted with the permission of Cambridge University Press.

In September 2009, Harvard University Press published *A New Literary History of America*, edited by Greil Marcus and Werner Sollors. The book is an anthology of original essays that kaleidoscopically comprise not only literature and fiction but many different fields from philosophy and science to political rhetoric, art and aesthetics, music, film, and popular culture. On 19 March 2010 we talked to Greil Marcus in his home in Berkeley. Werner Sollors we interviewed by email around the same time.

Werner Sollors: The topics are sufficiently varied to appeal to very broad general interests from the coining of the word "America" and the Puritan Jeremiad to the election of Barack Obama. The fact that each essay is only four to five printed pages long invites students and general readers to open up to topics they may never have thought they might be interested in. The volume rationale reminded contributors that essays were meant to be stimulating and provocative for both scholarly and expert audiences and for the public at large. An entry on, say, Faulkner or Stephen Foster does not have to rehearse the entire background story of the person in question, but should provide basic contextual information that can locate the reader in the entry. Keep the interested but general reader in mind, but do not ever feel you need to dumb down or oversimplify your arguments or your style.

Contributors were also assured that while they "should take cognizance of secondary literature on the given subject," there was "no need to get bogged down in critical controversies that will lead you and the reader away from the subject in question." We did not want writing that was predictable, but essays that would surprise even the authors of the essays themselves. Our goal was not to give readers a feeling that once they had read an essay about a subject they had acquired a definitive understanding of it. Much rather, our aim was to make nonspecialists curious to read, or look at, or listen to, works as if for the first time, intrigued by one of the essays. Hence we wanted not only academic specialists to write for us but also authors who had not previously published on a topic at hand but who cared about it and were curious about it.

Asbjørn Grønstad and Øyvind Vågnes: How did the idea for this anthology come about, and whose initiative was it? And what brought you and your coeditor Werner Sollors together? In short, why this book at this particular moment in time?

Greil Marcus: Lindsay Waters is an editor at Harvard University Press and has been for many years, and he is the editor who published my book *Lipstick Traces*, so I've worked with him for a long time. I've done other books with him too. A number of years ago he published a book called *A New History of French Literature* that was edited by Denis Hollier, and then a few years after that he published *A New History of German Literature* that both Werner and I contributed to. And they were both terrific books, and he wanted to do an American version, *A New History of American Literature*, and he thought that Werner and I—who didn't know each other, and I'm not sure that we were even aware of each other—would work well together. And so he arranged for me to come out to Cambridge so we could all meet. I mean, Lindsay had also published Werner's books at Harvard University Press, and we got along very, very well right away.

But what we realized immediately was that there was no way that any American book that would be even remotely equivalent to their earlier ones could follow the same format or the same ruling idea. With the German and French volumes you're talking about organic societies that developed through many, many very different dialects of German or French—some of them unrecognizable today—but there has always been a High German, there has always been a court French, there has always been an official language. And that has been the ruling language of those societies, and that language—in many ways—helped create those societies, and the societies long predate any modern political formations. These are histories of an organic literature, in both cases developing from at least 800 AD to the present, without significant invasions of other languages. America—you know there's just no comparison. When we're talking about America—obviously something of much more recent date—you have many different languages, you have people from all over, you have a constant battle, in a lot of ways, to even begin to create a national discourse. And in a lot of ways the political formation, with the Declaration of Independence and the Constitution, antedates the social world. The social world takes shape as a reflection of the political formation. The fundamental ideas in the Declaration of Independence and the Constitution shape and in many ways determine what the society is going to be, what its values are going to be, how they are going to be understood, and what the conflict, the intellectual, literary, social, and cultural conflict in the society is going to be, and that's going to be the history of the country.

So Werner and I, we just sort of immediately said that this is going to have to be completely different. And it cannot restrict itself to literature—it cannot be a history of American literature in any conventional sense. And we had a number of meetings where we really began to get a clearer idea of what this would be—but ultimately it was going to be the story of American speech, of American discourse, of people arguing with each other over what the meaning, purpose, reality of the country was and would be. And that would involve writing. But—in American literature, American speech—the first genre is the sermon, the Puritan sermon. Poetry comes not too long after that with Edward Taylor and other Puritan poets, but then you're moving out to political essays, satirical essays, and then you move in to the realm of rhetoric. Poetry doesn't begin to play a major role until the late eighteenth century, early nineteenth century. It's going to have to involve theater, it's going to have to involve music, inventions, creating. Werner's idea was always that this book was about making. It was about making America. And you made up, you invented America—you could do it in a poem, you could do it with the invention of a particular kind of rifle that would come to symbolize the whole American story, the American quest, its triumphant spirit, its imperialistic spirit. And all different sorts of things were going to constantly come into play—and what elements, what formations, what genres those might be—that was going to change over time as the story moved forward.

We also found—pretty quickly—that the story gains momentum and it becomes bigger and it becomes louder and more interesting in the nineteenth and twentieth centuries because it's in those centuries that the story of America becomes in a certain way the story of all different kinds of people who were previously excluded from the master narrative of the country. They begin to push in and take over that story themselves, so that—in the nineteenth century—obviously one of the towering literary figures of the whole era is Abraham Lincoln, as a literary figure. But also Frederick Douglass, just as much. And there are two entries on Lincoln, and there are two entries on Frederick Douglass. And of course, Poe and Melville and two fabulous essays on two different Emerson addresses, But it's then that other voices begin to come in, and this becomes a stream within a stream that widens within the greater river.

So both Werner and I, and I think Lindsay—once we agreed we would do this—just couldn't wait. We were just filled with a sense of mission. At Lindsay's suggestion we put together an editorial board of ten people. And these would be people who would have expertise in different fields—might be science, might be poetry, might be film—but who would also be the sort of people who had broad knowledge and broad interests, and could be involved in decisions having to do with any aspect of the book. It wasn't like the film person only was responsible for—or had to keep his mouth shut when we weren't talking about—film. So we convened this group, and we had a meeting in Cambridge to see if it would work, if this was going to be a good working group. And there were mostly younger academics—people in their thirties, maybe early forties. But also David Thomson, the great film historian, who's a bit older than I am; Gerald Early, who is a great Americanist from Washington University in Saint Louis, who's in his fifties. And we did get along, we did have an intellectual sympathy, except for one person, who just did not understand what we were doing.

So we ended up with a good group of people. And then, Werner and I asked each member of the editorial board to come up with suggestions for twenty or thirty incidents—events—happenstances that we should be covering in this book. Because the format was going to be as it was with the French and German volumes—turning points, moments when something happened that had not happened before—incidents where something that had seemed impossible the day before now seemed inevitable. Not necessarily for the whole society, maybe just for the individual involved, or a very small group of people who were aware of what might have happened. That could be the publication of a book, the starting of a newspaper, the delivery of a sermon, or a political event like an assassination or an election. It could be when two or more people met, and a certain kind of intellectual symbiosis took place that no one would have ever anticipated. It was all these sorts of events, and we were asking people: OK, find dates, find events, describe them and come to a meeting where we will decide what's going to be in this book, because we have room for about two hundred entries. We're going to tell the whole story from the beginning of literate America, which means the European discovery. We're going to tell the whole story from then to the present, and we only have room for two hundred essays. They're all going to be about 2,500 words.

I guess we had a total of about five hundred nominations—and most people nominated within their particular fields of interest, but not necessarily. Anybody could put forward anything. So Werner and I got this pile of suggestions. Some of them were just dates and names and some of them were lengthy descriptions of why we had to include this. And ultimately it meant that someone was going to have to play the grand inquisitor. And I took on that role, and that meant that I went through the whole list—we put together a master list—and before our meeting, where everyone was going to be present, I just checked yes and checked no, in the most fascist manner imaginable. Not discussing anything, not making any arguments, but saying, 1492—no, 1612—yes. Like that. People were encouraged to interrupt me at any time, like when I did something anyone disagreed with. We would argue about it. So it was a very intimidating procedure—because I just started: yes, no, yes, no, and nobody was saying anything. So I went back to the beginning and started over, and then: no. No? What do you mean, no? How can you say no? Do you even know what you're talking about? And of course, sometimes I didn't know what I was talking about.

We then really began to struggle and argue over this list, and the meeting began to generate its own new, and in some ways better, ideas, and we began to come up with all kinds of double entries, composite entries, where you're talking about two things at once—two things that maybe happened in the same year, that on the surface don't seem related at all, but in fact speak to each other, that are about similar things. They might not be in the same year, but they could be a thematic that encompasses certain things. For example, there is an entry on *The House of Mirth* and *Sister Carrie*. One published in 1900, the other in 1905. They are both novels about class anxiety, rise and fall—Carrie rises, Lily Bart in *House of Mirth* falls. And it just seemed like a natural. And it's a way of dealing with both writers and dealing with this greater theme that obsesses them both. So a lot of composite entries began to develop. And by the end of the day, or the second day, we had gone through this whole list, dispensed with many, discovered many in the course of the discussion. But we were down to somewhere around 240 entries. And we figured we could make that, we would find room for that, we would lose some along the way. We were there.

Then we had another meeting—again with the entire group. And the entire group included Werner and myself, Lindsay Waters, and a couple of other Harvard University Press people as well as the editorial board members. OK: who is going to write what? And what that came down to, what we wanted to do was to stay away from getting the main expert in this field or in this question, who would then recapitulate what he or she had already written about this subject. That was not what we wanted. We wanted people who would confront these questions as if they had never been asked—as if you bring your intellectual apparatus to bear on this question, but it's not a question you have really examined before. So we wanted that kind of freshness, and we wanted writers who were going to surprise their readers, and they were going to surprise us. But we also wanted people who would surprise themselves, who would be able to bring a sense of discovery into their own work. So we would take someone who was a great scholar of literature and ask her to write about Junius Brutus Booth, who brought Romantic acting from Britain to the United States in the nineteenth century. And it would be someone who was familiar with that period, and who certainly knew who Booth was, but hadn't really grappled with him before. That was how we tried to make this work.

Some of it was catch-as-catch-can. I happened to read an essay in the journal *Raritan* about Lincoln before the presidency, after he had been elected but before he took office. Things that were going on, things that he was trying to put in place. And the writing was so alive, and the thinking was so full of daring. I just said: this is the guy we want to write about the Lincoln-Douglas debates. Has he ever studied them? Probably, but not necessarily. But this guy could write, we have got to get him. Over and over again it became a question not of who would do the best job, or who knows the most but of what does this person think of such and such? That is how Ishmael Reed got the assignment to write about *Huckleberry Finn*. Because we said: I wonder what Ishmael Reed thinks of *Huckleberry Finn*—nobody had a clue. Well, let's ask him!

In some cases it was very easy to find the person we wanted. Sometimes we had to knock on several doors before we could get anyone to say yes. One of our composite entries was on *Gone with the Wind* and *Absalom, Absalom!* by Faulkner, because they are both southern novels and they were both published in 1936. Do they really have any affinity? Well, let's find a writer who could tell us if there is or if there isn't.

I remember I called Lee Smith, who is a southern novelist I know and whose work I love. And I asked her if she would do this and she said: "Well, of course I've read *Absalom, Absalom!* but I've never read *Gone with the*

Wind." I'm thinking: "You're a southern middle-aged woman and you've never read *Gone with the Wind*? Come on." But I wasn't about to say: and now will you please sit down and read this nine-hundred-page book? So I called Bobbie Ann Mason, another southern novelist who I know, and she said the same thing: "Oh, I've seen the movie."

Finally I realized I should have called my friend Carolyn Porter, who's an English professor at Berkeley, from Texas. And a downhome person, with no pretensions, and also a Faulkner scholar; she had just published a book on Faulkner. So I said, "Carolyn, I've talked to other people who claim they haven't read *Gone with the Wind*, have you read it"? She said: "Have I read it? I've memorized it!" And she had, I mean, she knew chapter and verse. Not only could she quote dialogue, she knew exactly where in the book it was. And *Absalom, Absalom!* was just as familiar.

So sometimes it was difficult to find the right person—sometimes easy— but it was a tremendous adventure. And there were very few situations— maybe one or two—where the person couldn't come through and didn't write anything. And maybe half a dozen or a few more where people turned in their essays and for one reason or another they were just unworkable. In most cases people understood the assignment, they were able to get some sense of the whole picture, even though nobody had the whole picture then. And in the cases where we got essays that were dull, or they were kind of programmatic, but that had passion and knowledge, we'd say: "Could you instead of going one, two, three, four, five—could you start with three, and then maybe go to five and then take us to one later? Just make this story a little less familiar, to yourself and to us."

Each member of the editorial board was responsible for between twelve and maybe eighteen entries. "You're the editor of these people, you've got to get them to turn their work in on time, It's gotta be good," and all of that. And Werner and I were each handling twenty to twenty-five apiece, and calling people up to say: "How many have you got?" and "When are you going to have everything ready?" Just that kind of housekeeping. That's a very long answer to your first question.

WS: Harvard University Press had published two earlier one-volume literary histories that provided models for an American volume. Denis Hollier's *A New History of French Literature* (1989) had introduced a kind of mock-chronological arrangement of single essays using an often arbitrarily chosen date and a tagline as hooks (e.g. "1922, November 18 Death of Marcel Proust, Death and Literary Authority"), and David Wellbery and Judith Ryan's *A New History of German Literature* (2004) had expanded the notion of texts and works that could be included as literature (with essays on Hitler's *Mein Kampf*, Edgar Reitz's film *Helmat*, and the falling of the Berlin wall); both volumes settled on fresh but provocatively short essays. Lindsay Waters and I had had regular e-mail contact since the 1990s, averaging perhaps a dozen messages a year. This changed radically in the second half of 2005 when I received over a hundred e-mails from him—most of them about imagining editing a new one-volume literary history of the United States and about who might be a good coeditor. After contemplating some other possibilities, in August 2005 Lindsay reported the exciting news that the famous music and cultural critic Greil Marcus sounded "interested" in becoming a coeditor, and we were soon all writing each other back and forth about the project, and at the end of September 2005 we had a long two-day brainstorming session in Boston at which a real book project began to take shape. Lindsay had known both me and Greil for decades, but Greil and I had never met. We liked the model of the two earlier volumes (all three of us had written essays for *A New History of German Literature*), but we thought that an American volume needed a different emphasis, and we settled on *poiesis*, "making" in the broadest cultural sense, as its overarching idea: works and things that have been made and that may also lead to the creation of other works and things. American literature would be the core, but it would be embedded in cultural history, not set off from it. We thought this a timely project for all sorts of reasons, including the postmodern anxiety about narrative, the availability of background facts on the Web, and the fact that while many works and objects created in America have had a resonance in other countries, today the whole globe consumes and debates, admires and loathes American culture. We wanted to produce "not an encyclopedia but a provocation" that would present American literature to nonspecialists, in a lively manner, following such classic examples as D. H. Lawrence and Leslie Fiedler. That would make it essential to get contributions not only by critics but also by writers and artists.

AG/ØV: How you describe the gestation of the book and the plan behind it ties in quite well with the impression that you have as a reader of a certain freshness and excitement. The unusual constellations.

GM: I'm thrilled to hear that. But when the essays were all in, and Werner and I began to edit the whole book, we realized that—either by luck or just because we really had chosen well in terms of entries, in terms of correspondences and affinities—there would be themes taking shape within a constellation of maybe three or four, or maybe six or seven, entries over a stretch of say twenty or thirty entries. There would be subthemes developing within that area, from one to the other that we had nothing to do with. It just had to do with the way the themes drew out certain subthemes from different writers, who were not aware of what other people were doing. And so we didn't have to draw linkages. We didn't have to edit—and we wouldn't have in any case—to make the book look more whole than it really is. It took on its own shape.

AG/ØV: How long was it in the making?
GM: I cannot believe we did this in three years, but we did.

AG/ØV: We are interested in this question of expertise versus writers exploring issues they would not necessarily be experts on.
GM: I don't mean that we wanted people who were ignorant, just the contrary, but we wanted people whose whole world was film, but who had never maybe written about or even seriously thought about *Some Like It Hot* by Billy Wilder. But who had the ability to then confront that movie and enter its world and create a larger world for it.

With the Linda Lovelace entry, which is one that came up during our original long list meeting, Gerald Early asked us near the end of the day: "Has anybody read Linda Lovelace's autobiography?" Nobody had. Then he starts telling us about *Ordeal*, her autobiography (written with somebody else, of course), about how she was turned into a sex slave in the pornography industry and all of this, and he said that the most dominant literary genre of the last forty years in America is the memoir. More particularly, the memoir of abuse, of survival of hideous circumstances. It's titillating; it's sensationalistic—and this is one of the first examples of it. Early claimed it was a completely gripping book, but most people had not heard of it. But he convinced us, although at first we all thought it was a joke.

So then the question is: who is going to want to write about this? Ann Marlowe—who did write about it—is someone who had written her own memoir—which is essentially about sex and drugs. And I thought, she can write about this. She can write about drugs, she can write about sex, she can write about domination, she can write about escape. Those themes are real to her. But like the women who had said they had never read *Gone with the Wind*, she said, "Well, I've never seen *Deep Throat.*" But she took the project on and she ended up knowing far more about it than anybody who assigned it. Then it turned out there isn't just one Linda Lovelace autobiography, there are four. So there is this sense of invention, of discovery, going on from place to place in the book.

AG/ØV: There is this energy that comes from that, like in the Jonathan Lethem piece.

GM: I don't remember who suggested that he write about Edison and the birth of the movies. Jonathan is someone I have known for many years, but didn't know he had any interest in that, or knowledge of it. It was someone else's idea. And it just turned out to be perfect. And he just immediately went for it. And it's funny—that is a controversial entry. A lot of people love it, some people find it completely dull and dry. But people talk about it.

AG/ØV: *A New Literary History* is rich with original and striking constellations, not least between writers and topics/thematics. It would be very interesting to hear a little about the process involved. Did you approach writers with specific things in mind, or were your invitations more open-ended? Was there stuff that you had hoped you would get in, but that for various reasons did not make it in this first edition?

WS: We were fortunate to receive funding to invite ten critics to a Radcliffe Institute Exploratory Seminar on 27 and 28 January 2006. Lindsay, Greil, and I had selected them in unanimity, and several of them we had already mentioned to each other at our initial meeting: literary scholars from departments of English and comparative literature, but also historians, interdisciplinary Americanists and African-Americanists, an art historian, a historian of science and technology, a film critic, a novelist-critic, and two graduate students. At this meeting we were ready to see the whole project radically questioned, perhaps terminated altogether, by the arguments of others. The first focused brainstorming session, based on some precirculated readings and presentations by Lindsay, Greil, me, and some of those who were present, moved from the question whether such a book should exist at all to the specific shape it should take, and we began to explore the topic of making and the question how far we could reach in describing things American.

For a second session we asked each of the participants to come up with a larger list of questions that could help generate a history of making in America. The assembled scholars enjoyed the chance to think about an American project more generally, far beyond their own backgrounds and areas of expertise. Most of the seminar participants (nine of the ten scholars and both graduate students) were excited enough by the discussions in this exploratory seminar to agree to form the truly interdisciplinary editorial board of *A New Literary History of America*, and another Americanist joined us a little later. The collective wisdom, imagination, and energy of these twelve immediately propelled the project onward. Each member took on the task to come up with a list of the twenty-five to forty most important American topics (by Ash Wednesday, 2006) that each believed would simply have to be included (with a brief rationale, outline, or listing of possible subtopics), regardless of individual specialties and disciplines, and trying to imagine the book as a whole, without territory to protect or turf to defend. And all lived up to that challenge.

A board meeting in the Harvard University Press offices brought all of us together a second time on 12 to 13 May 2006, armed with an elaborate composite listing of several hundred submitted topics that all of us now had to whittle down rigorously to about two hundred, while some new subjects also emerged at that meeting. Throughout, we were looking for points in time and imagination where something changed: "When a new idea or a new form came into being, when new questions were raised, when what before seemed impossible came to seem necessary, or inevitable." We asked board members before the meeting to trim their own lists somewhat and combine some of the more minute topics into clusters of related subjects. We asked, "Which twenty do you really want to see discussed?"—a question which led to spirited debate and quite a painful process of elimination, as all editors had to watch topics they had proposed, and with good arguments, disappear from the project. Among the many subjects cut were "1492 Columbus believes he finds honey and nightingales in New World: imports word *canoa*, the first American word to reach most European languages," "1640 Bay Psalm Book," "1774 Speech of Logan, Mingo Chief," "18—A fry cook at a remote lumber camp in Wisconsin overcooks some potatoes. These are the first potato chips," "1842 Dickens American Notes: Possibly a way to start an entry on foreign travelers writing about the US," "1862 Nathaniel Hawthorne, 'Chiefly about War Matters by a Peaceable Man,'" "1873 Levi Strauss and Jacob Davis put rivets in denim pants, creating blue jeans," "1874 'Catchphrase': the date of its first use in John C. Calhoun's *Works*, "1901 First refrigerated ship enables banana to reign supreme as favorite U.S. breakfast food," "1908 Ernest Fenollosa's widow meets Ezra Pound," "1930 *I'll Take My Stand*: The South and the Agrarian Tradition," and "1978 Publication of Edward Said's *Orientalism*." It is easy to imagine another book consisting only of subjects that did not make it into ours.

We also offered each member of the editorial board the opportunity to propose ideal contributors for each topic that remained active. They included the sadly unfulfilled hopes that Bob Dylan would write on Walt Whitman or F. Scott Fitzgerald, Toni Morrison on Lincoln's Second Inaugural or on Faulkner, Art Spiegelman on comics and graphic novels, Stanley Crouch on Edgar Rice Burroughs, Philip Roth on Hawthorne and Faulkner, Thomas Pynchon on Orson Welles, Don Delillo on Miles Davis, Supreme Court Justice David Souter on Madison's *Notes of Debates of the Federal Convention*, and a senator from Illinois on the Lincoln-Douglas debates. Even though such suggestions remained unrealized (the senator from Illinois, for example, was too busy because he was planning a campaign as presidential candidate), this only fired up the imagination of the editors who identified many other major authors and creators who did accept our invitation to write, and did come through with essays that help to deepen the understanding of making, of creating, of suggesting amazement at things that have been made in America: empty pages filled with memorable words, canvases on which unforgettable visuals took shape, or notes that turned into patriotic songs, popular tunes, and Jazz.

AG/ØV: The title of the anthology seems very apt; this really is not just a new history in the literal sense but, perhaps even more importantly, a new method or template for composing a literary history in the first place. Wes Davis in the *Wall Street Journal* enthuses that in *A New Literary History of America* "it's clear that nothing remains of the boundaries that traditionally separated literature, history, and popular culture." It might be interesting to know whether this dismantling of the boundaries was in fact a deliberate and carefully designed objective to begin with, or if it was something that just happened.

WS: We wanted to keep literature at the center but select works in all genres: not just prose fiction (which has become the preferred genre of contemporary American studies), but also drama, poetry, essay, autobiography, nonfiction, with some examples of writing in languages other than English. More than that, the notion of "Made in America" opened up the possibility to examine examples of a much broader array of subjects than earlier American literary histories, and not merely as backdrop for literature in the high-cultural sense but as central topics in the shaping of American culture: religious tracts and sermons, children's books, public speeches and private letters, political polemics, addresses and debates, Supreme Court decisions, maps, histories, travel diaries, philosophical writing, literary histories and criticism, folk songs, magazines, dramatic performances, the blues, paintings and monuments, prints, jazz, war memorials, museums, the built environment, book clubs, photographs, country music, films, radio, rock and roll, cartoons, technological inventions and innovations, pornography, cultural rituals, sports, and hip-hop. The hope was that the essays would illuminate each other—which would be a different mode of providing contexts than the more traditional literary histories' background writing on such topics as "the colonial era" or "the Civil War."

GM: I don't think it was a structural attempt to dismantle boundaries. It wasn't like, "Here's our chance to insert into the discussion of American culture all these things that are so often excluded, so let's shove all this in." It was more a sense, I think, on Werner's part and mine, that we didn't recognize, accept, countenance, respect, these boundaries, and we wanted to find people to contribute to the book who didn't either. Not who would set about breaking down boundaries, but who didn't see them and so they ignored them. That's what we were interested in.

There was a lot of discussion over what to call the book. We realized it could not be called *A New History of American Literature*, because it wasn't going to be that. And the question of America, rather than the United States. . . . The United States is this weird country, it's like the People's Republic of China, the Federal Republic of Germany—it's a bureaucratic name, it doesn't exactly have heart to it. And that's one of the reasons why the question of whether America exists or not—which is a fundamental question in our literature and our culture from the beginning to the present—is because the United States of America sounds more like a trade association than a country. It sounds like something that was just made up, which it was! That's the point. In terms of boundaries, in terms of how we were going to construct the thing, we went with America because it had more resonance than the United States. It seemed to be about something. Obviously the United States of America exists as a bureaucratic entity. But does America exist? And we know what we mean by America. Forget all this stuff about South America and Canada.

And then a literary history—not a history of the literary—a history that will have a literary engine behind it or within it. There will be a literary backdrop or a literary beating heart in a subject that isn't itself necessarily literary. Chuck Berry and Bob Dylan have entries, and obviously they're there primarily because of what they did as musicians, but a lot of what they did as musicians had to do with songwriting. But even more than that, we're talking about two people, Chuck Berry and Bob Dylan, who wrote absolutely singular, unique, revelatory autobiographies. There are no parallels to the books that they wrote. Both of them have left behind "documents not of edification but of paradox," as Hugo Ball once put it. So there is going to be a literary reflection, a literary echo—if not a fully formed literary body—in almost every entry in the book.

AG/ØV: The entry on Leslie Fiedler quotes him as saying (in 1979) that the function of English departments, and of freshmen composition in particular, is the constant bourgeois WASPification of all new Americans. What would be your thoughts about this quote some three decades later? Does *The New Literary History* cater to a new kind of English department entirely?

WS: At least one reviewer proposed that *A New Literary History of America* be given to new citizens as an introduction to America. The book is multi-voiced and does not offer one single storyline. Hence its goal is neither to WASPify nor deWASPify but to make its audience think. The reader will find Jefferson the political theorist and the Jefferson of the slavery issue; Emerson as "a self-defrocked minister turned freelance man of letters" and as the philosopher about whom Nietzsche said, "He simply does not know yet how old he is and how young he will yet be"; Truman employing the atom bomb, and Truman integrating the military; Elia Kazan turning Tennessee Williams's *A Streetcar Named Desire* into an unforgettable film and Kazan testifying on communists in Hollywood. Even though there is no party line in this book, and different, at times truly contradictory, perspectives emerge, reading more and more essays will generate a new and fresh sense of America. Together these essays illuminate the religious and heretical impulses in the culture: its Gothic and paranoid scenarios; its democratic promise; its slave narrative and persistent, though ever-changing, issue of race; its Indian, Western, and captivity narratives; its children's literature; the power of its sentimentalism: its love for the success story and its faith in self-improvement; its hard-boiled speech and sophisticated witty dialogs; its immigrant autobiography; its science fiction; its investigative reporting; its anthems, blues, and country music; and its tension between bursts of freewheeling creativity and repression, between experimentation and orthodoxy, between censorship and the broad laughter at any restraint. Gun culture and reform movements, hopes for regeneration and doomsday fears, loud exaggeration and quiet inwardness have been equally at home in America. What we hoped was to offer specialists and nonspecialists in the United States and abroad—including faculty and students in English departments anywhere—a strong and memorable reading experience. I can only hope that readers, whether they go through it from cover to cover or browse in it more randomly, will find this literary history in snapshots as thrilling as it has been for us to put it together.

AG/ØV: Let us throw a couple of quotes at you. In 1968, Hennig Cohen suggested in his preface to *The American Culture* that, although its origins "as a recognizable academic movement" can be traced to the 1930s, "for all practical purposes American Studies came into being shortly after World War II." He mentions among key events that the *American Quarterly* began publication in 1949, and that the American Studies Association was founded two years later. "Among Americanists a provocative assumption gained credence," Cohen wrote: "every aspect of the culture and all of its artifacts might be used to derive information about the culture . . . Disciplines were no longer secure behind impregnable walls; ideas, institutions and physical objects became 'documents,' the equivalent of inscriptions on vellum or bound files of newspapers, to be 'read' for clues to the state of the culture." And in the entry on Leslie Fielder, Carrie Tirado Bramen quotes Fiedler as saying, "I spent the first half of my career trying to break down the barriers between academic disciplines and the second half trying to tear down the walls between elite and popular culture." Although Fiedler presents these two concerns as distinct career stages, Bramen suggests in the entry, "they are in fact inextricably linked, bound together for his desire for opening up categories of any kind." Is your new anthology a testament to a persistent vision in the field(s) of American studies that hardly is provocative anymore, or does it represent something entirely new in its multidisciplinary breadth? Did the work with the book offer new opportunities to consider the "inextricably linked" barriers described by Bramen?

WS: I already mentioned the high esteem in which all of us hold Leslie Fiedler, and we were also inspired by the models of D. H. Lawrence and John Kouwenhoven. What we liked about their approaches to American literature was precisely their readiness to look at literature and culture, broadly defined, and to write in a way that would speak not only to academic specialists and graduate students but to a very broad general audience both inside and outside the United States. Hence—whether highbrow canonical or lowbrow popular—our topics had to be interesting and had to be presented in readily accessible prose, as free of academic jargon as possible.

GM: I don't know if I have a ready answer to that. I think that the mandarism in the academic world, the sense of knowledge that flows from those who have it to those who don't, from those who deserve to possess it to

those who perhaps don't, a sense of *droit de seigneur*, a sense of condescension, a sense of territory to protect . . . I think that has never gone away. I
don't believe it ever will. And I don't buy people who say the walls have come
down, there's no longer any differentiation between one form of culture and
another, one form of speech and another. I think that certainly the most em-
powered sectors of our society—whether that's government, whether that's
culture defined in any way, whether it's the academy, whether it's industry—have a tremendous interest in division, in separation, in a hierarchy of
values, of goods, of knowledge. I think there is a continual horror that goes
back to Andrew Jackson opening the White House to the rabble. Or maybe
even to the way seating was handled at dinners at the White House when
Jefferson was president.

But there is a horror of the invasion of those who don't belong, in every
field in our life. And I think if you look at the reception by official Washington—which is to say of the people who ran the newspapers, who ran the
news programs, the hostesses, people who ran the think tanks, embassies—
if you look at the reception of Bill Clinton and Barack Obama when they
assumed the presidency, it was all, "You're an outsider, you don't belong,
you don't know the rules, you have to show you can play by them, you have
to show you can learn them. And if you can learn them and you still won't
play by them—believe me—you'll never belong in this town." I think that
pervades all of our culture and always has. I think that there is a fear of democracy that is just as strong in the discourse that creates America—that is
just as strong as the lust for it, and there's a sense of entitlement—that "I'm
better than you"—just as there is a sense of entitlement in the American
character of "No one's better than I am, whoever I happen to be."

So I don't believe that the walls have come down, that there are no meaningful or enforceable or enforced distinctions. On the other hand, I think
that the first statement you read me from 1968 is absurdly parochial and
narrow-minded, to say that American studies begins with the founding of
this journal and the formation of this society. As a thinking person's disci-
pline, American studies begins in the teens and the twenties, begins with
Van Wyck Brooks and Constance Rourke and Edmund Wilson. People who
are saying: there *is* such a thing as America, it actually exists. There is an
American character, there's an American nation, there is an American literature. These were all controversial things. You have Constance Rourke
publishing *American Humor: A Study of a National Character* in 1931, you
have Edmund Wilson going back and rereading everybody all through the
1920s and '30s and '40s. Of course you have Mathiessen with *American Re-*

naissance which is the first magisterial academic work that is meant to be read by a broader audience, but that says, "This is inescapable, this is where it all begins. We're all part of this." But you can go back much further, and you can go to Melville's essay on Hawthorne's *Mosses from an Old Manse*, his manifesto. We have to study America, we have to *forget* about Europe, we have to claim that our writers are better than Shakespeare whether they are or not, because that's the only way we're going to convince ourselves that what we do is more important, because we're democrats, we believe in the liberation of all peoples. That therefore—as we have the greatest political idea and mission and obligation and burden—we have to have the greatest literature too. So we start by saying we already do and then we go out and make it.

You can cite the beginnings, or really the emergence of American studies there, and other people might place it earlier. In the 1960s, if you wanted to study American studies at the University of California, there was a sophomore honors seminar you could take if you could get into it. That was it— that was the single American class that carried the term "American studies." There was no major, there was no complex of courses you could put together, maybe drawing on history and English and art and music and economics and whatever. There is now, but there's still no such department. There are very, very few universities that have American studies departments—with their own faculty—today. It has to draw from all these different fields, which are protected, which are occupied. People don't want some generalist coming in, who just knows a little about a lot of things and not much about anything. That's the attitude. So essentially I don't agree with any of that.

AG/ØV: Thank you, that's a very fascinating answer. We could maybe stay a little bit on that subject and talk some more about American studies. The famous line from Springsteen's "No Surrender" comes to mind; "We learned more from a three-minute record than we ever learned in school." There is a vast terrain of texts, objects, and events in your anthology—the Stamp of God's Image, the Sacred Harp, the Winchester rifle, Preston Sturges, "White Elephant Art vs. Termite Art," and Linda Lovelace, to name a few—that are undeniably an important part of American culture but which nevertheless have rarely featured in American studies classes, at least not in your typical European English department. Rich as our education in American studies might have been, one can sense, retrospectively, how significant and nourishing that noninstitutional part (like listening intently and obsessively to Dylan and the Band records or watching Hollywood movies) has been in accumulating knowledge about, as well as generating insight into, the field. There seems to be something inherently eclectic and synoptic about American history that militates against expressive homogeneity. We wonder if you can follow up on that also in relation to the previous comments about American studies and the disciplinary problems and challenges . . . It's a huge question, we know.

GM: It is a huge question and in some ways I've written a lot of books either trying to address or transform or maybe just tiptoe around that question. I remember when I first heard "We learned more from a three-minute record than we ever did in school" and I thought, what a dumb comment. And I thought it was kind of a cheesy pandering comment, because in fact Bruce is a great reader. He may not have been a great reader when he was in high school, or grade school, but he is now. We get fundamental knowledge of life really early. I think it depends on what kind of reader you are. You can learn all you need to know if you are a person who reads with depth, any line in a book can then suggest whole worlds of curiosity and interest. You can learn everything there is to know about America by reading *Moby-Dick*. Not by reading it once, probably, but by returning to it, and using it as your fulcrum—as your power spot that will allow you to move out in any direction. "We learned more from *Moby-Dick* than we did from a three-minute record"—it just doesn't have the same ring, does it?

But on the other hand, there's no question that Bruce and I and countless other people learned things about America from listening to a single Little Richard record that we would never have imagined, could never have glimpsed, that were shocking and thrilling and mysterious and strange and threatening. There's a whole other country out there—that no one told you about! And you weren't going to learn all about that country from listening to "Ready Teddy," but you're going to learn it's there. And you're going to have to go out and find it for yourself. So there's different kinds of quests involved. One of the great things about school—grade school, high school, college—is that they make you read books that you would not have read otherwise. They are going to instill in you—they're going to make you read the classics, or, anyway, they used to make you read the classics. And if that didn't happen, then you wouldn't have read them. You would have heard about them. But you would have seen the movie and you never would have read the book. And I think that is of tremendous importance with regard to binding a society together, giving people a common frame of reference, giving people a common language. So I've always been a great defender of traditional education.

Just because we learned more from a three-minute record than we ever did in school doesn't mean that we ought to teach three-minute records in school instead of the other stuff we didn't learn anything from. Because people are going to discover that themselves. So I tend to be very hide-bound about this.

AG/ØV: The point that we were trying to make was mostly that there seems to be a discrepancy between the way in which knowledge of America is institutionalized in academic disciplines on the one hand and all the stuff that is not covered by disciplines on the other.

GM: The way American studies is taught at Berkeley today is not like that. It studies architecture, traffic, food—just countless different things are put forward.

AG/ØV: It's hard not to notice a persistent engagement throughout your work with the notion of secrecy, with underground histories and unmapped spaces, with the wonders of the invisible world and "the palavers with a community of ghosts," which is how you once described *The Basement Tapes*. Several of your book titles are revelatory in this respect. There is of course *Mystery Train*, the subtitle of *Lipstick Traces* (*A Secret History of the Twentieth Century*), *The Dustbin of History*, *Invisible Republic/The Old, Weird America*, and *The Shape of Things to Come*. To what extent would you say this trope, if that's what it is, of concealment or opacity has informed your work as an editor of *A New Literary History of America*?

GM: Well I hope *not*. I'm perfectly aware that there is this theme running through all of my work, and I know what its sources are. I mean I know what its personal neurotic sources are, and I've even written about that recently. It took me a long time. I didn't think that it was anyone's business or that anyone would care. But then there was an occasion to do it, so I did it. But for me to bring my own personality to bear on this enormous shared story of an infinite number of pieces . . . any two people would have come up with a very different book, even if they had been given the same charge by Lindsay Waters. It would be perverse to inflict your own personality, your own biases, on a story that is so much bigger than you are. All I tried to do—and I think the same is true with Werner and the members of the editorial board—all we tried to do was to help the writers who had accepted assignments to most effectively bring out what *they* wanted to say, what *their* understanding and *their* argument of a given situation was. So I hope—not at all. I totally know what you're talking about in terms of my own work, but all I brought to this project was some knowledge, a lot of ignorance, and some abilities as an editor.

AG/ØV: Several of the essays in the book establish resonant connections between the topic of any given entry and more contemporary concerns, thus situating the present in the past and past in the present. The essay "Limits to Violence" is a case in point. There is the impression that this work is more dialogical and contextual in a way than this particular genre has previously allowed for. So was this an intended objective when you set out to compile the anthology? To have the essays speak to the present?

GM: Yes, that certainly was something we talked about a lot. And I think it was more of a concern of Werner's than of mine. I think it was something that Werner thought—this is important, this is central, we should encourage this—more than I did, and that's all to his credit and the book benefits from that. On the other hand, the essay "Limits to Violence" was not one where we ever discussed with the writer: "Now, you know, there are these parallels with the present and you know, we'd really like to see you bring this out." I was just completely surprised when that entry came in. We wanted him to write about Grant, about the memoirs. We need an essay on Grant's memoirs. We didn't know what it was going to be. We didn't know what he was going to take up, or that he would end up focusing on brutality and torture, and draw these stark analogies with the Bush administration. The Bush administration was such a radical, antidemocratic, autocratic little *bunker* in the whole scope of American history, that it either overturned, denied, negated, or literally set itself against so many precedents, so many senses of limits in all areas of American governance, character, discourse. But this was a case where we can only really appreciate Grant and the depth of his character and his sense of what war is by comparing it to what we're going through now. That was just inescapable. If you take that away you don't have anything. But that's a tremendous essay, "Limits to Violence."

AG/ØV: His description in the beginning of the essay of Grant's final days is just astonishing.

GM: It is one of those signal moments in American history, like Poe's death, his lonely, miserable, forgotten death. And Grant saying, "I'm going to finish this fucking thing, I don't care if I die the next day."

AG/ØV: There are several entries in the anthology that reflect that a new literary history would have to approach what Leslie Fiedler called a "post-

Gutenberg" culture of the visual. In a recent issue of *The Believer* you describe what you call the "waiting images" of Haneke's *The White Ribbon*, suggesting that they change the way you look at Walker Evans's 1936 photos of tenant family shacks in Hale County, Alabama. This way in which images can have the capacity to transform how you look at other images seems to interest you (i.e. in your chapter about David Lynch in *The Shape of Things to Come*). Were you ever tempted to include a stronger pictorial element in your literary history, in order to address how such processes infuse cultural and mental histories?

GM: I think there are gaps or weaknesses in the book. We had to make choices. The book is somewhat longer than we anticipated it would be: counting the index and everything it's 1,100 pages. There are 225 entries in the book instead of the two hundred we were ultimately aiming for. There should have been an entry on *Mad* magazine, which would have opened up into Lenny Bruce, or there could have been an entry on Lenny Bruce which would have opened up into *Mad* magazine. But that kind of humor, that strain of American speech should have been in the book and isn't. And I think had there been an entry on—let's just say Walker Evans—that again could have gone in so many different directions and brought in so many other people. And that's something that isn't there.

The role of Walker Evans, particularly in *Let Us Now Praise Famous Men*, is really fascinating, and it tells you so much about what iconography is and how it affects a whole culture, and the way people understand who they are. *Let Us Now Praise Famous Men* opens cold with this portfolio of photographs. There's no title page, there's no nothing. You open the cover, and there you have these pictures. And you look and you think: Come on, when does the book start? And you finally get to the title page, and it starts, and you read James Agee's introduction, where he says, "The portfolio of photographs that opens this book constitutes a separate but equal statement." And you think: "Boy what a really bullshit modest thing to say." "Here's my friend's pictures and here's my five hundred pages of text." But who are you kidding? Obviously, the text vastly outweighs this little portfolio of photographs in terms of depth, reach, and intellectual claims to its importance.

The fact is—and I don't know if this was Agee engaging in a very complex joke with the future, or whether he actually believed what he was saying— that none of what he said there is true. As you read his book, you are constantly going back and looking at these pictures. You're trying to figure out who's who. And then you're just trying to see if what Agee is describing is captured in the photographs. You're trying to see whether he can match the impact of the photographs, or—depending on who you are—if the photographs can match the descriptions in his writing. So there's this tension set up, and it's just overwhelming, and it drives the whole book, the two parts.

Then he says that they are separate but equal, and we all know that's nonsense, because the text is so much greater. It's like saying the maps in the beginning of *Moby-Dick* present a separate but equal statement to the rest of the book. In many ways *Let Us Now Praise Famous Men*, as a piece of writing, is a landlocked *Moby-Dick*. But which has entered American consciousness? Which has had a determinant effect on our understanding of what the possibilities and limits, and depths and hellholes, of life in America are? Who has affected our senses of who we actually are? Agee or Evans? Obviously Evans. Obviously those images have traveled, have penetrated, in a way that the writing never has. There's a tremendous paradox there. Those are indelible images and they aren't documentary images either. They are constructed, they are selected, they are found. And yet they're also what they are.

AG/ØV: You've quoted Fielder's expression "imaginary Americans" a number of places, which you use with reference to the Beatles and not least in addressing the notion of America as an idea or a set of ideas. To what extent do you think that imaginary Americans have shaped and continue to shape this idea of America? We are certainly two imaginary Americans, and I think this would probably be interesting to American studies.

GM: It's a completely fecund notion. When I first came across Fiedler referring to the Beatles as imaginary Americans, obviously I said: Yeah, right. But I also thought that that was so limited—to refer to people who aren't Americans as imaginary Americans. Because all Americans of any interest are imaginary Americans—they are imagining themselves as Americans. You get a sense of the alienation or the strangeness of the notion of America, of a made-up country that essentially has no meaning except a few values, a few lines from the Declaration of Independence, a few principles you can derive from the Constitution. It's not just Ishmael who's an imaginary American, or an imagined American. Everybody who confronts this question, whether it's Chuck Berry who does so explicitly, whether it's Melville, and he does so explicitly, whether it's Jefferson, Lincoln—all these people do this explicitly, and many people do it implicitly. They're all saying, "What would it mean to be an American?" not "What does it mean?" It presumes that America has yet to actually take shape, come into focus, it's not completely real, it may never be. But you're going to have to act that out yourself, in whatever way it would be.

If you look at Coleman Silk in Philip Roth's novel *The Human Stain*—this is someone from an African American family in New Jersey, who's very light-skinned, who passes as white his entire life to absolutely everybody, including his wife, and all of his colleagues. This is someone who is asking this question in the most stark and in some ways perverse manner imaginable. What would it mean to be an American? One answer, the answer Coleman Silk is giving us, is that being an American means to be white. Philip Roth takes great pains to show us the real genealogical background of Coleman Silk's family, which includes African Americans, former slaves, Swedes, Jews. Essentially, Coleman Silk is the son of Sally Hemmings and Thomas Jefferson, he's that completely American. Or you can look at it the way Coleman Silk himself sees it, which is that he is fulfilling the American destiny more completely than anybody else ever could, because he has completely invented himself. Out of whole cloth, he has become someone he was not, and not only has he done so, he has inhabited that role so fully that his former identity has completely ceased to exist, just like a caterpillar sloughing off its skin.

So the question of the imaginary American is central, but as I said, Fiedler uses it much too narrowly. If you settle for what you are given, he claims, then you're not fully American. Now that is a parochial statement in its own right. Because most people who are born into poverty in America don't escape it. So do you want to turn to them and say, you don't really belong here, you're not really an American because you couldn't invent yourself, because you couldn't imagine a completely different destiny and then go on and live it out? That's stupid. I come from an educated middle-class background. I'm an educated person who lives a middle-class life. Have I escaped anything? Have I imagined a different destiny? Not really.

AG/ØV: With respect to the realm of literature and art—aesthetics—would you say that this process of continuous cultural reinvention is something that distinguishes the whole tradition of American literature from, say, the German, French or European equivalents?

GM: Yes, of course it does, it's our great obsession. Look at the Russian novel, which is about the inability of people to imagine themselves outside the worlds in which they were born and the horrible conflicts this creates. The one signal character in Russian literature who does escape is the killer

In *Crime and Punishment*. He commits this horrible, senseless crime in order to completely destroy the fabric of society, his own identity, and the destiny that it's presumed he will live out. And he fails! Right? Because he still essentially gets a pass. All literatures have their own ruling themes, and that is certainly ours.

AG/ØV: As a distinguished scholar of multiculturalism over the years, how did you decide to go into the word's early history in your entry?

WS: The format of each entry—a date, a newspaper-like headline, and a more dictionary-like title followed by a 2,250–2,500-word-long essay that would present a surprising creation, a turning point, a cultural momentum—intrigued me and inspired me to write on the little-known novel that, according to the *Oxford English Dictionary*, gave rise to the word "multicultural"—a word that had an astonishingly popular career half a century later. I drafted the essay in the manner of an entry and sent it to Lindsay and Greil—and they decided that it should become part of the book.

AG/ØV: "That was New Orleans," you write in your entry on Katrina, "but imagine now that it was any place, any great city, any small town, on which, for a moment, the attention of the nation was fixed. The place then becomes a mirror, the face of the nation itself. In the national imagination the place becomes the nation, or its negation—the face the nation faces, or the face from which the nation turns away." Moving from Faulkner to Neale Hurston and then to Thomas Paine and Melville—via Randy Newman—the entry seems a perfect example of how one can approach or address the present through prisms of the past, as well as past events through prisms of the present moment—and end up with a piece of text that addresses much, much more than a singular event or series of events. There are several such entries in the book—is this the result of an editorial strategy?

WS: Thank you for your kind words on this essay. From the very inception of the project we envisioned essays that would roam back and forward from a moment that provides its occasion to be included. Greil and I both thought of examples for the sort of pattern we had in mind. Greil: "An entry on Lenny Bruce, say, could move to Allen Ginsberg's *Howl* and to *Lolita*—and back to earlier gauntlets of twentieth-century legal censorship, as opposed to the social and self-censorship of the nineteenth century and before, as with *Ulysses*, *Lady Chatterley's Lover*, and Henry Miller—though in fact such an entry could begin with any of these specific items, moving forward in time, backwards, or sideways." Me: "e.e. cummings let typewriter keys serve as inspiration for a new kind of lower-case poetry; one could look at the stages of the invention of the typewriter that took on a new quality with the American patent in 1873 and the Remington mass production that followed it. Henry James typed many of his works and letters and used the phrase 'my Remington' with a certain fondness; there is a brass sculpture of Hemingway attached to his typewriter in the JFK Library; and the Beats are unthinkable without such keys as the ampersand &." Though neither of these samples became actual entries, they guided our process of imagining a good number of topics that did make it into *A New Literary History of America*.

20 Questions: Greil Marcus

Karen Zarker/2010

From *PopMatters*, October 25, 2010. Used by permission.

"Few if any American cultural historians take the great deep American Breath like Greil Marcus," writes Robert Loss in his *PopMatters* article, "Risk and Equilibrium: The Impact of Greil Marcus." "It's the breath of Whitman, of Ginsberg, of Little Richard and Dylan and Aretha Franklin—in scope and risk, at least, if not their artistry or forms."

Indeed, a skilled bridge-builder who spans the chasm between academia and pop culture, the critic who cut his teeth on *Rolling Stone, Creem*, and the *Village Voice* has another book out this month, *Bob Dylan by Greil Marcus: Writings 1968–2010*. We're pleased to have him back with us, this time in the playful framework of *PopMatters* 20 Questions.

1. The latest book or movie that made you cry?

Over Labor Day weekend at the Telluride Film Festival, I was introducing David Hoffman's 1965 film *Music Makers of the Blue Ridge*, about old-time country music in the North Carolina mountains. The great folklorist and singer Bascom Lamar Lunsford, then eighty-three, was the guide for a tour of the county—the best guitar player, the best clog-dancer, the best animal-sounds imitator, the best dulcimer player. I've seen the movie many times over the years, and after talking about it for a few minutes, instead of rushing off to another screening, I figured I'd just wait in the back and watch a few minutes. Of course I was pulled in and stayed.

There are two scenes, at the very end, that are completely devastating. Lunsford has been traveling through his home ground, bringing it to life, giving a deep sense of love for the place and the people and its history, and that drapes over everything. Still, after an hour, you figure you've got the picture. But then his tone changes slightly; he's going to take us to see a fiddle player, he says, someone named Jesse Ray—"Lost John." You get the feeling this is not going to be like anything you've seen before—as if he doesn't take just anyone to see this person.

Lost John turns out to be a moon-faced man who looks as if the top layer of skin has been peeled off of his face: a big grin, almost no teeth. It's hard to tell his age—somewhere between thirty and fifty. He picks up his fiddle and begins to sing "Little Maggie"—and suddenly you're no longer in a specific place, you're no longer looking at local culture, at folk music—you are in the presence of the kind of great artist no culture can account for, that no tradition can guarantee. You're swept up, swept away, dumbfounded, shocked, you can't believe how lucky you are to be in the presence of this man, you can't believe that this performance has to end, you're already afraid you won't be able to remember it in every detail, afraid that, somehow, this isn't real.

That brought me to tears—but then came the end of the movie. Lunsford stands on a hill, shot from a great distance, and begins to recite an old poem about a suitor at a garden gate, returning every day to win the affections of his beloved, and how she betrayed him, reciting the poem slowly, as if it's a memory he has never gotten over—even if being spurned ultimately led him to his true and faithful love. By the end of that, the tears were on my face.

2. The fictional character most like you?

Jason, the teenage son of the underground fugitive who goes by the name of Louise Barrot in Dana Spiotta's 2006 novel, *Eat the Document*. He's as smart as a fifteen-year-old can be, which is very smart. His intelligence is all obsession and play, and all devoted to '60s and '70s music—the music of his mother's never-explained, always shadowy past. His submergence in the Beach Boys and Funkadelic is his way of trying to figure out, if only emotionally, who she is, who he is—but it's thrilling to be brought into his quest, the love the music sparks in him on its own terms. The worry is there that this is a psychological diversion, that the music will vanish to him, cease to speak to him, if ever he does find out who his mother is.

I was never as smart as Jason—but I know the energy, the search, the sense of mystery that is in one's life and in music, and the delight of forgetting that there is any difference between the two.

3. The greatest album, ever?

Bob Dylan's *Highway 61 Revisited* (1965). No matter how many times you might have heard it, a different song will appear as primary, the star around which everything else revolves—it could be "It Takes a Lot to Laugh, It Takes a Train to Cry" one day, "Ballad of a Thin Man" the next, the title song for the next year, "Just like Tom Thumb's Blues" a year later, each different song casting all the others into a different relief. Then "Desolation Row" might make you forget that there's anything else on the album at all. But if the album were simply "Like a Rolling Stone" and thirty or forty minutes of silence, I still might pick it.

4. *Star Trek* or *Star Wars*?
   Never cared about either.

5. Your ideal brain food?
   Walking up Panoramic Way, behind the football stadium in Berkeley, up the steep street, not looking out at the Bay, not looking at much of anything except wild turkey if they're out that day, because I've done it truly thousands of times over twenty-five years or so—and without thinking, without intent, ideas arrive, bits of stories, phrases that carry stories inside of them that if you can forget yourself will tell themselves.
   One day, near the crest of the hill, the first two pages of my book *Invisible Republic* aka *The Old, Weird America* popped into my head, written word for word, in an instant—that's how it seemed. There was no chance of forgetting them. I went home and transcribed it all. It was perfect. That I didn't write another word of the book for three months was no matter. That beginning could never have come about any other way.

6. You're proud of this accomplishment, but why?
   Lipstick Traces. Because I finished it. Because I knew when I finished it that I would never write that well again, which was better than I ever imagined I could. It's the result of being caught up in a vision that refuses to come into focus, so turning to its smallest details, and finding whole worlds of conflict and desire in a gesture, a poem, a curse, and staying within those small worlds until they create their own gravitational force, until they are all spinning in harmony.

7. You want to be remembered for . . . ?
   Remembered by whom? I hope my children don't forget me as I am already forgetting my parents, and my father is still alive.

8. Of those who've come before, the most inspirational are?

Helen Hyman, my mother's mother. Ralph J. Gleason. Abraham Lincoln. Pauline Kael.

9. The creative masterpiece you wish bore your signature?

David Thomson's *Suspects* (1985). It's a novel based on characters from film noir, defined far beyond its normal boundaries: the central film is *It's a Wonderful Life*. Thomson takes, say, Rick in Casablanca, and imagines his life before and after the film. He does that for a whole constellation of characters.

It's a great game, you figure, for the writer, and for the reader too, until at some point—it could be quite early for some readers, very late for someone like me, who tends to forget plot even while reading a mystery—you begin to realize that this isn't a game, that the characters are being taken to a verge, that they have all been trapped in the same story, which is going to end—or be ended. Then the suspense takes over, and you can become afraid to keep reading. Imagine if a whole genre dreamed a dream of itself—this is that dream. But I don't wish it bore my signature, whatever that means—I wish I had the imagination to write something like this.

10. Your hidden talents . . . ?

I'm a good typist.

11. The best piece of advice you actually followed?

When teaching a seminar, and there's a point that rises out of the discussion that you think absolutely has to be made, wait. In five minutes someone in the class will say what, if you, the teacher, had said it, would have killed the discussion—but coming from a student, it will push the discussion forward, into richer territory than your own sterile interruption could ever have found. That was my own advice to myself, and every time I teach a seminar, I have to remind myself of it about every fifteen minutes.

12. The best thing you ever bought, stole, or borrowed?

A gold bracelet for my wife from I. Vittori on the Ponte Vecchio in Florence. There was something odd in the air, a glowing light in the overcast sky. The owner of the store wouldn't take a check. He said, I can trust you. Take it home, and if you like it, you can pay me then.

13. You feel best in Armani or Levis or . . . ?

I wear Levis almost every day, but I love my Miyakes. As for Armani—

one day in 2000, in New York, my wife and I went to a party at a private club in Manhattan held to welcome a new book editor from London, Frances Coady. I had heard about her and wanted to meet her. I was wearing a greenish suit and a gray t-shirt, but the club wouldn't let me in: ties were required, I was informed. And, the person at the desk said, ties were to be worn with a collared shirt—not tied around the neck over a t-shirt.

I was so incensed I stomped away raving and cursing. But my wife said, "You really want to meet this editor, don't you?" Yes, I did. "Well, there's an Armani store around the corner." We went in—and while I'd never been able to find a shirt or a tie that went with the suit I had on, this time we did. I put them on, went back to the club, met Frances Coady, and there was an immediate affinity. I knew I had to do a book with her.

That book turned out to be *The Shape of Things to Come*, and she turned out to be the best editor I ever worked with, someone who could see the whole arc of a book, what was part of that arc, what wasn't, and also say, "You know, you used a very similar phrase back on page 127 . . ."

14. Your dinner guest at the Ritz would be?

Is there still a Ritz? Where is it? To me the Ritz is the 1920s in New York. So I'd go back and sit down with F. Scott Fitzgerald. The food would be lousy, he'd get drunk, but every time I'd read him after that, each page would have a weight it would never have had if we hadn't been there.

Today I'd go to Chez Panisse in Berkeley with Pauline Kael. She'd be cranky and funny and outrageously cutting. The food would be simple, gorgeous, so full of flavor it would stop the conversation. We'd argue about movies, books, she'd tell stories of Berkeley in the '40s and '50s, we'd argue about our own writing—"I was reading your book, every word seemed to lead to every other, and then there was this thud—what happened? What is that terrible sentence about 'the catacombs of visible culture' doing there?" "But that was the sentence I was aiming toward all along—" "Your aim was off. Take it out. Believe me, you can live without it."

15. Time travel: where, when, and why?

I'd like to be in Montgomery, Alabama, just after the Civil War, when my great-grandfather Jakob Greil was building his liquor and grocery distribution business. I'd like to be in Hawaii in the 1870s, when my great-grandmother Belle Louisson was growing up. I'd like to be back in Menlo Park in the '50s, to see if it really was as wonderful a place as I remember it to be.

16. Stress management: hit man, spa vacation, or Prozac?
Hawaii, one of these days.

17. Essential to life: coffee, vodka, cigarettes, chocolate, or . . . ?
Gin.

18. Environ of choice: city or country, and where on the map?
I've lived my whole life in the San Francisco Bay Area: born in San Francisco, grew up in Palo Alto and Menlo Park, Berkeley since I went to college in 1963. My parents were born there—San Francisco and San Jose—and never left. I've never been anywhere where I wanted to live more than where I'm from.

19. What do you want to say to the leader of your country?
Don't let the bastards grind you down—and remember that they are bastards.

20. Last but certainly not least, what are you working on, now?
Earlier this year I published a short book on listening to Van Morrison—finding moments from throughout his career that seemed to catch the quest that runs all through it.

I'm going to write another short book, about listening to the Doors—but instead of having forty-five years to work with, I'll have four. Any day I drive over the bridge from Berkeley to San Francisco and back, I am all but guaranteed to hear the Doors at least three times: "LA Woman," "Roadhouse Blues," "Light My Fire" most often, a shuffle of half a dozen more.

I began wondering why they were still on the radio. I got lost in them every time.

Index

CPSIA information can be obtained at www.ICGtesting.com
Printed in the USA
BVOW081020250912

300512BV00009B/1/P

9 781617 036224